COMPASS *for* UNCHARTED LIVES

COMPASS
for UNCHARTED LIVES

A Model for Values Education

DONALD J. KIRBY, S.J.

Syracuse University Press

First Edition 2007

07   08   09   10   11   12   6   5   4   3   2   1

The paper used in this publication meets the minimum requirements
of American National Standard for Information Sciences—Permanence
of Paper for Printed Library Materials, ANSI Z39.48–1984.∞™

For a listing of books published and distributed by Syracuse University Press,
visit our Web site at SyracuseUniversityPress.syr.edu.

ISBN-13: 978-0-8156-3153-8

ISBN-10: 0-8156-3153-7

Library of Congress Cataloging-in-Publication Data

Kirby, Donald J.

   Compass for uncharted lives : a model for values education / Donald J. Kirby, S.J. — 1st ed.

      p. cm.

   Includes bibliographical references and index.

   ISBN-13: 978-0-8156-3153-8 (pbk. : alk. paper)

   ISBN-10: 0-8156-3153-7 (pbk. : alk. paper)

 1. Moral education.   2. Values—Study and teaching (Higher)   I. Title.

   LC268.K52 2007

   370.11′4—dc22

   2007028529

Manufactured in the United States of America

For my father and mother,

Donald (1915–2007) and Irene

"Those who are wise shall shine like the brightness of the sky,

and those who lead many to righteousness,

like the stars forever and ever" (Dan. 12:3).

• • •

Donald J. Kirby, S.J., is the founding director of the Values Program and professor of religious studies at Le Moyne College. He holds a Ph.D. from Union Theological Seminary in New York and has also studied at Woodstock College in Maryland and the Maxwell School of Citizenship and Public Affairs at Syracuse University. His teaching and research are in the areas of religion, ethics, and values with special interest in the ethical aspects of corporate policy. He is the coauthor of *Ambitious Dreams: The Values Program at Le Moyne College,* and his articles have appeared in *Change, Liberal Education, Journal of Business Ethics,* and *About Campus.*

Contents

Acknowledgments

While on sabbatical at Boston College I met Wil Derkse, a visiting professor from the Netherlands. As he listened to my story about creating a Values Program he said, "You have received a gift." My desire to share this gift is realized in this book. Now I want to thank those individuals who shared their gifts with me to make this book possible.

I express my gratitude to Andrew J. Brady, S.J., a man of profound intelligence and even deeper integrity and spirituality. Among his talents was the gift to discern the needs of the times and to know how to assist young people to meet those needs. From the beginning he recognized the importance of this educational effort. Before he died at the end of 1999 he encouraged me to publish what we had done and how we had done it so that this unique educational effort would not be lost. I want also to remember the late John Amos, the first and most faithful of donors, for supporting the program and the book project. He could always be counted on.

My special thanks go to Krystine Batcho, professor of psychology, who for nearly twenty years has made herself available for consultation and brainstorming. There is hardly a concept in this book that does not bear the stamp of her intellectual and deep spiritual acumen. Her book in progress, *Hollow Seed*, complements this book and breaks new ground in understanding and connecting spirituality and values education.

Through multiple revisions I was fortunate to receive feedback from Susan Thornton. A superb colleague, she combines the qualities of a confirmed advocate with the attributes of a fearless critic. With great skill she pushed and retreated as needed, and she helped me find my distinctive voice. Working with someone who is both gifted and committed is indeed a gift. Thank you, Susan.

To the Board of Directors of the Values Program I give thanks for their assistance with resources, time, and energy. If anyone influenced the daily hands-on building and completing of the book it was Nunzio Tartaglia. Together we spent long days in New York City and Boston wrestling with difficult concepts. Nunzio helped me sort out the possible issues and see the forest for the trees. For his financial, emotional, and intellectual support I thank him.

There is no one who can better bring a vision to reality than Donald LaCasse. For the style, tenacity, and gentle prodding that is Don LaCasse, I extend my gratitude. Michael Kinsella's humane wit, deep intelligence, and convivial hospitality helped keep my feet to the fire and my eyes on the prize. He introduced me to the right people and the right idea at just the right time.

When I needed legal counsel and the ear of a good friend, Bruce Collins provided his analysis both orally and in writing. I especially thank the Most Rev. Thomas J. Costello, auxiliary bishop of Syracuse, who served as chairman of our board. A former superintendent of schools, he was a strong advocate for our program and provided courageous leadership at a critical time. When I combine their gifts with the contributions of the other board members, Carol L. Lawyer, John W. Lawyer, Anis I. Obeid, Emil Rossi, Nancy L. Rossi, and the late R. David Carhart, I am most thankful.

The very nature of the subject matter of this book makes it impossible to cite every individual who made valuable contributions. The educational effort required to create and develop the type of compass we desired for our graduates' future uncharted lives involved literally hundreds of faculty colleagues, administrators, students, professionals, and other participants from a wide area. This book is based in large part on their practical lived experience, reflection, and evaluation. I cannot thank all of them personally. I do, however, express to them my gratitude.

My gratitude to Angela Albanese, Theresa Coulter, Mary Emily Alibrandi, Nancy Piscitell, and Nancy Wood for administering an office that reflected a welcoming atmosphere conducive to rich intellectual activity. Each in her own special way facilitated the synthesis of a myriad of pieces of a complex dynamic effort. Our graduate student Shannon Connerton assisted in preparation of the first draft of the manuscript by reading through the entire files and copying relevant materials for the chapter.

Partial funding to complete this manuscript came from the generous support of the Lilly Endowment, Inc., the U.S. Jesuit conference, and the faculty sabbatical program at Le Moyne College. Because of their support I was able to travel, learn from others, and receive valuable encouragement through conversations. These funds made possible reciprocal visits to and from the Netherlands organized by Wil Derkse and his colleagues at Fontys University of Applied Sciences and other institutions in the Netherlands.

I am especially grateful to Theodore Marchese, formerly of the American Association of Higher Education, the editor of *Change* magazine and the *AAHE Bulletin*. He is always a source of enthusiastic and practical support and encouragement. My professional colleagues at the Association of Practical and Professional Ethics gave me the opportunity to test ideas. Closer to home I am grateful to Patricia Schmidt for extending the values concern into the field of reading education. Also I would be remiss not to mention Edward Baumgartner for his support over the years as associate director. He was a source of humor and sanity, and especially instrumental in extending our efforts to science and mathematics.

I am grateful also to the Jesuit community at Le Moyne College and to the New York Province of the Society of Jesus for their financial assistance as well as their intellectual and spiritual support. More particularly, I thank Patrick Lynch who suggested changes and new directions to early drafts. James Woods brought his wisdom to bear on certain aspects of the prospectus and early drafts, especially the chapter on acquiring resources and assistance. Paul Naumann provided daily encouragement, Terrence Fay wise counsel, and Donald Zewe unflagging support. Thanks also to my faculty colleagues at Le Moyne and elsewhere.

Thanks to Glenn Wright, acquisitions editor at Syracuse University Press, for his support and intelligent involvement in the book project.

My family and friends listened to the narrative of this book many times and offered continuing encouragement and support. They have my profound gratitude.

COMPASS *for* UNCHARTED LIVES

Introduction
Churning Still Waters

Mixing the Surface and Bottom Waters

One morning I hiked at Green Lakes State Park not far from my home in central New York State. At the park, I walked around its two sparkling jewels, two glacial lakes surrounded by upland forest. They are as rare and unique as their emerald-colored surface water. Both Round and Green Lakes are meromictic lakes, which means that there is no fall and spring mixing of surface and bottom waters. Such lakes have a high potential for evidence of ancient plant and animal life.

The awesome beauty so moved me that I was caught by surprise. I found myself wondering about a similarity between the makeup of these lakes and their environment and the composition of the collegiate campus, medical school, and high-tech medical-corporate environment that is so prevalent in contemporary society. Some campuses and professional schools, like meromictic lakes, seem also to have little or no fall and spring mixing of surface and bottom waters. Much sediment remains at the bottom.

Do we hear echoes of this lack of mixing when educators refer to "the silos and mine shafts" of the collegiate campus that remain virtually untouched by each other? The official description of a meromictic lake says:

A meromictic lake is one which lacks complete circulation. In meromictic lakes the deepest water contains no dissolved oxygen. Sediments are relatively undisturbed and therefore offer a detailed record of the history of the lake. The monimolimnion is the deepest part of the lake, it is the most dense and is not involved in annual circulation. The increased density is due to the accumulation of salts. During spring, summer, and early fall, decomposing organic matter produces a gradual elimination of the oxygen. The anaerobic zone moves upwards during the summer. (Hilfinger and Mullins 1997)

These relatively undisturbed sediments offer a detailed record of the history of the lake and are thus treasured primary research resources for geologists. It fascinates me that the usual renewable energy resource, which is the oxygen, does not have an opportunity to mingle throughout the lake. Because I was working on this book at the time, it occurred to me that the lack of oxygen in these lakes may be a metaphor for a dangerous trend in higher education. Could the higher-education bias toward leaving itself relatively undisturbed by the values and spiritual dimension of issues be harmful? What happens if educators neglect a necessary, critical, and perhaps most important dimension of reality? Is it possible that we are not providing our students with enough oxygen? Is it possible that they need the values and spiritual dimensions of issues?

The challenge is to create a process that has the dynamism and the power to mix the surface with the bottom waters. In a college climate where values are not discussed, where students are given no framework for learning values formation, the deepest dimension of reality is ignored. The Green Lakes are perhaps misnamed. Without oxygen, they cannot grow. They need the mixing of the different waters; they need oxygen.

Historically, it has been thought that it was unprofessional or inappropriate for a teacher or professor to address the values and spiritual dimensions of issues. However, we now know that as educators, we need to assist students in dealing with the deepest issues in their personal and professional lives.

I believe that the values dimension is a critical catalyst for this circulation, just as oxygen is critical for circulation in the environment. The values dimension is like oxygen: unless it is circulated completely throughout the system, unless there is a fall and spring mixing of surface and bottom waters, there is a serious problem.

A Critical Need to Discover and Implement

What drew me into these thoughts was that I was participating at the time in a critical journey of discovery that had engaged colleagues from near and far. In the beginning we were drawn by an ambitious dream to make a major difference in values education and values development. We had realized that an increasing number of students were prepared to tackle technical tasks but not prepared to meet the moral and spiritual challenges of their professional and personal lives. We felt an urgent need to work with educators to fashion a collegiate environment where we could enhance the values, spirituality, and moral sensitivity of students and their commitment to ethical decision making.

Rather soon we realized this goal involved the challenge of churning the still waters of our college environment, injecting oxygen into an anaerobic environment. We would need to discover and implement ways to engage in an institution-wide educational effort, to engage the faculty and others, to "train the trainers" and then discover how to circulate this energy into the classroom and the surrounding community.

This book presents our process and methodology, our approach, techniques, and reflections. I pull together the hundreds of conversations and meetings in which participants across the institution and locally, regionally, nationally, and internationally became engaged in our effort.

Each institution and its constituencies will discover how it ought to proceed, depending on the mission and purpose of the institution, its location and geography, its culture and its civilization. No one can tell you what your experience ought to be; only you can discover it. What I can give you is a vision.

The Values Program is a journey of discovery. This effort is designed to assist students to develop for themselves a framework of values that is consistent, coherent, and defensible with the best of the philosophical, religious, and cultural traditions. What distinguishes this journey of discovery is its vision of both what is needed and how best to achieve it. Making this vision come alive presents difficult and practical challenges. How do you create a collegiate environment that enhances students' values, spirituality, and moral sensitivity and their commitment to ethical decision making? How do you educate students who spontaneously, with no prompting, give priority to the values dimensions of issues and have the skills, judgment, motivation, and expertise to deal with those issues? At its core, the Values Program creates a change of consciousness. My goal in this book is that you will understand and appreciate the fundamental insight behind the workings of this whole operation, that you will come to believe that it is possible for your educational institution to aspire to the same goals, and that these models, guidelines, and examples will give you the courage to implement it.

The final product is called the Values Program. The dynamic instrument that ignites the process is the Center for the Advancement of Values Education (CAVE) model, a process that is accessible and adaptable for anyone, no matter what his or her religious, philosophical, or cultural background. It is unlike most attempts that reach only the already converted or those individuals of a particular philosophical or theological approach. This approach and model will be welcome on not only the higher-education and professional levels but also at the secondary-education level.

The goal of this whole operation was to create and discover "ways" of achieving our mission at the institutional, departmental, academic, and student-affairs levels both in and beyond the classrooms. This book grows out of practical experience.

The Values Program developed in central New York State, a region renowned for its innovations. In this region the Erie Canal became a practical school of engineering for building canals. Close by, the Oneida Movement, a nineteenth-century experiment in social and religious organization, flourished. To the west, less than an hour away, is Seneca Falls, the base of the women's suffrage movement. This area is also where Tom Watson transformed his Binghamton business machine shop into the international giant IBM. In the air is the culture of combining the practical with the theoretical, the prophetic with the profitable, and the spiritual with the modern world (Kephart and Zellner 2000).

In this same spirit a group of faculty colleagues (together with staff, administrators, practitioners, professionals, students, and parents), beginning in a Jesuit college in upstate New York and soon working together with colleagues nationally and internationally, struggled to create and implement a model. This model began by addressing the complex and controversial problems of values development and values education and went on to tackle the issues of spirituality and religion in higher education. For more than fifteen years we engineered an educational effort to discover ways to meet this challenge. This book is about that proven method of values education. After fifteen years of development, research, and fine-tuning, I am now able to describe and clarify this evolving, effective, operational process that we developed and other institutions can use.

From its very beginning the CAVE model and the Values Program have been structured so that they could develop within the context of a wide variety of institutions and professional schools. It became clear we had achieved this goal when Wil Derkse, former director of the Radboud Foundation in the Netherlands, called it a gift. He has since worked to integrate the process into the Fontys University of Applied Sciences in the Netherlands, where our program thrives. That the founders of the Values Program created it under the demands of teaching full-time with minimal initial support from the institution perhaps speaks to the very giftedness of the concept and the idea. The outside support and encouragement of professional and educational organizations and foundations such as the Amos Foundation, Consortium for the Advancement of Private Higher Education, Lilly Endowment, National Science Foundation, and other foundations that wished to remain anonymous and many smaller groups also helped us to hone our skills.

In other articles and presentations (aside from the book-length study *Ambitious Dreams: The Values Program at Le Moyne College* [Kirby et al. 1990]) it was possible to do little more than a superficial description and analysis. Now, by doing a more substantive, analytical description, it is possible to grasp the accomplishments of the program's inventors.

One of the reasons for writing this book is to carefully explain our process and methodology, so that it will not be misunderstood or misinterpreted. I want to present this information so that others can continue the process and assess and research what we have done. Also, because the field of values education and spirituality continues to evolve, the publication of this book will enable others to take our creation and situate it within contemporary research and action. The major accomplishments of this program will become more evident. Also, it will become clearer what major questions remain.

Ambitious Dreams: The Values Program at Le Moyne College is a collection of essays. It set out the seminal ideas for the program and introduced the model's structure and components. Faculty who were cofounders, coordinators, directors, and participants in the 1988 and 1989 Summer Institutes and Academic Forums contributed chapters. Two students who were actively involved in the early years of the program also authored chapters. Given the diverse authorship, the chapters function independently and offer different perspectives on the early years of the program.

This first book was well received. It introduced the program in an engaging manner both within and beyond our institution. Faculty and others from diverse institutions nationally and internationally made inquiries and requests for information. We received a number of invitations to assist other institutions in adapting the Values Program and the CAVE model to their own institutions.

The style, structure, and content of this book are very different. There are advantages to being the sole author. First, I am able to provide unity and coherence and can speak with a single voice. Second, as a cofounder and director of the program since its implementation in 1988, I am the only person who has been involved in all aspects of the program and its development both within and beyond its founding institution.

There already exist excellent theoretical and academic studies on moral and spiritual development and the foundational issues of knowing and valuing. However, these works are not practical. They omit or do not recognize the challenges involved in creating and implementing a comprehensive and holistic educational effort that seeks to engage as many individuals as possible in an institution and beyond. Other excellent books deal with learning communities, service learning, and ethics across the curriculum. These programs and initiatives, though, address only a portion of the academic community, whereas the challenge of the CAVE model approach is to involve the entire institution.

Primary-Source Material

My primary-source material for this book is my own practical lived experience and reflection and the experience of countless participants from very diverse backgrounds. These participants learned by "doing" and by paying attention to the feedback and reflection process. I will also draw on conversations with deans, students, faculty, academic departments, student affairs personnel, human resources offices, development officers and grant writers, public relations, admissions, alumni, the wider community, and the town-gown connections. My sources also include hundreds of interactions with foundations, conferences, seminars, international and national presentations and symposia, visitors, phone calls, and representatives of the media. Because the CAVE process engages participants from throughout the educational and professional communities, it draws on a broad range of experience. The biologist, psychologist, philosopher, theologian, historian, accountant, and engineer and education major all contain a vast store of theory and experience. As our program developed, we welcomed and included those abilities.

One of our guiding principles in the design of our instrument was, "What works?" Our goal was to design and create a program that would be both useful and capable of continually renewing itself. We were not interested primarily in the theoretical principles of values. Rather, like the Wright brothers or the engineers of the Erie Canal, our goal was to discover what design features were necessary to bring about the desired goal of values education. We faced several challenges. How do you engage and commit an institution to the mission of values education? How do you get the faculty involved, and how do you keep them involved? How do you provide faculty with the legitimacy, technique, and content necessary for values education? How do you manage to impact nearly every student in your institution? How do you engage students in real-life experiences? How do you create a community of learners with both students and faculty coming together? How do you keep this program at the center of the academic enterprise so it is not just a marginal program?

With the participants it is not just a question of getting them there. When you have them present, you need to find a way to keep their focus on values and the spiritual dimension. How do you keep the focus on discovering and implementing ways to assist students? How do you help students to make connections, to achieve integration? How do you cross discipline boundaries, and, when you do, how do you intertwine content, pedagogy, and learning?

We certainly took advantage of the established theories and practices of values education. Creating the Values Program demanded that we be able to move back and forth between the abstract and the concrete. The

Wright brothers were masters of this process. They were able to take abstract concepts about wings, winds, weights, and lift and turn them into workable machinery. In our case the abstract theories became concrete in our models of:

- the theme
- a working group on values
- an institute (summer or otherwise) for faculty and staff development
- the Academic Forum to mediate the connection between the Summer Institute and the academic year
- building bridges across the institution.

The information yielded by these program elements could be incorporated directly into the design of the Values Program and the CAVE model.

We believed no specific component to be more important than any other. No matter how creative the theme, without a way to integrate it throughout the institution, the Values Program would not work. No matter how effective the Summer Institute, without a soundly designed Academic Forum, the Values Program remained stuck on the ground. Moreover, realizing that both the students and the faculty are integral to the system, the founding faculty devoted as much attention to learning to be values educators as they did in designing and building the program.

A result of this practical experience and learning is that we came to learn better ways to assist the students in the valuing process at the collegiate level. Parker J. Palmer, a respected writer and presenter of workshops, lectures, and retreats in the United States and elsewhere, pointed out that our model is able "to bring students into truth by teaching them how to participate in humankind's endless, demanding, and exhilarating conversation over what commands our commitment and care" (Palmer 1990, vi).

Many authors have used the metaphor of a stone or a pebble being tossed into a pond. This simple action creates numerous ripples. These ripples spread far and wide from the initial point of contact, and create effects all along the varied shoreline of the lake into which the pebble is cast. The Values Program was "tossed" like a stone into the pond of a particular institution of higher learning, and its effects touched many different shores. First to receive the ripple effect of values education were the people at that institution, and then through them and from them the ripple effect of the values program reached out nationally and internationally.

Application of Practical Experience and Reflection

My perspective as a cofounder and director of this educational effort from its beginning enabled me to observe all aspects of the program's development. That experience puts me in a unique position to recognize and describe important insights derived from the accumulated practical experience and learning of the many participants. I am also able to recommend guidelines for individuals and institutions looking to implement such an approach.

By emphasizing this praxis (doing and reflecting), this book tells the story of how this pioneering model for values education was instrumental in discovering and implementing strategies to meet the changing needs of students over and over again in diverse situations. The book is helpful to those individuals asking, how do you create and sustain an institution-wide educational effort that can continually evolve? The list of institution-wide themes over the years reflects this program's ability to deal with complex and wide-ranging issues. Themes have included "Science, Technology, and Values"; "Economic Justice"; "Peace and War"; "Ethics Across the Curriculum"; "Action for Justice in a Changing World"; "The Student Connection"; "Education and Public Policy"; and "The Spiritual Dimensions of Higher Education."

The Values Program approach has the ability to remain current by being adaptable to different constituencies and needs within the institution and other educational contexts. A question frequently asked is, "How do you maintain such flexibility and adaptability?" As students, faculty, staff, and administrators changed and grew and as new needs surfaced, the approach's design was a catalyst for the discovery of new ways to assist students whether inside or outside the classroom. Whether related to issues of peace and war, economic justice, education and public policy, or the spiritual dimension of higher education, this approach proved able to discover and implement a plan of procedure to meet changing needs in changing times.

By adding our own insights and intuitions to well-accepted educational techniques we have created a model or process that is specifically useful for values and spirituality. This freedom of exchange has allowed for creativity for all participants throughout the program's implementation.

To be effective it must assist students, faculty, staff, and administrators in keeping their focus on the values and spiritual dimension of issues. For instance, in Chapter 4 I describe how the program, no matter what the content and theme, continually kept in focus during the Summer Institutes that its primary purpose in "training the trainers" was to give them the techniques, legitimacy, and content to deal with the values dimensions of issues with their students. The Values Institute facilitators and participants needed to work hard so that they never lost sight of their goal: to provide collegial support and resources. Each time the institutes' participants struggled to discover and implement ways to assist their students with the values dimension, the program's structure provided needed support both during and after the institutes and into the academic year.

I am also able to describe and analyze the practical experience and reflection flowing from the constant activities of the Working Group on Values (WGV). In many ways this WGV is the heartbeat of the whole procedure. It is the Working Group's task to help integrate a particular values theme, Values Institute, or Academic Forum.

Selection of the Term *Values*

Why did we decide to use the term *values* rather than *morals, ethics,* or *culture*? As I mentioned earlier, our initial aim was to help students integrate their professional interests with the college's liberal arts and religious tradition. The more sensitized and aware we became of the complexities involved in the search, and the more conscious we became that the urgent need was not just a local problem but much larger, we searched for a language that would speak to the historical specificities of our environment yet would also be applicable to any collegiate and university environment.

We sought to address the fundamental struggle between the individual and the common good. At issue was the quest, "What kind of actions ought I to do?" "What kind of society and community ought we to create?" These are fundamental values questions. Other programs reach their objectives by asking questions such as, "What is the role of the college in forming responsible citizenship?" and "What is the responsible citizen, and how do you form responsible citizens?"

Personal Components

For me this journey began in 1969. I was a second-year master of divinity Jesuit theologian at Woodstock College in Manhattan living with other Jesuits in an apartment on 102nd Street and Riverside Drive. One morning at breakfast, I observed the heavy traffic on West Side Drive as many thousands of commuters rushed into New York City going to their jobs on Wall Street and in the financial and media centers of the world. I began to think, "What is the connection between what they are doing and what I am studying?" This nagging concern surfaced later at Columbia University in one of the first interdisciplinary courses in the new field of biomedical ethics. The team-taught course under the auspices of the Hastings Center consisted of faculty and graduating students in the medical, law, and humanities Ph.D. programs. When I was in class with that great variety of students I was struck by their thoughtful integrity. I asked myself, "How do they have so much insight and wisdom without going through the rigorous spiritual and educational formation I have had?" This question surfaced again when I worked at the Children's Health Center on the Upper West Side, a neighborhood with the largest ethnic mix in New York. Here I wondered, "What is the connection between the lives of these people and what I am doing in theology and my sophisticated education in the humanities?"

These thoughts germinated within me, and when it came time to decide where to pursue my Ph.D. in theology I chose Union Theological Seminary because there I could combine its rich ecumenical faculty, the Jesuit faculty at Woodstock, and the urban environment of the city of New York. I knew that it was the place where I had to do my theological studies.

So in theology I spent a lot of time trying to crack the nut: How are the secular and the sacred related? What is the relation of nature and grace, the history of humankind, and the history of salvation? I also thought a lot about how religion, faith, values, spirituality, and morality connected, how they developed in persons, and their usefulness and effectiveness for people.

I did not understand it then, but these gut-level questions, these nagging concerns that vexed me in my late twenties, were provoked by my experiences. I was being provoked because something that I could not grasp had taken hold of me, had grabbed me and invited me in. William Dych, a Jesuit author, describes this experience in a powerful image. It was not like a flashlight shining on an object so that I could see it, but rather it was as if I were burning inside with a new kind of knowledge that changed my relationship to what I was seeing. As the disciples at Emmaus asked in the New Testament, "Were not our hearts burning within us as [Christ] spoke and unveiled the scriptures before us?" (Luke 24:32). Somehow I had become one with the object, but we were not identical; we were separate. I was learning something in a profound way that touched my heart as much as my mind. I was beginning to consciously experience a new knowledge, a new "way of knowing" that was different from my formal studies.

But I also realized that I felt I had to do something about it. What was there about this knowledge that called me to action? Something was compelling me to search into this further, to open myself up to these new realities, to try to understand them. I did not know how to answer these questions because I did not have the necessary background, intellectual categories, or information to think through these issues. I would need to go to school. A resolution to these concerns was going to come from joining together the questions of my experience and the inherited teachings of our religious, philosophical, and cultural traditions. I was aware that these experiences were forcing me to question things I once held with certainty. The experience focused the question, "In what way is what I am doing and studying related to what most of the people in the world are doing?" Under the tutelage of the director for my Ph.D., Dr. Roger Shinn, the Reinhold Niebuhr Professor of Social Ethics at Union Theological Seminary, I began the search.

The Need for the Values Program

The world has been profoundly changed by the terrorist attacks of September 11, 2001, and the 2003 invasion of Iraq. As the twenty-first century unfolds we face an unsettling world. Fast-paced changes have moved us quickly into a world where we are losing the ability to deal with each other as persons. We no longer foster the interconnectedness and interdependence of all persons. We are increasingly isolated by the technology that is supposed to unite us. We are becoming withdrawn and alienated. Perhaps worst of all, we risk becoming comfortable with this symptom-plagued society.

In what ways should we be preparing our youth? Decades of research have yielded an image of the college graduate as an intelligent, verbal, knowledgeable, and questioning adult. The ideal graduate is prepared to apply reason, technical knowledge, and skills to professional problems. But aren't there other important attributes that college graduates should possess? Prior to the development of the Values Program at Le Moyne College, psychologist Krystine Irene Batcho reviewed national research on this subject and remarked to me prior to the first summer Values Institute, "What remains unclear is whether the college experience yields a graduate who is sensitive to the values dimensions in problems, and perceives the values questions as at least as important as technical questions."

She had put her finger on two questions that most people were not yet asking. In the mid-1980s few people were convinced that it was legitimate or even possible to make sensitivity to the values dimension of issues a concern among students. And the second question, to give priority to the values dimension and to suggest that students ought to perceive that values questions are at least as important as technical questions, was to ask for a deep shift in priorities for most people. It was to meet the implications of these two questions that a small group of faculty colleagues embarked on what would prove to be a very difficult but also highly rewarding journey.

Today the question is reflected in books such as *The Decline of the Secular University: Why the Academy Needs Religion* (Sommerville 2006) and *Excellence Without a Soul: How a Great University Forgot Education* (Lewis 2006). The need for values education confronts not only colleges, universities, and professional schools but also the educational programs sponsored by corporations and not-for-profit institutions of all types and the advances in long-distance learning and the Internet.

As contemporary literature makes clear, universities, colleges, and professional schools are in danger of losing their voice as a prophetic moral consciousness in the community and are also in danger of selling their souls in order to maintain their institutions in the face of great fiscal challenges. Twenty-five years ago such calls were often ignored, but now those calls for some sort of appropriate resolution of the challenge are heard loud and clear. Unfortunately, I believe, there are not many manageable and effective proposals for change.

It is into this environment that I present this book. This book provides, however, not only criticism. Nor is it simply a call for deeper awareness. There are already plenty of those types of books. Instead, I present an approach to meeting this challenge, an approach tested and won through more than fifteen years of hard work.

This book is a report of a real-life experience that is grounded in quantitative as well as qualitative analysis. A full report of the analysis and the assessment is prepared, and a manuscript is awaiting to be published in a companion book by Dr. Krystine Batcho.

This chapter presents an introduction to the beginning of the Values Program. Since the beginnings of the model's story contain certain key experiences and insights into the essence of the Values Program, I will briefly recount how it came about.

There is another reason for identifying certain characteristics and insights that were developing within the institution and at the earliest beginning of the CAVE model. These traits eventually became significant, even though we did not recognize their power at the moment they were happening. As so often happens, only after we began our journey to discover and implement ways to assist students in dealing with the values and spiritual dimensions of their personal and professional lives did we recall and recognize the importance of those experiences. I encourage readers to look more closely at their own institutional environment in order to discover possible building blocks within their situation. My purpose is not to ask readers to reinvent the wheel but rather to discover what might already exist in their own institutions that can give energy to such an educational effort.

The challenge now before institutions of higher learning and the wider society is to find out "What works?" The need is for models that faculty and administrators at any institution can adapt and implement so that they might discover for themselves the best ways to do so. What is needed is a process of serious inquiry, not indoctrination.

Weaving a Durable Fabric

Family, church, school, and community have traditionally woven a durable societal fabric. That fabric has now become frayed, and the power it once had to instill and maintain the values of personal and social responsibility in people has been diminished. We know we need to strengthen this fabric, to re-create powerful connectors, but how can we reinforce the threads that bind us together?

We are confident that we have developed a proven, effective, evolving process and model of values education and spiritual development. This confidence in our model is grounded in the more than fifteen years of practical lived experience, feedback, and reflection by numerous participants and colleagues locally, nationally, and internationally. Our tested program is a model of teaching and learning that addresses the dualism of the mind and the heart and does so in a language that is accessible and effective within all the disciplines.

Our goal is to equip young men and women with the tools and the deep desire to foster the pursuit of moral inquiry and growth as a lifelong process. We wish to assist them in developing a framework of values crafted in dialogue and questioning and including elements of the best of the philosophical, religious, and cultural traditions. We also want to give them the motivation to address the moral and spiritual challenges of their professional and personal lives.

A Brief History of the Values Program

The Center for the Advancement of Values Education is confident that it has fashioned, implemented, and thoroughly assessed a process to equip people to develop a framework and the skills and motivation to respond to these problems.

The Values Program happened quite by accident, and the beginnings can be traced to a certain amount of serendipity. The impetus occurred at a conference at the University of Southern California in 1983. I happened to be seated across from David Smith, executive director of the Society for Values in Higher Education (SVHE). Six months later he called to ask if I would be interested in being part of a pioneering "values audit" project that was being initiated by SVHE. I told him it sounded like an interesting project. Accordingly, in 1984 Le Moyne joined seven educational institutions nationwide to undertake "values audits" as part of the pilot project sponsored by SVHE. Participating institutions were Susquehanna University; the University of Tennessee at Knoxville; Centre College, Kentucky; California State at Long Beach; the University of Wisconsin at Green Bay; Willamette University; Southwest Texas State; and Le Moyne.

Under the aegis of the Values Audit, the Le Moyne College Values Group began to diagnose gaps between the college's assertions and its realities. The Values Audit put difficult issues on the table in 1984–1986 such as: "The college says its mission is Jesuit and Catholic; in the college's actions, is that assertion true?" "The college says it integrates its academic affairs with its student-life activities outside the classroom; does it?"

The second impetus was the 1986 core curriculum–revision process at Le Moyne College. The *Report of the Humanities Core Committee* stressed that one of the essential features of the revised core should be the constant encouraging of students to explore the connections that courses have with each other and with life outside academics. It further emphasized that core courses are intended to be instrumental in helping students to shape their attitudes and values (Le Moyne College, 1–3).

The Values Audit and the core curriculum–revision process cleared the air, allowing faculty members to put forward tough questions, which could be discussed without rancor or personal conflict. People who had retreated into their closed offices began to come out; new life percolated throughout the campus. We discussed issues that are today at the heart of the controversies within all education: the vocationalism and insularity of students, issues of mission and identity (Steinfels 2004), social responsibility (Colby et al. 2003), and connections between what one learns and one's personal and professional lives (Putnam 2001). The audit's process and methodology gave us hope.

Student Vocationalism

Students at Le Moyne, presumably like students everywhere, possess a strong career drive, which translates into an overwhelming desire to become certified for a particular career, get a job, and make money. In 1980, freshmen at the college admitted with some embarrassment that they attended college in order to "make as much money as possible." By 1987 the embarrassment was gone, and they were proud to give this reply. This type of thinking became only more prevalent in the ensuing boom years of the 1990s. Educators at Le Moyne realized that they had to engage students in issues and skills beyond concerns of becoming certified, getting a job, and making money. They began to see afresh that students have difficulty making connections between what they learn in college and their lives after college. The challenge was to discover how educators could awaken career-oriented students to the full potential of a liberal arts education and thus revitalize their commitment to social responsibility.

Two issues related specifically to students will illustrate the magnitude of the challenge that we faced. First, how do you get them interested and engaged in issues and skills beyond getting a job? How do you get a twenty year old to commit to acquiring the skills and frameworks for which she may not explicitly feel the need for at least twenty years? This task was made difficult because students would hear their professors say, "Put your effort into your bread-and-butter courses such as accounting and finance. The others are not important." Second, students see no need to make connections between their courses and their personal and professional lives. The midlife crises are a long way off.

A number of important seeds were planted in these early days that later blossomed into key characteristics of the Values Program. First, the Values Audit demonstrated that it was possible to engage the wider community of faculty, staff, and administration in common concerns such as mission, education of the whole person, and governance. It can be done in a credible and trusting manner. Second, the core-curriculum revision highlighted the necessity of exploring the connections between inside and outside the classroom and also the notion of core courses being "instrumental in helping students to shape their attitudes and values." Third, this experience gave us an insight that the language of "values" could be an accessible and effective instrument for dialogue among diverse groups. Finally, because nearly every significant item recommended by the audit was put into place, we learned that change was possible.

The Working Group on Values

What happened next was also serendipitous. In an offhand comment, the director of alumni relations asked me if I would be interested in applying for a small seed grant to examine some of the issues raised by the Values Audit and curriculum reform; I agreed.

This five thousand–dollar grant from the Raskob Foundation provided funds for the working group to create a seminar designed to help students integrate their professional interests with the college's liberal arts and religious tradition. Discussions about what this seminar ought to do led into the Values Program.

During 1985–1986, six faculty and one administrator at Le Moyne College met to create a senior seminar that would help students integrate the liberal arts and the Jesuit emphasis on socially responsible values into their major disciplinary field. I organized the group, whose other members were William R. Barnett, also of religious studies; Mary Ann Donnelly, business administration; Edward J. Gorman, director of admissions; John W. Langdon, history; Bruce M. Shefrin, political science; and Krystine Batcho, psychology.

Background and Inspiration

Through the fall of 1985 and the spring of 1986, this group met every two weeks to discuss the ways and means by which college students could be alerted to the values-laden components and consequences of their actions. *Habits of the Heart,* a 1985 best-seller by Robert N. Bellah and others, provided a set of perspectives critical of the self-centered individualism that characterizes much of current American life. This work and other readings provided the background and inspiration as we began to discuss possible courses of action.

By the spring of 1986, the group became convinced that a capstone seminar to help students integrate their professional interests with the college's liberal arts and religious traditions was not going to be enough. A more substantial change was needed. Attempts to address the need for values education would be ineffective if they consisted of isolated courses or programs. Instead, we needed to involve the entire community in an experience that would enable students to integrate their learning and values.

As we understood the problem, it became clearer that the symptoms of vocationalism that bothered us among our students were not confined to our particular group of students or only certain majors; instead, it was a societal problem at the core of American culture.

A Critical Turning Point

Thomas Curley, a professor in the Philosophy Department, provided the necessary spark when he said, "Even though others have tried and failed, we must do something. We have these students here, and it is our responsibility." This instant was perhaps the most critical moment in the early process. We committed ourselves to a process of dialogue and discovery. Not only did we arrive at a consensus, but we would actually create, implement, follow through, and assess a program that would begin to resolve the issue.

During the spring of 1986 the Working Group on Values began to dream an ambitious dream: to have a major impact on values education and development at Le Moyne College and beyond. Could it transform the culture of the college? Could it weave a new fabric? How could that ambition be accomplished? The Working Group did not know but committed itself to a process of discussion and discovery. This process was challenging and fruitful. As Parker J. Palmer wrote in 1990, the people at Le Moyne "are willing to walk into their fears for the sake of a more humane vision. . . . [T]he result is an increase of vitality, humanity, community, and a sense of purpose on the Le Moyne College Campus" (vii).

For the next two years we struggled with what ought to be in our plan, how we ought to express it, what our goals and objectives should be, how we would organize it, how we would fund it, and how we would attract others to the project. After the first year we knew what we did not want to do, but we did not know what to do. So we got a second grant, this one for ten thousand dollars, and committed ourselves to finding a solution.

An example of a critical problem was determining how we could introduce this issue to the disruptive faculty in such a way that they would not break and run. I had learned as a Jesuit that my mission as a Jesuit and the Jesuits' corporate apostolate is not necessarily shared by the faculty, nor should it be. I had to let go of my suppositions and listen to and cooperate with my faculty colleagues.

At first we struggled with whether the need should be framed in a Jesuit, Catholic framework. After many days of discussion we rejected this idea because we knew the faculty would reject this approach. What kind of language did we need to use to get at this problem? The term *values* was the best entry point because people were more open to it and it did not turn people off.

We had begun to plan the foundation of what would become the Values Program but still did not know what the plan would look like. In the summer of 1986, we employed two grant writers and set about applying for funding for a project that would consist of a "summer institute" for faculty on a values-laden theme, to be followed by an "academic forum" that would involve the entire campus in values exploration throughout the year following the institute.

By the summer of 1987 funds had been secured to launch the 1988 Summer Institute on the theme "Economic Justice" and the 1989 Summer Institute on the theme "Peace and War." By 1987 the Working Group had expanded to include Thomas V. Curley, philosophy; William Miller, mathematics; and William Holmes, who assisted Krystine Batcho in the evaluation and assessment process. Undergraduate students also became involved, and several administrators facilitated the efforts of the Working Group on Values.

From the beginning, an empirical research and assessment component contributed to a deeper understanding of the moral and spiritual development in college and monitored the continuing effectiveness of the program. At critical junctures, quantitative and qualitative self-reporting and task-performance data enabled us to explore faculty and student perspectives on values and spiritual outcomes. Perceptions, attitudes, pedagogy, and abilities were investigated using social science methods and instruments developed for our purposes.

Three Questions

There are three questions that we faced early on. First, what is values education? Second, should colleges and universities be involved in values education? And third, what role do families, religious groups, and other community members play in values education? Our question has always been, "Is there such a thing as a values-free education?"

The professionalism of graduate schools makes many educators fearful of dealing with values in the classroom. They face a flurry of difficult questions: Are all positions of equal value? Should teachers admit their feelings or beliefs about an issue to students? Should teachers respond differently according to whether their students are predominately Catholic, Jewish, Protestant, or Muslim?

Many of those individuals involved in education wonder whether members of college or university communities should accept the responsibility of promoting values. This question points to the fear that a small group or an entire college will impose its beliefs on impressionable young minds and hearts. The Working Group on Values agrees that no one person, group, or institution should impose its values on anyone. But strong value positions are already being subtly communicated to students and parents by the courses, professors, sports programs and dormitory lifestyles available, requirements demanded, and rewards and promotions offered. By ignoring the fact that, however indirectly, all institutions and systems already impose their values, one risks fudging crucial issues.

Another question is whether values education should be the exclusive province of parents, families, and religious groups. But these institutions, which traditionally transmitted societal mores, have lost much of their influence. Although we are not denying that parents and other caretakers have responsibility, we also believe educators share that responsibility. Students are going to live and work in our colleges and universities for four years. We need to discover how best to serve those students who, during these formative years, will in any case absorb the values inherent in all colleges and universities. The Values Program seeks to increase values sensitivity, to educate students in values-related skills, and to connect what students learn during their education with how they live after graduation. As this text will illustrate, our program is different from others in that it is institution-wide, involving faculty, students, administrators, and staff—virtually every aspect of the academic community.

Inquiry, Not Indoctrination

Although some might worry that the program engages in indoctrination, it in fact initiates a process of serious inquiry. Our aim is to help students fashion frameworks of values that are consistent, defensible, and in keeping with the best of philosophical and religious traditions. The program's primary goals are to create an atmosphere that promotes the serious reflection of values issues, to encourage faculty and staff to explore the relationship between teaching methods and the development of moral sensitivity in students, and to involve students, faculty, and staff in an ongoing analysis and criticism of values.

The Three Components

Three major components constitute the program: the Working Group on Values, the Values Institute, and the Values Forum. These components work as interactive forces in an integrated, dynamic system. Each component serves a particular purpose and supports and strengthens the function of each of the other components.

▼   ▼   ▼

We are confident that we have a proven model of values development and spiritual development. We have fashioned, implemented, and assessed a process and methodology to create a college environment designed to enhance students' values, spirituality, moral sensitivity, and commitment to ethical decision making. Our goal is to equip and give people a new compass, a tool to foster the pursuit of moral inquiry and growth as a lifelong process.

As the title of Martin Luther King Jr.'s book *Why We Can't Wait* (1964) implies, the time for more talk and analysis, criticism and negativity, fear and throwing up of one's hands is over. The question raised by Krystine Batcho twenty years ago about whether the college graduate was prepared to deal with these types of issues has been answered. Dr. Batcho joined hundreds of educators and professionals to create an instrument to begin to address that concern. This book presents a model of values education and spirituality that we know works and we know is adaptable and transferable to many other institutions.

By looking at the very earliest moments of this model's birth, we can now see many of the major requirements and characteristics that were already present at least in seminal form. I present some of these qualities to you so you can begin to pick out and identify certain key threads and watch their development throughout the book. I suggest that many of these threads are the same ones you will discover in your institution.

From my perspective, these very early years uncovered certain characteristics that are necessary to meet this need. First, it is necessary to engage as many members of the community as possible in this educational effort to discover and implement ways to assist our students in this project. I believe that if there is to be an adequate model, it will work best if it finds a way to engage the entire institution in a mission of values education and spirituality. Second, the educational effort needs to be an open, free, and trusting process of discovery and serious inquiry. It cannot be a process of indoctrination. Third, a way must be found to conduct continual faculty and staff development, a way to train the trainers. Thus, a way needs to be discovered that will motivate the best of the faculty to want to begin to learn how to deal with this issue in their own personal and professional lives. It will mean learning how to bring this new awareness and consciousness into the classroom in forms of pedagogy and ways of interacting with students. Undergirding this need always is the concern of how to engage faculty, students, and staff in an ongoing dialogue about the critical moral and values issues of the time. Finally, this process will involve bringing the model outside and beyond the classroom, into the student affairs programs, residence halls, athletics, and the wider community.

That the impact of the CAVE model has expanded well beyond its initial setting should give you inspiration and courage. I suggest you take this book as a guide for your journey. Reading about it is just the beginning. My goal is to get you actually engaged in the process itself.

Distinguishing Between the CAVE
Model and Four Other Approaches

There is a plaque in a canal park alongside the Erie Canal towpath just east of Syracuse, New York. It tells in simple language the story of how a discovery and the efforts of thousands of unknown, creative, everyday folk brought off one of the engineering marvels of its time. The story has always inspired me.

> When work on the Erie Canal began in 1817, little was known about canal engineering, and construction depended on the ingenuity of many persons. Canvass B. White (1796–1834), a surveyor, greatly facilitated canal construction by perfecting hydraulic cement. White discovered in 1818, near Chittenango, a "meagre limestone" which could be used to form a mortar which hardened under water. His discovery of an abundant, easily prepared, waterproof cement immensely improved construction techniques.
>
> The Erie was a practical school for acquiring engineering knowledge. Resourceful contractors, surveyors, and local workman planned the canal through a wilderness. They drove stakes, bored holes, felled trees, pulled stumps, blasted rocks and dug in swamps. They built canal banks, tow paths, waste weirs, culverts, aqueducts, locks, hand gates.
>
> When they finished in 1825, they had constructed a 363-mile canal across the state. It was considered the foremost achievement of the time. Western New York flourished with new, cheap transportation. The canal insured the place of New York City as the nation's greatest port and city, and it hastened development of the mid-west.

During the construction of the Erie Canal engineers, craftswomen, and craftsmen experimented with different approaches along the 363-mile canal corridor. One size did not fit all. Practical and ingenious designers developed machinery and equipment, locks, and water systems interdependent and integrated into the terrain, the climate, and the purpose of that particular stretch of waterway. It reminds me of the creative and persistent individuals and groups laboring in institutions of higher education and the wider society to discover what approaches best prepare our students to meet the moral challenges of their personal and professional lives. These approaches developed day to day and institution to institution, inspired by the commitment and creative work of many people who will never receive recognition. They did it because they had an opportunity to make a difference. They did it because it needed to be done. They did it because they were fired by a vision that it was possible to change the status quo.

Before I explain the purpose of this chapter I would first like to situate it within the organization of the rest of the book. In the previous chapter I highlighted that today's graduates are in even greater need of assistance in meeting the challenges posed by the values dimensions of their personal and professional lives. I discussed how now is the time for action, not the time for more talk and more analysis. In Chapter 3, I lay the foundation for the rest of the book. I do so by recounting an experience at an annual faculty convocation assembly that symbolized the engagement of an entire institution in an educational effort that had struggled to discover and implement ways to meet those challenges of values education. I relate that moment because it functions as one of those rare moments in institutions of higher education when most of the elements that are needed in higher education seemed to come together. It is important because the project had managed to engage the majority of the faculty, administration, and staff in a demanding and challenging endeavor of values education and the beginnings of reflection on the place of the spiritual dimension in higher education. Within institutions of higher education and professional learning there are different approaches and different ways to address values and moral sensitivity among students. There is certainly more than one way to enhance students' commitment to ethical decision making.

Four Approaches

My intention in this chapter is to explore and offer a summary description of four other well-known approaches that many think address this concern: Values Clarification, Learning Communities, Service Learning, and Ethics Across the Curriculum (EAC). They are all powerful pedagogies that have been able to attract all sorts of allies.

I would like to delineate what aspects of the need are addressed effectively by these approaches. All address values education needs. There are different ways to effect different ends. But not all approaches accomplish the same aspects of the need for values. I will discuss the various approaches and delineate how they use different ways to effect different ends. Finally, I will highlight some of the distinctions between the CAVE model and the other approaches.

Values Clarification

Why do I include Values Clarification in this comparison? Didn't the Values Clarification movement reach its peak in the mid-1970s and then fade away along with the hippie and the human-potential movements? Wasn't it pushed aside by the moral majority and the religious Right? This belief is only partially true. It may be subtler, but it is nevertheless still present within our cultural life. A more concrete reason for including this approach is that people sometimes assume that Values Clarification and the Values Program are similar. They unwittingly confuse the differences and the strengths and weaknesses of these two initiatives. In actuality, however, the goals and objectives, methods, outcomes, and adaptability of Values Clarification and the Values Program have many more differences than similarities.

Like most educational change, Values Clarification came into existence to meet a particular set of needs and challenges. Once these needs are understood, Values Clarification's objectives, methods, intended outcomes, and challenges become clearer, and then I am better able to clarify how the programs differ. By the latter part of the 1950s and into the early 1960s confusion about morality and its foundations began to surface within educational institutions and individuals. They became less clear as to what is meant by morality and even more confused about where to go to find an answer to that question. The bonds once assumed within the family and religious, cultural, educational, and political institutions were beginning to fail. Religious traditions and the moral traditions resting on them no longer spoke plausibly to young people and culture in general. Many people found a more humanistic approach to be much more appealing. Institutions and other traditional modes of transmission were losing their ability to transmit values from one generation to another.

An Alternative

Values Clarification offered an attractive alternative in this time of uncertainty and confusion. Its approach was to give students the skills to become conscious of and clarify the values they held and cherished, so they would be able to provide the answers themselves. With so many voices from many sources vying to be heard, including traditional religious and cultural values, it no longer made sense to look to traditional cultural and religious values as such. Given all the uncertainty and confusion, it seemed to make more sense to place the emphasis on the process of valuing that each individual goes through to discover, explore, clarify, and become more aware of her basic values. Values Clarification sought to provide a process to give people the skills to get in touch with and become aware of, to approach seriously and justify, the values they had, and then to challenge them to cherish and act on those values (van der Ven 1998, 236).

The needs and challenges just discussed remind me somewhat of the backdrop of a conference I attended in Taiwan in 1992. Its title was "Values Education in the Classroom." The participating sponsoring countries were the Asian nations of Japan, the Philippines, Taiwan, Korea, and Malaysia. These educators faced a serious challenge as their countries rapidly moved from traditional societies to capitalistic market economies. Their question was what content, principles, rules, values, and norms should be transmitted to students in the university and K–12 classrooms. In this age of the global market economy, do you do justice to young people by passing on the traditional cultural values of their grandparents, or is it best to transmit the traditional and modern mix of their parents, or do you focus on the market-driven capitalistic individualism of contemporary society? The moral pluralism that permeated these new Asian countries reflected in some sense what was happening in the United States in the late 1960s. To whose values do we educate our young people and why? Values Clarification seemed to be a good alternative in these times of the declining influence of churches and social, political, and economic institutions. Neither religious traditions nor the moral traditions of those religions would provide the foundations for Values Clarification. Instead, it would be built on a secular foundation; its origin would be humanism, "humanistic education, the human potential movement, and humanistic psychology" (237).

Influence of Values Clarification

Why has Values Clarification continued to exert influence? As I mentioned earlier, many believe that the Values Clarification movement faded away along with the human-potential movement, humanistic psychology, and the hippie movement. The rise of the moral majority and the Christian Right and the emergence of cognitive psychology all over the world have also given rise to the perception that Values Clarification has faded away. But the lasting influence of Values Clarification in society and higher education remains. Milton Rokeach, who criticized Values Clarification for its inadequate explanation of what a value is and for its value neutrality, admitted in 1975 that the Values Clarification movement was responsible for the broadening of educational objectives to include values considerations.

Today's Culture

A powerful reason for Values Clarification's continuing influence is that it is in tune with today's cultural atmosphere. Its residue is reflected in students' resistance to anything being inculcated from the outside. In today's culture everything is meant to grow and ripen from within. Students want to decide for themselves what is good and bad, right and wrong. In the 1985 best-seller *Habits of the Heart*, Robert Bellah and his colleagues note this fact when they reflect on how people's individual contemporary ethics are reflected in the therapeutic approach. "The therapist does not transmit values and norms, but listens empathetically in order to help the client allow those values to emerge from within" (238). Our vocabulary today uses phrases such as "clarifying questions" and "the clarifying interview." We also recognize the importance of emotions. These characteristics are all part of the lasting influence of Values Clarification.

Now that we have some sense of the environment out of which Values Clarification grew, it is easier to understand the reasons behind its goals and objectives, its methods and challenges. It will also make it possible to distinguish between Values Clarification and the Values Program. One technique that often works in breaking down the meaning of a term is to begin by first defining, for example, *values* and *clarification* and then combining the two. This approach will not work in this case, however, because the advocates of Values Clarification are interested not in the term *values* as such but in *values* only inasmuch as it stands for "valuing" as a process. The terms *valuing* and *clarifying* are closely connected. In fact, *valuing* almost equals *clarifying* (240).

It may be beneficial to examine what within the framework of Values Clarification is and is not meant by values. Values does not refer to institutionalized and culturally fixed principles, rules, and norms that can be transferred from one generation to the next in the context of family, the school, or the religious community. Nor do values have an ontological, objective, or even societal status that causes them to exist autonomously and precede the individual person's choice and commitment. Values have nothing to do with one generation passing on to the next a specific moral system. Proponents of Values Clarification do not deny that such things exist, but the word *values* does not refer to this meaning in the Values Clarification framework (240–41).

Nor can a value be understood to "equal a goal or a purpose, aspiration, attitude, interest, feeling, belief or conviction, activity or worry. All these things do have aspects in common with values but are not themselves values. For instance, a goal can be merely a stated goal, not a goal one lives by or acts on, which is necessary for it to be considered a value. An aspiration is a value only when it is put into practice in daily life according to certain criteria" (241). One of the criterion that determines whether something is a value is whether it has been carefully considered.

Seven Elements

What, then, in the positive sense is a value? Louis E. Raths, Merrill Harmin, and Sidney B. Simon understand values, or rather valuing, as based on three processes: choosing, prizing, and acting (1966, 28). Under choosing there are three elements: (1) one chooses one's values freely, (2) from among alternative values, (3) after thinking over any consequences. The process of prizing consists of two elements: (1) one appreciates the choice that has been made, (2) and one is willing to affirm that choice in public. The third process, acting, contains two elements: (1) one acts on one's value choice and (2) does so repeatedly, thereby establishing a pattern. Therefore, a value is something that one freely chooses, prizes, and practices. It consists of three processes and seven elements (van der Ven 1998, 241–42).

The focus of Values Clarification is "valuing" and "clarifying," not with "values" as many understand the word. Its emphasis is primarily on the process used to clarify a student's values and in coming to understand the valuing process. Its focus is more on the process of valuing than on the actual content of the values.

Goals and Objectives

Values Clarification's goal is to encourage young people and others to become aware of their values, to give them the skills to consider and reflect on their values, and to learn tolerance of the values of others. The faculty member's responsibility is to be the facilitator of Values Clarification. As she works with students to become more aware of their own values and to tolerate and treat with respect the values of others, at no time should she attempt to directly inculcate or instill values. In addition, she is to conduct a group or classroom such that a sense of psychological safety permeates the group's atmosphere. Given the emphasis on helping young people develop their own values, the teacher needs to be careful never to impose her values on her students.

Within the culture of the 1960s and 1970s it was hoped that this process would bring more personal satisfaction and effectiveness to the student. More concretely, it was hoped that students would become less apathetic, less flighty, less overconforming, less overdissenting. In positive terms the hoped-for qualities in students were that they would be more zestful, energetic, critical in their thinking, committed, consistent, and likely to follow through with their decisions.

Four Main Ingredients

Howard Kirschenbaum describes the Values Clarification approach as it might be used in the classroom as being made up of four main ingredients. First, "a value-laden topic or moral issue is selected" (for example, family, friendship, health, work, drugs, or politics). The teacher, student counselor, club leader, or parent may select this topic. In the second main ingredient, "the teacher, counselor, or group leader introduces a question or an activity, sometimes known as a values clarification 'strategy,' to help participant(s) to think, read, write and talk about the topic." The third ingredient insists that "during the course of the activity and discussion, the group leader ensures that all views on the topic are treated with respect and that an atmosphere of psychological safety permeates" the group situation. Fourth, "the activity itself and the discussion leader encourage . . . the participants to use the seven particular 'valuing processes' or 'valuing skills' while considering the topic" (2000, 5).

Criticisms of Values Clarification

The critics of Values Clarification point out that "such education is little more than propaganda, and propaganda that does not work, because the opinions or values arrived at are will-o'-the-wisps, insubstantial, without ground in experience or passion, which are the bases of moral reasoning. . . . The new moral education has none of the genius that engenders moral instinct of second nature, the prerequisite not only of character but also of thought" (Allan Bloom cited in van der Ven 1998, 238–39). The authors of *Habits of the Heart* wrote about the dangers of stressing what they called the "therapeutic ethos" (Bellah et al. 1996), and this insight helped our founding Working Group on Values consider the contemporary celebration of the self and the growing proclivity to forget our interdependence on one another.

A criticism frequently leveled against Values Clarification is that it leads to indifference about values or to total value relativism. Adjectives used to describe the process include *superficial, relativistic, value-free,* and *devoid of any cogent theoretical base* (Kirschenbaum 1977, 7; see also Kirschenbaum 2000). Critics have recognized that if you stay within the Values Clarification framework, anything, regardless of its nature and content, can be considered a value as long as it has been chosen, cherished, and acted upon by the individual. Another question is why in reality this "values-neutral" process for achieving value clarity and consistency is not capable of producing a Hitler as well as a Gandhi. Couldn't this process be used by the good and the bad, the just and the unjust?

To these criticisms the advocates for Values Clarification respond that the process "does not propose to answer all questions of human existence, including the origin and design of the universe. It does attempt to describe a valuing process and to say that if people use the process they will experience more positive value in their living and will be more constructive in the social context" (Kirschenbaum 1977, 13). This statement raises another fundamental question. "What does it mean to experience 'more positive value' in one's living and to 'be more constructive in the social context'? What beliefs about human life and its relation to values or valuing, are implied in these statements?" (van der Ven 1998, 243).

In Values Clarification the student's task is to choose the value freely, having looked at the alternative values and thoughtfully considering the consequences. Within its framework, what does this technique tell us about the ultimate aim of Values Clarification? The influence of Carl Rogers on humanistic psychology and education is sometimes cited as the very basis of Values Clarification. When looked at from the Rogerian experiential perspective, some scholars have noted that "values become your own when they emerge from your own experience instead of being socialized from the outside and then internalized" (van der Ven 1998, 252).

Philosopher Charles Taylor positions this meaning within contemporary understanding. For him, "the source of the modern self is no longer to be found in some transcendental reality (i.e., God) or some other reality that is outside human existence (i.e., nature)," notes Joannes A. van der Ven. "Neither the nature of God nor the nature of cosmic creatures but the nature within, the human soul, is the source of the moral self," van der Ven writes of Taylor's insights. He continues, "We find truth within us, we hear our inner voice speaking, we listen to our experiences, and we take seriously what our feelings tell us about life." When we look at Values Clarification, however, "this experiencing from within as a source of the moral self takes on a specific character: it is not the content of our experiences that is important, but the fact that they are ours: coming from within, emerging from inside, that is all that counts. Not substance but emotion counts. In a way the emphasis on experience qua experience re-duces ethics to aesthetics" (1998, 253–54).

Important Strengths

There are important strengths within the Values Clarification framework. Most important is its emphasis on the need itself for clarifying values. The attention to the first mode in the process, "choosing," also makes a contribution. But its scope needs to be broadened so that the focus is not just on the individual but also on the institutional, social, and cultural values, especially in situations where they are related to one another. To bring about such an awareness and understanding of these connections is very difficult. It requires substantial help and support from the teacher and professor. It is also important to stress the notion of freedom, but this concept must also be related to the traditions and societal forces that the students have been exposed to in their lives. The student needs to learn that his or her own traditions ought to be the subject of critique and study just as much as the alternative values of others. Students need to under-stand that making choices involves serious inquiry that is a difficult and ongoing process.

If we examine a gap between the intended outcomes and the actual outcomes of Values Clarification, we recognize a weakness in the ap-proach. For example, Values Clarification advocates a valuing process by which if students follow it they will experience more positive value and effectiveness in their lives. There was something important that the approach's advocates were not able to see. The process claims to be val-ues-free and values-neutral. But critics soon began to recognize that this characterization was not an accurate description of what was happening. What the proponents of Values Clarification had difficulty seeing was that there actually was a value-laden context implicit in the Values Clarification process. This approach was taking people's fundamental values for granted. There was an assumption that there is enough basic goodness in people that their intuitive understanding and goodness of character will ultimately bring them to make the most responsible choice among the alternatives. Experience has shown most of us that it does not always work that way. The approach also finds it difficult to acknowledge that what today we would call the hidden curriculum is implicitly transmitting certain fundamental values; it is just not being acknowledged.

Shared Goals

Values Clarification shares some of the goals and objectives and some of the processes and methods of the Values Program. It does give a proper focus to the values dimension of issues and makes an important contribution by stressing that facts and skills are not the only important dimensions of an issue. Second, it makes a contribution in stressing the modes of choosing, prizing, and acting. Third, it is correct when it says the role of the teacher is to be a facilitator, not an indoctrinator. Its idea of using a value-laden issue or topic can be an effective suggestion, especially when combined with Values Clarification strategies, and the emphasis on getting the student to go through the process. As a critique I would say it ignores the social dimension of reality.

Some Distinctions Between Values Clarification
and the CAVE Model

I would like to highlight some distinctions between our model and the Values Clarification approach. The first distinction I would make pertains to comprehensiveness. The Values Clarification approach performs an important function by helping students raise their sensitivity and awareness of values issues. The insight of the Values Program, however, is that clarifying values needs to be part of a comprehensive program of values education and development. If it exists by itself, it is inadequate. The Values Program includes clarification of values, but it is part of a comprehensive system.

A second distinction concerns Values Clarification's taking people's fundamental moral foundations for granted. In doing so, it fails to acknowledge the traditional moral training that young people already have.

It is their very training in traditional values that has helped them develop their sense of right and wrong, conscience, empathy, and responsibility to a sufficient degree that Values Clarification techniques can work. A major distinction in the CAVE model is that we do acknowledge the foundational moral training that our students bring to the table. Many students have excellent backgrounds and caregivers that have worked very hard to help them grow in wisdom and humanity. The challenge is that these students do not know how to take this earlier training and make the connections and the adaptation to the major problems and dilemmas that are out there in science, technology, and the larger world.

A third distinction concerns the research and assessment mechanisms of the approaches. Values Clarification articulates its goals and objectives, but it is not always able to develop adequate instruments to measure how well the outcomes match the objectives. On the other hand, the Values Program is cited in the Middle State Accreditation Report as having "clearly defined goals and a very sophisticated approach to assessing them" (Middle States Association 1996, 18–19).

Another distinction deals with the scope of the approaches. The Values Clarification focus is on the student and classroom or group. There needs to be a greater institutional effort to connect those individuals or classrooms to the larger community. The Values Program, on the other hand, is a process that engages the community in an institution-wide educational effort to discover and implement ways to assist students in becoming more aware of values and spiritual issues, to establish frameworks to deal with those issues, and to give students the courage to act on those truths.

The most important distinction between our model and the Values Clarification approach is in the latter's relativizing approach to values and its reluctance to assist students in acquiring a clear idea of right and wrong in relationship to other approaches and traditions. Given the pluralistic nature of the Values Program's approach, it is easy to see that this same concern might arise. But in fact the Values Program "steer[s] a middle course between relativism and its usual alternative, dogmatism," according to Jack Carlson, academic vice president and dean at Le Moyne. "Key to avoiding these extremes," he noted, are "clear articulation of issues, the search for consistent frameworks, attention to the best in human traditions, and openness to new evidence as well as to the insights and arguments of others. As long as they embody these traits, the Values Program encourages a deep respect for the opinions and perspectives of all—students, faculty and staff, and on-campus visitors. Such respect is quite compatible with commitment to one's own views" (1991, 13).

Even though the Values Program, according to Carlson, "does try to help students achieve a clear idea of right and wrong," he is quick to point out, however, that such clarity—especially regarding concrete issue—does not come without cost. "Moreover, since the contours of values issues change with changing circumstances (e.g., recent developments in biotechnology), the search for clarity must be ongoing" (13).

The Values Program recognizes that our students and faculty come to us already deeply formed in their values and traditions. We acknowledge and respect who they are and what they bring with them. The Values Program builds explicitly on the background of our students.

What is needed is not so much a program that "teaches" values (in the sense of inculcating a particular set of moral views). As Jack Carlson, who is both a college administrator and a philosopher, recognizes, it must include a comprehensive effort that effectively works to enliven in students an awareness of values questions, the ability to deal critically with such questions, and the courage to act on judgments made. Both in the classroom and outside the classroom teachers and the institution need to bring a variety of resources to bear on the values questions being studied. Students and faculty need to examine these issues from a variety of perspectives, but in the end students, whether they are Jews, Protestants, Catholics, Muslims, or nonbelievers, must "own" their moral views; they must prepare to participate in a modern pluralistic society.

Learning Communities

Learning Communities have a particular focus: create community and bring about an enriched curricular experience.[1] Often the interdisciplinary

---

1. My intention is not to give a literature review with major references for these approaches and others, as doing so is beyond the scope of this work. These references can easily be found, and periodicals such as *Change* and *About Campus* are ready resources. A

aspects add a new dimension to what students and faculty are doing. Even though Learning Communities are present in more than five hundred institutions, it is possible to give a general definition of what the term *Learning Community* refers to:

> [It is] the purposeful restructuring of the curriculum by linking or clustering courses that enroll a common cohort of students. Learning communities are a variety of curricular approaches that intentionally link or cluster two or more courses, often around an interdisciplinary theme or problem, and enroll a common cohort of students. This represents an intentional restructuring of students' time, credit and learning experiences to build community, enhance learning, and foster connections among students, faculty and disciplines. At their best, learning communities practice pedagogies of active engagement and reflection. On residential campuses, many learning communities are also living-learning communities, restructuring the residential environment to build community and integrate academic work with out-of-class experiences. (Smith et al. 2004, 58)

Goals and Objectives

The goals and objectives of Learning Communities in their essence are to form communities by attempting "to create curricular coherence and connections among courses and ideas, and to teach skills in meaningful contexts." It is hoped that the more students are together and the more classes they take together that they can create both academic and social connections so that they become "both autonomous and independent learners" (68).

The literature shows that the goals and aims that can be realized from Learning Communities are diverse indeed (70; see fig. 3.1). Multiple

---

good place to start for general information on the Learning Communities is http://learningcommons.evergreen.edu. Other good sources are "Realizing the Potential of Learning Communities," a keynote address delivered by Barbara L. Smith, codirector at the Evergreen Learning Communities Dissemination Project, Evergreen State College, March 1, 2002, available on the Internet. See also "The Challenge of Learning Communities as a Growing National Movement," pts. 1 and 2, *Peer Review* 3, no. 4 (Summer 2001); 4, no. 1 (Fall 2001). Other sources can be found in this work's bibliography.

layers of Learning Community outcomes are being considered, articulated, and assessed by the creators of Learning Communities. Students, professors, and institutions can all realize goals from the Learning Community experience.

Learning Communities came into being because of a variety of practical, bread-and-butter challenges such as student retention, incoherence within the curriculum, the loss of faculty vitality, and the need for building a greater sense of community within our colleges and universities. The rallying themes around which Learning Communities have evolved are democracy, access, and classrooms as community. Like the classic American artists and musicians, these themes speak to the American ethos. Learning Communities' existence is partially a response to the question, "What role should schools play in preparing for responsible citizenship?" Always looming in the background is the question, "Education for what?" Given this historical context, Learning Communities are an effort to develop students' capacity to make both academic and social connections and to create an intensified learning environment and an academically and socially reinforcing experience.

Method and Process

What is the method or process of Learning Communities? At their best they promote pedagogies of active engagement and reflection. They do so by a purposeful restructuring of the curriculum, usually by linking or clustering courses that enroll a common cohort of students. There are three general structural frameworks followed in the creation of Learning Communities. From among the many different varieties of Learning Communities, there are numerous specific examples of how these frameworks have been adapted on a variety of campuses. There are also a "number of similar broad intentions and goals that recur in all learning communities" (70). The variable in these three basic structures is the degree to which the Learning Community teaching teams work to foster connections between or among their courses.

The first type of Learning Communities include courses that are unmodified. It is the simplest type of Learning Community and often involves students in two or three standing courses that are taught autonomously without any modification. A small group of students (generally ten to thirty) enrolls as a cohort with two or three of the classes taught by faculty members who do not modify their teaching or syllabi. However, this sub-group of students is also enrolled in an additional course as a self-contained group, and it is within this important additional course that the community building and connection making can occur. This type of Learning Community structure has two major adaptations: the freshman seminar or interest-group Learning Community and the community with an integrative seminar or colloquy.

The second type is called "linked or clustered courses." This structural format involves the effort to link explicitly two or more courses. At the same time, the teachers collaborate with each other. Classes linked are usually an introductory skill-building class and a content-heavy class (for example, a student's major introductory course, minor, or general education course). Three or four classes offered as Learning Communities are called a cluster. Most Learning Communities will try to create a pure cohort of students who form the entire enrollment of the two or three courses. For these courses the class size is twenty to thirty-five students. This pure cohort of students is an advantage in two ways: the students and their faculty become a community of learners having a common experience, and everyone is taking both (or all three) classes, so intellectual connections can be drawn and integrative assignments created.

Some Learning Communities are also living-learning communities, restructuring the residential environment to build community and integrate academic work with out-of-class experiences. Most frequently, the additional course in this type of framework is a freshman year–experience course. Key to this structure are the connections, social and curricular, both for students and for teachers. The advantages of this system are, first, that students have a common experience and become a community of learners and, second, since the same students are in both (or all three) classes, there are more intellectual connections because integrative assignments may be created. The disadvantages are that a pure cohort is an ideal, but frequently Learning Community students are put in with regular students for scheduling purposes. Also, if there are two to three faculty members involved, it is often difficult for them to meet and overcome severe scheduling difficulties.

The third type of Learning Communities is called "team-taught communities." These programs bring together the equivalent of two, three, or even four classes that faculty members adapt to create a common syllabus around integrating themes or projects. Interdisciplinary questions and problems, some timeless and others contemporary, animate these Learning Communities. Thus for the students, what is at the forefront is often not the English composition and the European history course they are taking, but rather the program's theme (for example, "The Fall of Empires," chap. 3).

Challenges

As mentioned above, pure cohorts are the ideal, but frequently non-Learning Community students are put into the classes for scheduling reasons. This dilution of the Learning Community can risk lowering the bar for faculty members on taking seriously and fully the Learning Community intentions of community building and curriculum integration for all. If these practices become regular, broken cohorts inevitably lead to reductions of quality. In some institutions only a handful of students are coregistered in both classes of the Learning Community, thereby creating no incentive for faculty members to make any linkages at all. Learning Communities recommend that planners and teachers be sensitive to the implications of broken cohorts, to avoid them if possible, and to agree to let in non-Learning Community students only in special situations.

When non-Learning Community students are put into the class, or there are few Learning Community students in a class, the faculty have little incentive to make the connections and integration. Most of the linked cluster courses involve two or three classes and therefore two or three faculty members. Although many campuses put together communities of four or even five classes in a semester-long, full-time package of credit, planners for these more ambitious constellations often face daunting enrollment and scheduling problems. When four or five faculty are involved it is difficult to schedule time for them to communicate. Also, some students like to have the opportunity to mingle with different students and environments outside the small Learning Community group.

Distinctions Between Learning Communities
and the CAVE Model

If I use the rationale behind setting up a freshman Learning Community for science majors, for example, I may be able to communicate a distinction between the approaches of the Values Program and Learning Communities. A reason Learning Communities would establish a community for freshman in science is that science majors often learn better in a group with different perspectives. The Learning Community breaks down barriers so you not only think as a chemist but also learn to understand how a biologist or a physicist thinks. This kind of skills-based community has its purpose, place, and value. All sorts of honors programs, junior year–abroad efforts, groups, and clusters of majors gather together to enrich students' knowledge and skills. The result in each case may be community, but you have arrived there from different directions.

The important difference between the Values Program and Learning Communities in regard to these same science majors lies in the purpose for which the teaching faculty work to foster connections. Both groups are concerned with fostering the social connections necessary for learning, but with the Values Program the goal is to facilitate students in learning to connect their thought and their action within a whole new horizon. Can students develop the sensitivity to see value priorities and to sense the importance of making ethical decisions? Can they develop the ability to make ethical decisions?

Barbara Smith and her colleagues (2004) point to an important critique of Learning Communities when they discuss "linked or clustered courses." They say that if no intentional effort is made to foster community (through a residential, living-learning community, for example) or to take advantage of the curricular connections that the related courses invite, the learning and the community often remain in the shallows. Therefore, campuses offering these types of programs need to invest resources in creating both time and faculty-development support for teachers to engage in collaborative course planning, to take greater advantage of the obvious opportunities already in place with block-scheduled students.

An important distinction between Learning Communities and the Values Program is the expectation of who will participate in faculty development and why. Think of this situation: Students who have had good experiences in Learning Communities can find themselves literally trapped in classes where the faculty are not prepared to handle what these students need. Because of the very nature of the Learning Community and how it is structured, students have an experience of community that many of their regular faculty often have not experienced. "Training the trainers" is an intrinsic part of the Values Program. Our supposition is that every professor and person must have struggled with the values dimension of issues in their own personal and professional lives before they can guide the decision-making process for students. In our Summer Institutes faculty experience once again what it means to be a student as they learn from and with their faculty colleagues. Because they themselves have had the experience of learning within the context of creating a community in the summer seminar, they are better able to transmit their experience to their students.

The Learning Communities' central intention is "the building of community." These specific communities and structures enhance students' knowledge and skills by having them interact with the knowledge and skills of others. Other skills such as "communication," "learning," and "fostering connections" are to follow because one is participating in the community. This issue points to another major distinction between the approaches: the Values Program's central intention is to discover how best to assist the student in learning the values dimensions as well as the technical dimensions; this learning process brings the person into real communication and struggle with others, and out of this encounter will eventually come real community.

Service Learning

Service Learning is a widespread, diversified movement of more than five hundred colleges and universities of all types initiated in the mid-1980s. It can be defined in various nuanced ways. A helpful definition of Service Learning is "a method under which students learn and develop through thoughtfully organized service that: is conducted in and meets the needs of a community and is coordinated with an institution of higher education, and with the community; helps foster civic responsibility; is integrated into and enhances the academic curriculum of the students enrolled; and includes structured time for students to reflect on the service experience" (American Association for Higher Education 1993, 15).

An example of an important vehicle for research and dissemination for Service Learning is Campus Compact, a "top-down" effort created by three university presidents from Brown, Georgetown, and Stanford in response to the recognition that many students desired to serve their larger communities. The goal of strengthening the role of higher-education institutions in fostering responsible citizens also motivated these university presidents.

Service Learning touches on many of the issues surrounding the discussions and research on learning versus teaching, especially how we learn and where we learn. Campus Compact and similar movements recognize the need to broaden our understanding of learning to include the experiences of students who learn by engaging in service. By acknowledging that the formal classroom is not the only place where education takes place, Service Learning raises the question of whether learning takes place primarily in the classroom or both in and outside the classroom. It also raises the question of what kind of learning takes place and by and for whom.[2]

A Top-Down Program

The Campus Compact approach is an example of a successful movement, mandated and initiated from the top down. It has been able to gather support among other presidents and boards. In addition to acknowledging the generosity of students and highlighting the fact that higher-education institutions have a responsibility as community members, it also raises issues about the students' and faculty's relationship to the community and

---

2. There is a great amount of literature on Service Learning. Resources can be accessed through Campus Compact. Especially helpful is Edward Zlotkowski, "Mapping New Terrain: Service Learning Across the Disciplines," *Change* (January–February 2001): 25–33. The article gives an overview of the American Association for Higher Education series edited by Zlotkowski, Service Learning in the Disciplines, 18 vols. (Washington, D.C.: American Association for Higher Education, 1997–2000).

to the people in the community. Most educators are careful to avoid any semblance of using the community and its needs as a tool for providing young people from more prosperous neighborhoods with another item to put on their résumés.

It is interesting to note that in 1994 Krystine Batcho and I were invited to Georgetown University to give a daylong workshop on the Values Program and its possible relationship to Service Learning. For the next year's conference, the organizers invited Professor Batcho to give the keynote address at the Georgetown conference. These invitations indicated to me even then that significant, well-administered approaches were beginning to ask if the concerns of values education were adequately integrated into Service Learning.[3]

Goals and Objectives

The goals of Service Learning, when it is functioning well, are to improve student learning, to address community needs, to facilitate public debate and dialogue, and to create campuses that are true partners with their communities. With funding from the Pew Charitable Trusts and other foundations, Campus Compact's goal is to engage students so that they will become educated and responsible citizens in democracy.

It is important to understand that Service Learning is not just community service. Service Learning differs from community service because it is both intentional and situated learning. The service experience is intentionally incorporated into a course, into traditional papers, exams, and other forms of pedagogy within the course. One of the vehicles for

3. For more information, please see Richard Devine, Joseph A. Favazza, and F. Michael McLain, eds., *From Cloister to Commons: Concepts and Models for Service Learning in Religious Studies,* Service Learning in the Disciplines (Washington, D.C.: American Association for Higher Education, 2002). (This volume is published in cooperation with the Wabash Center for Teaching and Learning in Theology and Religion.) Other books include Janet Eyler and Dwight E. Giles Jr., *Where's the Learning in Service Learning?* Higher and Adult Education Series (San Francisco: Jossey-Bass, 1999); Barbara Jacoby et al., *Service Learning in Higher Education: Concepts and Practices,* Higher and Adult Education Series (San Francisco: Jossey-Bass, 1996); and James Youniss and Miranda Yates, *Community Service and Social Responsibility in Youth* (Chicago: Univ. of Chicago Press, 1997).

learning is that the course is community based, that is, the learning space is situated in the community. On the institutional level these institutions are very concerned about addressing the role of institutions of higher education as responsible citizens and creating campuses that are true partners with their communities. One way to accomplish this goal is to facilitate public debate. On the wider level it is hoped that doing so will begin to address the larger community needs.

Challenges

Service Learning shares some of the same challenges faced by other approaches. One challenge relates to how accessible and available are the courses in which Service Learning is an option. Institutions of higher learning can provide only a limited number of courses with the Service Learning component. This limited availability obviously means a certain proportion of the students on a campus do not have access to Service Learning. Also, overloaded student, faculty, and staff schedules put great stress on all educators today. This pressure makes incorporating Service Learning especially challenging. Some students and faculty very much want to be involved in Service Learning, but when they discover it to be time-consuming, difficult to schedule, and applicable to only one or two of their courses, they are sometimes required to reexamine their priorities. The issue of support and time for faculty development and community mentor training is also a major challenge. In a 2003 presentation at Cornell University, Edward Zlotkowski noted that the number-one predicator of success for a Service Learning initiative or for any learning initiative is that the faculty need to know that they will be successful (Zlotkowski 2003a).[4] Failure is their greatest fear. The reward structure in the academic institution for faculty promotion and advancement, which is usually tied to the salary structure, needs to include a faculty member's efforts in Service Learning. If it does not, it will be very difficult to attract the best of the faculty. Other challenges include how the faculty and the students learn to transfer their insights from the service component to the rest of the

4. I am grateful to Ed Zlotkowski for many ideas and clarity on the issues in a phone conversation on May 1, 2003.

class content. How do you make the experience relevant to the student? Finally, when you involve the student in grassroots community issues, there is always the question of intellectual honesty and public-policy perspectives on the issues. Finding the time and energy to assist students in integrating and getting critical perspective on their experiences can be very challenging.

An example from the Values Program is the Town Meetings, created under the Values Forum (or the Academic Forum) of the Values Program. These meetings enable both intellectual honesty and policy perspectives. They also become vehicles for showing that the community's goals are just as important to the college as classroom goals.

Differences Between Service Learning and the Values Program

The core learning objective in Service Learning is not charity or philanthropy but citizenship. Edward Zlotkowski in his workshop "Integrating Service with Learning" at Cornell University explained that Service Learning's main ethos is to develop citizens who are responsible in and through their skills. He pinpointed that ethos by explaining that "students no longer conceive of themselves as knowledge consumers (banking education) but rather as knowledge producers" (2003a, n.p.). He gave as an example a group of students in an English literature course who became involved in a service project. During the course they took on the process of writing grants to fund the project in the community they were serving. Thus, their knowledge led to action.

This illustration is a good example of how both the Service Learning and the Values Program approaches can sometimes share the same goal and use some of the same methods. One of the Values Program's main objectives is to "enhance students' courage to act on what they see to be true." In certain contexts this mission could be the same as saying that students become "responsible citizens in and through their skills."

Many of the important concerns expressed by Edward Zlotkowski are not unique to any of the approaches that are available. At one time or another my colleagues and I have struggled with the same challenges. I know that Learning Communities and Ethics Across the Curriculum ask the same questions. I point this reality out to highlight the fact that even though approaches might share the same techniques and methods, they are not necessarily accomplishing the same objectives. For example, I am a member of the Association for Practical and Professional Ethics. When we directors of centers meet at a colloquium designed to address our special concerns, we find that we share many of the same challenges:

- How do we keep the focus on the common good of the community?
- How are we training students to help with reflection?
- How do we empower students?
- What do we do about site supervision?
- Who are the student leaders on campus? Which of them ought we to tap?
- How do we engage the administration in the center's concerns?
- Will this impact promotion and reward issues?
- How do you get the faculty involved?
- What do you need to do to keep them involved?
- How do you adjust the demands of the teaching load, the necessity for scholarship, and tenure and promotion issues?

When evaluating the various approaches it is critical to recall that some approaches share the goals of values education and differ in their methods. In the case of Service Learning I think they share many of the methods that we use in values education but only some of our goals. For example, in Service Learning it could happen that for many students the concrete experience they get from community service is the experience of being in the community. These experiences often give rise to reflective observations within the students, and once they do, reflection is hard to control. One challenge faced by this approach is that it is sometimes very difficult for educators to get a chance to raise public-policy issues. Frequently, there is little or no time for active experimentation with public policy and alternatives.

No Explicit Attention to Values

By definition the experiential learning strategy of Service Learning does not necessitate an explicit attention and awareness to the values dimension of issues. In fact, I suspect many public and private colleges and universities in the current situation might be reluctant to touch the values dimension given all the various values in the community. The aim of the Service Learning approach is to add an experiential component to learning by bringing campuses of higher education into partnership with the community. It seeks to develop students into responsible citizens, but what ensures that this service assists the student in developing a moral awareness and moral framework? It may or may not. In many courses and programs this development of a moral awareness is not intentional to the program of Service Learning. Service Learning skirts the issue but does not address it. The program does not include an explicit moral-values purpose. One of the fears may be that in a multiethnic community, doing so could cause difficulties.

Transforming the Teacher-Student Relationship

To distinguish an initiative such as Campus Compact and the Values Program, I will use an example. Its point is to illustrate how when a faculty member becomes committed to the legitimacy and necessity of values education and decides to join the discovery process with her students, it will transform the faculty-student relationship. If I am an instructor in a government course, I can teach you about the structure of government. But when the class evolves to the question of, "What is the best form of government?" then the discussion moves into another realm. Now the students and I have a values decision to make. I can take the opportunity to make clear to the students that we are now dealing with another realm of issues that are values questions; for the class, a response will depend on where it wants to go as it defines its government. Then I can discuss various questions such as, "Where do you want to go with your government?" and can discuss the pros and cons of various forms of government. I too now face a values question. Even with my long years of expertise, I am now just another individual making a values decision about what is the best form of government.

When we assist students in values development, it raises new questions about the traditional teacher-student role. In many courses a teacher is seen primarily as one who imparts information and skills. If I as a faculty member trying to tell you what values are appropriate and what is the moral thing to do in a given situation because these issues are important moral dimensions, then I do not understand that values cannot be taught. The word *teach* is defined as "to impart knowledge or skill to somebody by instruction or example, or to bring understanding to somebody, especially through an experience." A teacher's role is to impart information. Once you transfer into the values dimension, you become a guide, a facilitator. I cannot build your moral framework for you. I can only help you go through the issues and dimensions that it takes to build one.

I will apply what I have just said to this example. In my class I have two groups of students who, using Ed Zlotkowski's words from his work on Service Learning, are moving from being "knowledge consumers" to "knowledge producers." I ask the students to imagine that they are instructed to form two groups. One study group imagines that it is now at the place where it can put its energy and expertise into creating weapons and bombs. The other imagines it can put its energy and expertise to work on medical problems, such as a cure for a major disease like AIDS. What is the difference between these two groups of students? They are both producers. I then engage them in the discussion and ask what their products are good for. They have consumed the knowledge and now are using the knowledge, but we are not yet into the values dimension of the issue. We sometimes assume that certain actions, such as Service Learning, can lead to the building of a more strengthened moral framework. An action in and of itself does not do anything. What is crucial is what the individual does with knowledge. You have to address that point explicitly. Once the teacher says, "What should we do with our knowledge?" we have begun to enter the values dimension. Faculty need to learn and understand the connections between their pedagogy and the development of moral sensitivity and priorities within their students. A Ph.D. does not usually teach graduate students how to do so.

Another distinction between these approaches is in the number and percentage of an institution's students who are reached by the approach. In Service Learning the students impacted must be in a course with a Service Learning component. The Values Program approach is that its goal is to reach *all* students and not just the elite few. The Values Program, by contrast, becomes intrinsic to every course, as every faculty member becomes a values educator. It is important to note that the Values Program is not a component to a course; instead, it is a transformative element in that course. Also, values concerns become catalysts for discussion both inside and beyond the classroom. And the faculty has gone through the process themselves of learning how to develop a values framework before they attempt to guide the students through this process.

The Values Program addresses the values dimension explicitly and develops methods to learn how to do so better and continually. Some Service Learning professors and courses may do this work some of the time, but the CAVE model's process calls for this dimension to be present in all elements of the course. Our goal is to raise students' awareness of the fact that they are making values judgments in everything they do. Our goal is to illuminate this process and bring it to the students' conscious awareness. Then we seek to give the students the tools with which to work, to form their own judgments. We have discovered that students learn to make values decisions by practicing. It is not exactly like practicing a golf swing or putting, however. For most people, practice in golf is related to the fact that one wants to improve one's score. In values education there is no score to keep. The entire effort is grounded in the belief that the person has to learn by practice to continually readjust all the factors to learn and do what is most fitting in a particular situation. As in learning golf, you learn only when you swing the club. Our program teaches students these skills and motivates them to use their skills.

Faculty development is critical in our program, as it is in Service Learning. If critical values issues are being raised by the experience of the students, it is necessary that the faculty and staff are trained to deal with those concerns. Would you want to be on a baseball team where the coaches have never played baseball? You want to be on a team where coaches know how the game is played because they have played it before.

Why is it that when people talk about politics they get such strong feelings? When people argue about politics, they become fully, totally, and emotionally immersed. In the Values Program that reality needs to be focused on and not allowed to run loose. Students need to realize that the reason for their emotions is that these convictions are coming from deep within themselves. Is that where you want it to be coming from? Do you want your values to reflect only a gut-level feeling, or do you want to be able to articulate the method you used to come to your beliefs? Do you reflect only your upbringing or your peers' opinions? Or do you want to develop the skills to create your own values?

The goal of the Values Program is to create an environment in which students feel the freedom to experiment with deeply felt opinions and ideas. In the Values Program, we create a space where students will not to be mocked or criticized. We create a reasonably trusting environment where they can try to grow. This trusting environment is needed for any personal development.

Ethics Across the Curriculum

Since many colleges and universities use the Ethics Across the Curriculum approach for values and ethical education, it is important to discuss it here. Ethics Across the Curriculum can be defined as a wide-ranging effort to bring together scholars who focus on ethics, both practical and theoretical, to encourage the teaching of ethics, and to bring about an exchange of information about teaching ethics across the disciplines.

I will use the EAC approach at Utah Valley State College (UVSC) as my primary example. In terms of its goals and methods it seems to most resemble the Values Program. My hope is that by comparing these two seemingly similar programs, the unique aspects and distinctive characteristics of the CAVE process become clear.

I will first clarify the EAC goals and objectives. Its primary purposes are to promote and instill ethical thinking and decision making within students. This program renews and reenergizes the faculty as scholars and teachers by establishing a faculty-development program centered on the shared study of ethics. It creates an atmosphere of openness and impartiality by providing a college or university forum for discussing a variety of ethical issues. The goal of this program is to lead participants to the ability to evaluate the complex moral problems facing society and to respond to these problems in light of alternative approaches begging for a hearing.

The EAC effort began at UVSC in the mid-1980s with the objective of bringing an ethics component to the curriculum. Adding a core course, Ethics and Values, accomplished this goal, and this new interdisciplinary humanities course was required of every student for the associate in arts and associate in science degrees. In 1986 UVSC received a three-year National Endowment for the Humanities (NEH) grant to implement this course.

Five years later, in 1993, Utah Valley State College's commitment expanded into a schoolwide project titled Ethics Across the Curriculum. It was funded by a grant from the Fund for the Improvement of Postsecondary Education, a scholarly agency in the U.S. Department of Education. In 1996 Utah Valley State's reach extended into the wider community when it was awarded funding from the NEH for a community project titled Teaching Critical Thinking in Ethics, K–12. The Utah Valley State program has received national awards for teacher development (Hesburgh Award) and for outstanding curricular development (American Council of Colleges, 2001).

The EAC goals and objectives include a strong student orientation. Like the Values Program, Ethics Across the Curriculum believes that ethics is a dimension of academic inquiry rather than an isolated philosophical discipline. The EAC program explains what it means to promote and instill ethical thinking and decision making, that is, the abilities to accomplish the following:

- recognize ethical issues
- develop critical thinking and self-confrontation skills
- cultivate tolerance toward disagreement and the inevitable ambiguities in dealing with ethical problems
- elicit a sense of moral obligation and develop a personal code of ethics

The faculty objectives include the following goals:

- Integrate the subject of ethics into vocational, technical, nursing, business, and liberal education courses
- Challenge students to understand the basic principles of ethics, to think and write critically, and to confront inconsistencies in their own ethics and values systems
- Establish a faculty-renewal program through shared study of ethics, so the faculty may reenergize as scholars as well as teachers

Beginning in 1990 the goals and objectives of Utah Valley State's EAC approach expanded beyond the classroom into the college community and the wider community. The vehicle for doing so was the Center for the Study of Ethics. The center is an academic organization that seeks to provide a forum for discussion of a variety of ethical issues within an atmosphere of openness and impartiality. Its inspiration is the Jeffersonian ideal that democracy requires "educated citizens." The center brings together diverse voices for what it hopes will be thoughtful and productive dialogue designed to evaluate the complex moral problems facing society. The center also encourages response to these problems in light of alternative approaches.

Among the methods used by Utah Valley State's EAC, beginning in 1993, two that are important for our purposes are the summer institute for faculty and the required ethics course across the curriculum. One of the objectives of the EAC at Utah was to reenergize the faculty as scholars as well as teachers. The method that EAC used to accomplish this goal was a faculty institute conducted in the summer or at the semester break. Here faculty came together for a period of somewhere between two and five days to undertake a shared study of ethics. Utah Valley State College institute leaders have included Robert Solomon, Martha Nussbaum, James Sterba, and Janet Kourany. Faculty are paid a stipend for participation in the summer seminars, and books and other materials are provided. Now that the original grant monies from federal agencies have expired, the UVSC administration supports the continuation of the program.

In many ways the EAC at UVSC has evolved in a direction very similar to the one established by the Values Program, even to the extent of our Center for the Advancement of Values Education. Over the past fifteen years, the EAC program at Utah Valley State has evolved from a collegewide course in values and ethics to Ethics Across the Curriculum, offering a series of discipline-specific courses in ethics. The program has also created the Center for the Study of Ethics to organize events, including conferences, symposia, guest lectures, radio programs, and faculty seminars.

I would like to mention two areas where I think the CAVE model can be distinguished from this EAC model. First, "a critical discovery for us has been the value of a common ground of experience and base of knowledge" (Kirby 1998, 21). In our model the instrument for accomplishing this goal is an institution-wide annual theme that connects the three components of the CAVE model. Anyone who works in education has felt the burden of this deficiency among our students. "The college wide theme presents the content as a bridge between student affairs and academic affairs, and provides the community with an opportunity to gain knowledge and experience in a central question of life." The collegewide theme working together with all the elements of the program "focuses this dialogue and gives participants a trusting, intelligent, and caring environment within which they can grapple with tough issues from the world outside the college community" (21). We feel this dynamic element is important because it is only through dialogue between individuals and the community that individuals' true values are discovered.

Second, that the CAVE model was a grassroots movement that engaged the community in an institution-wide educational effort has important ramifications and distinguishes the CAVE model's way of proceeding. That the faculty initiated it themselves with no orders from the top speaks to the commitment of the faculty. That this grassroots movement created, implemented, funded, and maintained this effort since 1986 speaks not only of commitment but also of patience and long-term perseverance. These same grassroots beginnings were also instrumental in making it welcoming and nurturing to everyone. It also provided a vehicle for those individuals who seemed to have no other way to accomplish their values education goals.

Finally, the CAVE model transformed the institution's culture. The program functions as a catalyst to effect a cultural shift in an age of cultural drift. Our hope was to reinvigorate undergraduate education by permeating the culture of the institution. Rather than reinventing the wheel, we set out to transform what was already there.

Conclusion

Within institutions of higher education and professional learning there are different approaches to values education and spiritual education; different ways to address the values, spirituality, and moral sensitivity of college students; and more than one way to enhance students' commitment to ethical decision making. Books such as *Educating Citizens: Preparing*

America's Undergraduates for Lives of Moral and Civic Responsibility (Colby et al. 2003), *Where's the Learning in Service Learning?* (Eyler and Giles 1999), Thomas Groome's *Educating for Life* (2001), and Parker Palmer's *Courage to Teach: Exploring the Inner Landscape of a Teacher's Life* (1998) and books described in *About Campus* and *Change* magazine and the approaches I describe point to diverse efforts to address the need for values and spiritual education. Not mutually exclusive, a variety of approaches and movements can coexist within the same institutions. Part of my thesis is that the CAVE model can coexist in an institution with approaches such as I have described and others. The Values Program can enrich efforts focused on other goals, such as student retention, critical thinking, faculty renewal, and creating intensified learning environments with academically and socially reinforcing experiences.

Since there are different ways and levels to understand and implement moral and values sensitivity and development, I have worked to find a way to distinguish among and between these varied approaches in order to better understand some of their more significant aspects. I hope this explanation of the distinctions will also begin to give a clearer understanding of the Values Program's approach.

As I explain in this chapter, each movement has its own goals and objectives, methods, intended target audiences, challenges, intended outcomes, and applicability to other situations and institutions. In addition to the four well-known and widely disseminated methodologies reviewed here, Values Clarification, Learning Communities, Service Learning, and Ethics Across the Curriculum, I could have selected a number of other initiatives. The same systematic analysis could be applied to each of these approaches.

My first observation is that each of the four major approaches I have discussed can be implemented in different ways appropriate to the nature of the institution and the specific objectives of that particular program. We have seen some of the different ways it can be done. For instance, Service Learning is integrated within many different disciplines and courses ranging from chemical engineering to women's studies. Its service might include projects to enhance the living environment of physically handicapped people or working in shelters for battered women. Ethics Across the Curriculum studies will range from required courses to freshman discipline-specific courses and the use of case studies. Course content varies if used in a school for mining and engineering versus a nursing program. Learning Communities can provide focus in a living-learning community or can be adapted to large community colleges with a focus on creating community amid large numbers of commuting students, with a focus on student retention.

The specific objectives and goals of such programs can vary greatly, as can be seen in the wide diversity within the Learning Community approach. Service Learning will vary depending on the faculty member involved, the quality of the service site, and the training and competency of the site mentor. Required ethics courses are often among the ways that professional and other schools seek to provide values education and spiritual development. It seems to be generally true that, in every case, for an approach to be effective it needs to be tailored to fit the mission and purpose of the institution and the specific objectives of the program.

A second observation is that the methods one uses do not define or determine an outcome of values education. The dictionary defines a method as "a way of doing something or carrying something out, especially according to plan," as well as "the body of systematic techniques used by a particular discipline" and an "orderly thought, action, or technique." Nothing in these definitions implies, requires, or determines a particular outcome.

Frequently, people become confused when they observe that the ways and methods utilized in values education are often very similar to the methods used in other programs and initiatives. What needs to be recognized is that groups frequently adopt and implement these ways to accomplish different goals and intentions. For instance, many of the initiatives in higher education and the professions use the same methods: summer institutes, faculty-development programs, campus- and community-wide events, clustering courses together, building community, integrating academic work with out-of-class experiences, and using pedagogies that actively engage and work toward reflection. More specifically, faculty-development programs are very popular with many groups, but only one of these approaches might be specifically concerned with the values dimension. It is important to understand that using the same methods does not necessarily create the same outcomes.

The outcomes depend on the goals and objectives and the substance and matter, the stuff of the activities. For example, anyone who has ever played on a team is not surprised that most coaches run warm-up drills. What they do in those drills, however, depends on the sport and the positions played by the athletes. The same applies to institutes. Institutes can address many different goals and objectives. Some exist to teach Writing Across the Curriculum, others to transfer information about science and the technology of cloning. Others are formed to teach graduate students issues related to research ethics. One might be designed primarily to give information and content. Another may be created to form an interdisciplinary community among faculty to discuss issues such as cloning. Or as in the case of the Values Program, the aim might be to lead the faculty to the understanding of the importance and the necessity of attending to the values dimension so that they are willing to be part of the discovery process of learning how to assist others in dealing with the values dimensions of issues. So methods that look the same might accomplish different objectives.

Some approaches share our goals of values education but differ in the methods they use. For example, a Learning Community at Bowling Green State University integrates its learning around the theme of "values" in order to promote and instill an awareness of values issues and to help students recognize and act on the moral dimensions of both word and action in their learning and lived experiences. The Ethics Across the Curriculum program at Utah Valley State College publishes a journal titled *Teaching Ethics* as a method for advancing ethical awareness. At the University of San Diego, the Institute for Faculty is designed to last two days. At other institutions, such an institute might last a single day or three days.

Others approaches may share some of our methods but not share our overall goals. So, again, the same methods might accomplish different objectives. For example, various groups share the method of integrated learning, but that method does not necessarily accomplish values education. Many groups use integrated learning, but the goal or intention of the integrated learning determines what the outcome is or ought to be.

For example, Learning Communities can sometimes integrate a cohort of students or a cluster of courses around a theme such as "Science and Creativity" or "Revolution and the Marginalized." In these situations the goal might be to assist the students in seeing the interrelatedness and connectedness of disciplines. A living-learning community might have a cohort of students taking both a chemistry course and an ethics course or a course in medicine and healing. You can integrate chemistry with another course, you can have students live on a common floor and set up arrangements for discussion and common teaching, but it does not mean that there will be increased moral sensitivity. It depends on the goals that motivated the integrated learning. The values dimension may not be involved.

Freshman orientation plays an important role in all institutions. When you compare the methods that institutions use to orient new students, it is clear they use many of the same ones. But their goals and objectives for using those methods can be quite different. They have very different expectations. For instance, both the Learning Communities and the Values Program can integrate freshman orientation into their methods. In one approach the objective may be to increase freshman retention by building connections among entering students. In the Values Program approach, however, freshman orientation is designed to impress upon the students that in our institution, values education is a priority. The message to the freshman and the new student is that they should expect the values and spiritual dimension of issues to be central to their classes and beyond the classroom. It is not something for just a few select students.

Purposeful restructuring of the curriculum is another method commonly used. Groups accomplish this goal in all sorts of ways. Learning Communities link courses and ideas and enroll in the classes a common cohort of students. Service Learning intentionally integrates the experience of service in the community into one or two courses; Learning Communities have a variety of curricular experiences depending on the degree to which the teams work to foster connections. Different groups may do the same things, use the same methods, but their goals may be very different. One group may desire an intensified learning environment and community, another may desire a community experiential factor, whereas still another may look to have students understand the moral and values connection between issues. All are very different.

Finally, methods can be used to accomplish other or additional objectives. For example, when Dr. Ed Baumgartner in the Mathematics Department at Le Moyne College creatively designed his courses and activities to integrate the study of math and values education using our method, he struggled to discover ways that students would be involved in values education and also learn math well. Eventually, he was able to make connections with faculty in the natural sciences. Together, they developed a multimedia student symposium that generated student interest beyond the classroom.

Criteria to Be Considered

If you are interested in values education and perhaps also the spiritual dimensions of higher education and want to find a model, there are ways of evaluating any plan you are thinking of implementing. I will suggest certain variables you ought to consider.

There are some preliminary steps you can take. First, recognize that each approach has its own goals and objectives, methods, intended target audience, challenges, intended outcomes, and potential for applicability to other institutions. It will be a great advantage to you to study these differences carefully. The material is quite readily available. Our practical experience taught us the value of clarifying and understanding terms before choosing and acting.

A second premise is something that is becoming more and more self-evident: "You are doing values education, regardless of whether you think you are." Whether the faculty member, the department, or the corporation acknowledges it, there is a values dimension in every choice, action, pedagogy, planned event, athletic or academic program, new building under construction, itemized budget, and admission policy. In every instance we are acting on some set of values; we are thus being values educators. Therefore, there is high probability that your institution is already engaged in values education. I suggest you investigate and get a sense of what aspects of values education, or the spiritual dimensions of higher education, are already present in your institution, its classrooms, and beyond the classroom. Once you have begun to think in this way you will begin to understand the importance and the necessity of meeting this critical need.

I will limit my remarks to what I consider to be key variables: the objectives and the methods. I will look especially at the characteristic of inclusiveness and the need to engage the whole institution. I will also look at the seriousness of the inquiry for values. These variables are points where the rubber meets the road. This discussion is important because it is here that the objectives are given form through the vehicle of the substance and matter, the stuff of the activities.

A key characteristic you should be looking for is adaptability to the ever evolving changes in personnel and environment within your institution. An approach's objectives and methods must be capable of being tailored to fit the mission and purpose of your institution.

I suggest you make inclusiveness a very high priority on your list. If your program is going to be adaptable to the ever evolving needs of the student body, faculty, staff, administration, and wider society, I would look very carefully for simplicity of design. Whatever design you choose needs to have the potential to include and encompass all the essential facts and facets of the institution. It needs to function efficiently yet always be ready to adapt. It needs to be clear as to the purpose and function of each of its components and must be able to support and enhance the functions of the other components. The totality of the experience needs to be more than the sum of the parts. The design should function as a dynamic, integrated system.

Second, its design must be such that it respects what is already functioning in place within the institution. Its objective is to be a "catalyst," a force to enrich and enhance what is already there. If it is perceived as trying to take things over, "to reinvent the wheel," the forces in the institution will reject it. Ask yourself, Does this approach respect what is already in place? Is it welcoming and accepting to all elements within the institution? Does it encourage widespread participation?

Another variable I suggest you consider is the program's ability to engage the entire community. The critical need today is that the members of the institution rediscover its communal responsibility to discover ways to help students deal with the values dimensions in their personal and professional lives. You need to ask if this approach provides a way that has potential to help bring about such an institutional commitment to the mission of values education. That is, does it engage the faculty, staff, administrators, and students? It needs to be so designed that members of the community with diverse backgrounds and expertise can participate in and work to make the program successful. Why do I think an institution-wide effort is needed? In an age of cultural drift, your design should encourage cultural shift.

It is not enough that an approach has a faculty-development component, a service component, or a learning-community component. Using these methods does not necessarily mean that you will want their values education approach. Many institutions of higher education use the same methods of faculty and staff development such as Summer Institutes. You need to examine these options carefully.

Look at your faculty development and staff programs. Do they stand alone, or are they integrated into the larger design of an educational effort devised to enhance values education and perhaps approaches to spirituality? Is the educational effort for values education perceived by the educational community as being at the very core and center of the academic enterprise in your institution? Does this approach attract the best of the faculty? Is the institution's promotion and reward structure thoroughly integrated into the design of the approach? How effective is it in maintaining the interest and commitment of the best faculty? Is your program a one-shot deal, or does the approach have staying power? Does it provide reasonable assurances that the faculty and staff will receive adequate research and development funds for this endeavor? What sort of a priority is it in the institution?

For the very complicated pedagogical issues that the faculty will face and for the equally complicated connections between pedagogy and the moral and spiritual development of the students, very serious demands are made on an approach. Does the approach have very clear goals, and has it developed and successfully implemented sophisticated instruments to assess and research those goals? How does the approach begin to engage the faculty and the staff in these very difficult tasks? Are the design of the process and its content capable of successfully addressing the barriers that institutions and higher education throw up to block or negate legitimate values education? How does the program prepare faculty, staff, and students to see it as a legitimate task of higher education and professional schools? How do you give the faculty the necessary credibility among their colleagues? Are there careful efforts to ensure that the faculty are given techniques and institutional support on all levels before, during, and after to carry these efforts out in and beyond the classroom?

Another variable to carefully examine is to what extent this educational effort is a process of "serious inquiry" that has the power and the dynamism to engage the community in an institution-wide educational effort. The key words are *engaging the whole community in an educational effort.* Is the program inclusive? Does it engage all aspects of the community in the values education dimensions of the issues? Is it welcoming and hospitable to members and elements within the community? Is it sensitive to and aware of the needs of the students, the faculty and staff, the administration, and the community? Is it perceived as being owned by a particular contingent within the institution? It cannot be relativistic, nor can it seek to indoctrinate. Instead, it must be a process of serious inquiry. I think this idea means that its objective is to assist students in developing for themselves a framework of values that is consistent, coherent, and defensible with the best of philosophical, religious, and cultural traditions.

I will close with two examples that pull these variables together in a concrete manner. I began my discussion by saying that you need to ask of every pedagogical strategy and approach, "What kind of values education is happening? Is it what we want?"

For example, an engineering school has a requirement that freshmen take a course on ethics and the engineering sciences. I believe it is possible that, even though the course might be rigorous and of the highest quality, students might well conclude for all sorts of subsequent and subtle reasons that the values and moral and ethical dimensions are not as important as the technical side. What might be some of those subtle signals picked up by the student? One issue might be the fact that the values and ethical dimension are explicitly raised in only one of fifteen courses required in the chemistry curriculum, conveying the message that the values dimension is not significant to professional or academic chemistry. Or it could be that the professor teaching the course is from the Philosophy Department, and the student may perceive that the professor does not have the credibility and reputation among the other chemistry and engineering faculty in the profession to give the student a sense that this facet is a priority. Even though the course being taught by a chemistry professor is an excellent example of integrating the moral dimensions into chemistry, the student may get mixed signals. She likes the course, it is at the highest level, but at the same time she feels it is an isolating experience. I wonder how lasting and effective that impression is on the student as she participates in other courses with the rest of her natural-science professors. That course's insights could become an example of an isolated, lonely attempt within the Chemistry Department.

On the other hand, if this same course is tied into Service Learning and the student has quality exchanges with teenage mothers and young men living in poor neighborhoods near the chemical plant, what sort of values education is going on in that experiential learning? Or when this same class is part of a tightly knit cluster group from a Learning Community who lives together on campus, who share high ideals and work habits and compare themselves to other students, what kind of values education is going on? I recommend that all approaches ask themselves that question.

The premise of the Values Program is that the values dimension is at least as important as the other dimensions. I recommend this dimension be given more priority and that faculty, staff, and students be given the wherewithal to deal with it. For those individuals who agree, the educational approach offered by the CAVE model will give various educational strategies and ways to discover and implement how to make the values dimension as important as the other dimensions.

Advantages of the Values Program Model and Process

I recommend that the reader investigate and study the process we have developed and its concrete realization as it came to life in one particular institution of higher education. Having studied these other programs, I would like to suggest certain unique advantages of the model and process we have developed. My hope is that you will consider it worthwhile enough to do further investigation and study and possibly implement the process in your institution.

First, the Values Program process offers an umbrella-like structure under which all or most elements within the institution can find a welcoming place. Its dynamic structure and organization are grounded in a vision big enough to engage the entire institution and the communities beyond; it can provide the wherewithal for a flexible, welcoming, and open environment. Under the umbrella structure a space is created that allows members of the community to initiate whatever is needed to provide an environment capable of enhancing what we think is important. The program has shown its adaptability across time, student cohorts, current events, and changing institutional needs and resources. Out of it could come a Learning Community, Service Learning, retreats for students, out-of-class activities, orientation creativity, student-personnel changes, changes in teaching pedagogy and course syllabi, and connections within departments, areas, and college constituencies. The dynamic umbrella structure did not dictate a particular agenda or thing to do but instead allowed for creativity and inspiration, as all involved sought to discover and implement ways to enhance values education and values development. This goal is always sought within the larger framework of recognition of the interdependence and connection among so many aspects within the institution. For example, from this process some of the institution's memberships were able to begin to map out the issues behind the theme "The Spiritual Dimensions of Higher Education: Attending to the Sacred in Our Midst." This type of issue did not evolve from the other approaches we have studied. In fact, not every program even addressed spiritual development at all.

Second, this dynamic, alive, and ever evolving structure also provided continuing support for participants. It is not enough that participants and the institution see and understand the values and moral issues; unless resources in terms of both personal and professional reward structures and staff- and financial-support systems are supplied, very little will be done. The process worked to create concrete resources within the societal structure to make real the prioritization of the values dimensions of issues.

It worked to raise awareness and consciousness at every level; we successfully wrote grants and helped the institution to see the importance of hiring an institutional grant writer. The Values Program created, funded, and implemented faculty- and staff-development programs. Coaches, secretaries, residence-hall directors and staff, vice presidents, and academic and student deans worked together with faculty to create the necessary resources for values education: legitimacy, content, and technique. Our goal was eventually to get the commitment of all of these people to become part of the discovery process and to train their students in values and spiritual development.

The issue of expenses and resources can be seen if we consider what is involved in the creation and sustaining of the approach called Learning Communities. Learning Communities can be very expensive for an institution and raise challenges such as, How do you get faculty to live on the corridor? Who pays for construction, housing, and stipends? How do you keep a faculty member after she has a husband and a family with young children? Where does this type of experience fit into the faculty-promotion and -reward structure? It is much easier to achieve the goal of learning communities if you have an environment where many other things in the institution are working to make all of these goals happen.

The Values Program's Summer Institutes gave to the faculty content, legitimacy, and technique. They also worked with the faculty to develop ways to make concrete changes in their pedagogy, departmental structures, and priorities. Most important, they provided a community of support and worked to change the reward environment to make the latter realistic and desirable. Built into the system is ongoing faculty, staff, and administrative development. It is critical to create an environment where these efforts will be supported (as will be shown in Chapter 6).

Third, the Values Program worked to make the experience of students going through college more connected. In this chapter I developed the example of a student being exposed to different levels of interconnectedness. A student can take a course in urban economics and write a paper on the issue of women and the economy. That same student can take the same course that is also a Service Learning course and as her service work volunteer at a home for battered women. That student can also be attending the course as part of a cluster group that is part of a living-learning community centered on the issues of poverty, families, and the community. And that same student can also be taking any of those courses in a institution that has a two-year institution-wide theme of "Economic Justice" or "Families and Public Policy," where most of her faculty, dorm meetings, and student clubs and activities have creatively tried to address the issue from various perspectives. The connectedness of the Values Program process is more far-reaching and also touches the student at the level of her own needs and interests. The mechanism of the institution-wide theme and the Academic Forums and Summer Institutes is capable of transforming what might be a traditional content-centered course in biology, nutrition, theater, or philosophy into an experience connected to an institution-wide theme that helps students to see the connections among history, philosophy, business, accounting, and biology. For instance, when the Le Moyne College theater program decided to experiment with staging a production related to the institution-wide theme chosen every one to two years by the Values Program, suddenly a whole series of connections began to develop among stage design, music, costumes, publicity, intended audience, connection with specific courses, campus dialogues on the performance, and so on. Students and faculty began to experience with their colleagues and peers the interconnectedness, dependency, and interdependency of individuals and communities embarked on a common educational experience. They experienced education as connected, in and out of the classroom, within and among the disciplines and college activities.

Finally, whenever possible the process is grassroots. The Values Program's energy, vitality, and equilibrium are generated by its ability to tap into a sense of ownership of the issues and the methods to address those issues. If participants in a program own the theme and create a strategy that is meaningful to them, it will have very strong legs and durability. The various Town Meetings generated tremendous energy and commitment because they always grew out of the grassroots interest of the participants. A Town Meeting on education and public policy drew state officials from Albany and local and regional superintendents, principals, faculty, union members, parents, and neighbors who struggled with the issues of equity and distribution of resources. The institution's staff, secretaries, and office personnel, for instance, came to life when they were asked to become involved in creating a strategy to make real the theme "The Spiritual Dimensions of Higher Education: Attending to the Sacred in Our Midst." As one secretary said, "In all the years I have been here I have never before been asked how I think we ought to do something." This woman had been a secretary for the faculty for many years and had a profound sense of the deeper needs of the students and faculty from her unique perspective. A unique strength of this program is that it taps into the grassroots needs and energy of the many aspects of the institution, especially its students. All too frequently in other programs, students are presented with a program, a course, a schedule. For example, a freshman going into a Learning Community may or may not have a choice as to what cohort group, class sections, or professors he will be assigned. The freshman in the chemistry course with the ethics connection does not have an option as to which course or what type of cases will be used. Students often are forced into one-size-fits-all situations. In most programs the student, especially the freshman, usually does not have an option. She is selected or invited to join a Learning Community; the Service Learning opportunities are all set up for her to choose from; the Ethics Across the Curriculum is imposed from the top down. How do these programs attend to the needs and interests of the students? How do we know what their needs are?

With the Values Program, the structure and specificity of the learning situation grow out of the creative discoveries of the participants as they reflect on the theme and decide how they will integrate that theme into what they do. Everything from the selection and implementation of the biannual theme to the planning for an implementation of the Summer Institute and the Academic Forum is done if possible with grassroots input. Successful events included "South Africa Week" and "Let's Talk," a mock late-night dorm session presented at the Faculty Convocation on the theme "What Were We Students Promised When We Came to Le Moyne? What Did Le Moyne Deliver?" In all these respects, grassroots input is critical to the process.

The CAVE Model
Like Ripples in a Pond

A Story

A senior biology major and cocaptain of the college's swim team sits with six upper-class students talking. It is like a late-night "rap session" in a student dormitory room. The students are engaged in a heated exchange concerning "promises made, promises kept, and promises broken." But this session has evolved to, "What did this college promise us when we applied and were accepted, and what it has actually delivered during the past four years?"

The other students' professional and personal interests run across the arts and sciences and professional fields. Some live on campus, others commute, one is married with a family; all are motivated and fired up because they are about to graduate. It is truth-in-advertising time. The mix of students guarantees a multifaceted perspective. Present are a record-holding swimmer, an honor student biology major, a commuting student who is staying overnight with her friend, a nontraditional-age student-parent who is part of the senior-course study group, an accounting major interviewing with large public accounting firms, a math major who is working toward certification to teach math in high school and the starting catcher on the championship women's softball team, a faculty member who is doing a late-night course review, and a commuter who is also a member of the student senate and editor of the college newspaper.

What is highly unusual about this "student dorm rap session" is that representatives of the entire institution are listening in and watching the exchange. The whole faculty is there; so are the vice presidents, academic

and student deans, student personnel, admission and financial aid officers, librarians, institutional development officials, campus ministry, and,
of course, the students.

Convocation Day

Convocation Day is a collegewide yearly event at the start of the fall term.
It is a day dedicated to the core of the institution's identity and mission; it
is a day at the core of the academic enterprise.

The students are on a raised platform in the middle of the assembly.
The room has been dimmed except for the lights that focus all eyes on the
student discussion. Surprisingly, the students appear at ease. The atmosphere is one of trust, of freedom to experiment and to make a mistake,
one that can accept trial and error.

An Institution-wide Event

How did something like this event ever come about and why? It is happening within the fall semester faculty development day after the college's
traditional opening of the academic year with Mass of the Holy Spirit.
Some faculty members and students who are active in the Working Group
of the Center for the Advancement of Values Education had suggested the
idea to the academic vice president and dean and to the executive board
of the faculty senate. They liked the idea, and the Working Group came up
with a plan for the afternoon. The two centerpieces of the event would be
a student dorm rap session on promises kept and not kept and a report to
the institution's faculty and other interested personnel on the finding of
the ten-year pioneering program on values education. It was all part of an
institution-wide educational effort designed to discover and implement
ways to assist students in meeting the moral and spiritual challenges of
their professional and personal lives.

As anyone in any institutional setting, whether a university, a medical
school, or a nuclear power plant, will recognize immediately, an event like
this one would never have happened unless the soil had been prepared
carefully in advance. In fact, the event was symbolic of what had been
happening during the past ten years. It is noteworthy that the entire institution was listening in.

The agenda had been set not by the administration or even the academic dean, academic vice president, or the faculty senate but by a grassroots group called the Values Program. It had established sufficient credibility and esteem within the institution that the faculty, administration, student body, and staff trusted its competency and judgment of what is good for the institution. Its reputation is something like C-Span or *The News Hour with Jim Lehrer* in the television market; it is not perceived as having a biased agenda, nor is it perceived as pushing one perspective. It is all-inclusive and welcoming. The time, place, participants, and content were serving as a self-renewing energy resource.

Following the student "rap session," witnessed by the entire audience, Krystine Batcho, professor of psychology and director of research and assessment for the Values Program, delivered the major address at the fall faculty convocation. There she reported on the findings of a ten-year institution-wide values program whose major goal had been to give graduating students the skills, motivation, and knowledge to deal with the moral and spiritual challenges of their personal and professional lives.

Krystine had just completed a sabbatical studying and analyzing this material. It is empirical knowledge, based on an assessment of the actual needs, wants, and accomplishments of students and faculty. Her objective was to provide the faculty with this empirical and relevant conceptual material. This gathering offered the community a time for reflection on the data. Much of what she fed back to the faculty, the key decision-making people, and the grassroots group in the community would, it was hoped, find its way back to the classrooms and beyond the classrooms.

Krystine Batcho held the faculty, administration, students, and some staff spellbound, and they recognized that she was reporting on a process in which most of them had taken part. For more than ten years most had been engaged in this institution-wide process. Many of them had worked their way through a process of trial and error; they had tested techniques, contents, and other approaches. Now they were hearing what they had been promised at every juncture of the program: there will be feedback on progress made and opportunities missed. Krystine was giving the report to the college on its efforts in assisting students in their search for meaning and value: where had we been, where are we now, and where ought we to be going?

A Process That Is Chosen by Faculty

The people who would be making college policy were all in the same room together; they were all hearing the same report, getting the same content, having the same experience. They were all adjusting their vision, and slowly and imperceptibly most would be beginning the academic year on the same page. It was not required that these people were in this room together; they had come there freely because they wanted to participate. Most faculty in the room had chosen over the years to participate in the process. So had many of the staff, deans, directors of housings and continuous learning, and coaches. Because the process engaged so many different people who wore different hats in the institution, it was easier to obtain resources to continue the project. This important dynamic had been built into the process itself, as I will explain in a later chapter on acquiring resources. What was happening on this day also points to another barrier that we were successfully removing. It concerned important issues such as: How do you get the faculty engaged? How do you engage the entire institution? How do you engage the student body in the process?

Also significant was that this process had credibility among students who were the real leaders among the students, not just the student senate presidents and the official leaders, but the students whom the students themselves considered to be the leaders. In this case the group represented the leading academic students, athletes, opinion makers, and typical students, including the continuous-learning students. The Values Program process had been able to engage the student body at all levels. The program had shown itself able to reach out and engage not just an elite group of already recognized and highly motivated students but also the normal student, the one who had to also work at a job to pay tuition, the one who came to class but was not always active in student or college activities. The program's goals had been to engage the entire institution in the values and moral and spiritual dimensions of issues. In this institution it was not perceived as unusual to be raising issues such as these students were raising.

The content and the feedback delivered by Krystine Batcho were followed by questions and open discussion. The faculty, administration, and decision makers in student personnel and other offices were on that day getting a reading as to where the institution had been, where it was at present, and where it intended to go.

A Grassroots Effort

The energy for this event came from the very grassroots of the institution. The sense of ownership of this institution-wide educational effort was felt throughout the room and the institution. The students wanted to do it, the administration wanted to hear about it, and the faculty and some of the staff and student personnel people who had been integral to the creation and implementation of the effort wanted to hear the results of their endeavors. Because people felt ownership of the project, they wanted it to succeed. The unique strength of the whole process was its ability to tap into the grassroots needs and energy of the many aspects of the institution, especially the students.

The CAVE Model and Process

This chapter presents an overview of the CAVE model and process, our approach and our techniques. The model has three main components: the Working Group on Values, the Values Institute, and the Academic Forum. I also provide reflections on our achievements gained through dialogue, discovery, and implementation. I provide these impressions so that others will have a better understanding of the model and an adequate sense of why it is a good approach, why it works, and how to think about adapting and implementing the model in their own institutions.

A Three-Legged Stool

The CAVE model has three main components: the Values Institute, the Academic Forum, and the Working Group on Values. The story at the beginning of this chapter that tells of students, faculty, and staff speaking and listening to each other is a vivid example of the CAVE model in action. A helpful image to understand the model and its inner dynamics is the notion of a three-legged stool. Like the stool, the model has three components, or legs, designed to be connected by a carefully chosen values-laden theme. An effectively functioning three-legged stool must keep all three legs in first-class condition, each supporting an important area yet always seamlessly connected to the whole. The stool's structural integrity, what you might call its content and its process, works best when the design is clean and simple. We have tried to make the design of our model just that clear; simplicity of design is our goal.

The model's material content, the values-laden theme, is vitally important to the CAVE model and became the responsibility of the Working Group on Values. As the brochure for the Values Program stated:

> Each year the Center for the Advancement of Values Education brings together a working group of campus educators comprised of faculty, administrators and staff. Among their tasks is to select and prepare a values-laden topic which will be the Values Program's theme for the ensuing academic years (e.g., Science and Technology and Values, The Spiritual Dimensions of Higher Education, etc.). The Working Group is responsible for conducting a thorough research of the selected values theme preparing for the Values Institute and Academic Forum. ("Values Program" 1998, n.p.)

The CAVE model is more than the sum of its three component parts, just like our stool. The model is a dynamic system whose components work together to make an institution-wide educational effort. If you have only the faculty- and staff-development piece of the Values Institute, you do not have the CAVE model. If you have only the Academic Forum and the Working Group on Values and emphasize the "beyond the classroom" activities and programs, it is not this model. You must have all three components and the theme. All the components must work together in an interdependent, interconnected, dynamic system. Faculty development is certainly a major force within the mission of the Values Program, but the faculty are only part of the college and university. Just as the challenge faced by the Wright brothers was to design not just wings and an engine but an entire plane that could become airborne, so too our task is to understand the CAVE model as a dynamic combination of all the parts functioning together, each part reinforcing and supporting the others.

This pioneering project evolved in a collegiate, university, professional school environment. But it can just as easily be understood within a business, professional, or corporate environment—for example, law schools, hospitals, or medical services. Our central aim is to assist individuals, in our case students at our college, in establishing for themselves a framework of values that is consistent, coherent, and defensible with the best of the philosophical, religious, and cultural traditions.

As busy professors and faculty members in a small to medium-size institution, we worked initially without assistants, graduate assistants, or staff. Everything we did we had to do by ourselves. At all times we were responsible for our regular teaching, research, committee service, and publication obligations. We were always more practical than theoretical.

The Process

One of the major contributions of the Values Program to higher education and the wider society beyond may be the model and process it developed. The image of the seed and the sower provides a way to observe the tasks of the various components of the CAVE model. In response to the questions, "How do you prepare the soil? How do you create an environment?" our model has proved to be an effective tool. The process followed to execute this model is one of the most significant outcomes of this educational effort. I will now describe some of that process and offer guidelines, models, and examples that may be helpful.

The Working Group on Values

How do we begin to glimpse the process that gives the CAVE model life? Part of our answer is found by examining the praxis and process of the Working Group on Values. I think it is fitting that this group that was part of the original founding group eventually became a main component of the model. This group, in cooperation with many other colleagues locally and nationally, struggled to create and articulate some of the ideas and strategies that would eventually emerge as the CAVE model. In fact, the praxis of the WGV provides an excellent mirror with which to observe the beginnings of the model in action. We discovered with time that the model we had developed had been so engineered that our experience was capable of being replicated by others. It can be handed down to others; if they follow the outlines of the model carefully, it can become for them an instrument imbued with the power to assist them in recognizing that there are value and spiritual dimensions to their professional and personal lives. And it can help them replicate the successes we have had in their institution or environment. Let us look at how the Working Group on Values functions.

At the beginning, the Working Group on Values was concerned with how to identify and address the deficiency growing within our societies and institutions that could have important and critical consequences. At first, our sense that something vital was missing was quite vague. Within six months the Working Group would come to realize that it had something to do with values and that one challenge was how to describe and analyze the symptoms of a profound critical need for both higher education and the larger society. Eventually, we would have to articulate this problem before a very skeptical group of faculty colleagues and attempt to sell them on a strategy and plan that we called "an ambitious dream."

The format that would eventually be called the Values Program and would be administered by the Center for the Advancement of Values Education touches something basic. Even though it was created in a particular college and institution, it is repeatable in a great diversity of environments. Without realizing it, we designed the CAVE model and process so that any participants would be able to replicate the experiences of the original founding group. In doing so they will come to understand and experience the critical importance of the values and spiritual dimensions of issues and will be given the skills to learn how to deal with the moral and spiritual challenges we all face in our personal and professional lives.

It seemed so simple back in 1985. Gather together five to six faculty colleagues from diverse academic disciplines and perspectives. Meet twice per month for a year to create two or three capstone seminars. Get a few members to volunteer to teach the seminars. And bingo, our students will learn how to integrate their professional and career-oriented studies with the college's liberal arts and science curriculum and its Jesuit and Catholic traditions. It wasn't that simple, but it sure has been rewarding.

The Beginning

In September 1985 six faculty members and the director of admissions met to test my hypothesis. We had a five thousand–dollar anonymous "seed grant" from a major foundation to get us started. When I had invited my colleagues to participate I explained that my proposal involved working with them to create and implement a choice of two to three capstone seminar courses that would be integrated into the college core curriculum and become an option for the senior required core courses. The seminars' aim would be to assist graduating seniors in meeting the challenges of integrating the liberal arts and sciences, their majors and future career and professional commitments, and the college's Jesuit and Catholic traditions.

Looking back now I can see that we began with a vague proposal. But what we did have was commitment. At the time, I was a recently tenured member of the Religious Studies Department and a Jesuit, hardly even part of the midechelons of the college's power and decision-making structure. I met with each colleague individually and explained what and why I wanted to do this project and why I thought he or she would be good for the task. The only leverage I had was that this project could be interesting and useful. With some I used my trump card: that I was asking them on the recommendation of Andrew J. Brady, S.J., one of the founders of the college. I could see they believed that if Father Brady had recommended them, this project must be worthwhile. I also explained that we would each be paid a five hundred–dollar stipend and that we would also be accountable to a national foundation for the project. Every person on my list said yes. They joined the group freely, for their own reasons. They had not felt coerced, forced, or mandated by a dean, department chair, or college president. We became a grassroots group working within the institution, accountable only to ourselves. Everything was now in place.

The Team

Being for the most part professors with from ten to twenty years' experience and having held every major position of authority and committee service and faculty chairs that were open to the faculty, this group, I could tell right from the beginning, was going to make this endeavor a serious project and meant business. I functioned as the facilitator of the meetings and the group, but we ran the Working Group the same way that Red Auerbach coached his championship Boston Celtics basketball teams: Even though the team included stars such as Larry Bird, Bill Russell, and Kevin Hale, Auerbach made it clear that there were to be no individual stars. The focus would be the team, the Boston Celtics. All the teammates worked together for the good of the team. This outlook is the attitude that permeated our deliberations and discussions.

As the group struggled with my proposal, looming in the background was the beginning of an understanding that the challenge was actually much bigger than we had imagined and that it was not just a problem at this one institution but a problem that challenges all of higher education and the wider society. We had begun our discussions with some unexamined assumptions:

- We would concentrate our energies on creating courses
- These courses would be required for seniors
- The symbolism of the course in the catalog was important
- A single course could pull together four years of nearly 120 credits in areas as diverse as science, literature, philosophy, religion, math, history, and psychology
- Any one of us would be able to teach that course

In the end none of those assumptions proved to have any legs. Instead, we began to understand the following:

- Creating a course or working to make this part of the curriculum as a course or requirement would not work
- Our target should be the entire student body
- No single course could bear the weight of carrying what had been lost in the cultural transformations during the twentieth century
- The faculty would need careful and consistent development and training if they hoped to succeed

A Serious Setback

After one year of working together, we also realized that our original proposal was not going to work. We began to perceive the outlines of ever strengthening dark clouds of a much more systemic and deeply ingrained challenge to our very society. At the end of this year I had learned three important things. First, as a Jesuit and as an ethicist in religious studies, my way of looking at things was one way to perceive things, but it was not the only way. Second, the commitment and moral conscience of my colleagues were at least as strong as mine. Third, I had to learn to listen and to facilitate this group. I could not impose myself on them; they now had ownership in the process and the project.

Together we had realized the original proposal was not going to work. But we had not really rejected it. Rather, we began to transform it into something like we had never seen, and, in the meantime, we ourselves were being transformed.

During the experience of working together we were getting to know and trust each other in ways that we had not beforehand. The experience was also giving us a new understanding of a challenge that we had not been sensitive to or aware of. We were ourselves beginning to understand the importance of the values dimension, or the moral and spiritual dimension, not just in an abstract, theoretical, and universal manner but also in a way that was actually touching us in our professional callings as professors and professionals in our given fields. We were no longer struggling with a vague issue. We now had before us a deep conviction that we had the responsibility to assist our students in meeting this profound challenge. We did not yet know how to do it, but we committed ourselves to a process of dialogue and discovery. For the next two years the Working Group on Values would struggle and live with this challenge.

Our Mission

In an article I published in *About Campus,* I described the mission of the Values Program:

> The mission of the Values Program is to engage the college community in a campus wide education effort designed to discover and implement ways to help students heighten their awareness of values issues, develop a comprehensive framework for addressing these issues, and strengthen their moral courage to act on their principles. Although some

might worry that the program engages in indoctrination, it in fact initiates a process of serious inquiry. Our aim is to assist students to fashion frameworks of values that are consistent, defensible, and in keeping
with the best of the philosophical, religious and cultural traditions. The
program's primary goals are to create an atmosphere that promotes the
serious reflection of values issues, to encourage faculty and staff to explore the relationship between teaching methods and the development
of moral sensitivity in students, and to involve students, faculty and staff
in an ongoing analysis and criticism of values. (Kirby 1998, 16)

It took nearly ten years of lived experience and reflection on the total lived experience of many participants and colleagues before we were
able to understand and articulate this mission that I have just quoted.
The Working Group on Values worked to develop and articulate this understanding in its earliest versions. This mission statement has had vital
importance to us. The material above is only a brief sketch of how the
Working Group on Values grew and developed over its first year, and into
its second and third years. I will discuss other more recent aspects of the
Working Group later in the book. What is important is that it planted the
seed and sketched the main outlines of this mission statement and that
the CAVE model began to take form in word and in deed both in a particular institution and already beyond its borders. Every institution will
need to adopt some form of Working Group as it begins to discover and
implement ways to accomplish these goals.

An Inclusive Design

By design our mission and our programmatic activities became inclusive
of the entire college community and did not focus on only one or two
courses. We rejected our initial idea of a capstone senior seminar because
we believed that creating one or two courses was a little like an emergency
room doctor applying a Band-Aid to a hemorrhaging patient in system
failure. A capstone seminar theoretically works best when the faculty, the
institution, its students, and the wider culture reasonably share common
values and priorities. Our own experience and our professional backgrounds loudly proclaimed that the traditional carriers of values, beliefs,

and ideology could no longer transmit their cargo. The very culture was in deep trouble.

We had experienced this insight firsthand. In 1984–1986 the college conducted a Values Audit, part of a national pilot project shared with seven other colleges and universities and sponsored by the Society for Values in Higher Education and funded by Arco. Through this experience we had begun to understand how an institution might have significant disparities and gaps between its assertions and the realities within the institution. For instance, even though a college can resolutely make claims to be Jesuit and Catholic, do those assertions hold up when compared to what actually happens within the institution? A college may assert quality interdependence and connections among and within most aspects of academic affairs and student affairs and between what goes on in the classroom and what happens outside and after class. But in reality, what does actually happen? The college might claim to govern itself according to certain policies and principles. When you examine how the institution is governed, what is the difference between what is said and what is done in governance?

Our first year together as a Values Group did produce foundational understanding and insight. We recognized clearly that an educational effort to meet this challenge must necessarily involve the entire community. All parts of the institution, not just the faculty and the administrators, would need to be engaged in the educational effort to discover ways to weave disparate threads "into a new fabric of experience" that would enable students to integrate their learning and their values. As students left for the summer in May 1986 we began to dream an ambitious dream: to have a major impact on values education and development at Le Moyne and in the wider educational community. Could we transform the culture of the college? Could we weave the fabric we desired? How could it be done? We did not know, but we committed ourselves to a process of discussion and discovery.

During the summer of 1986 two questions would not go away: How do you begin to involve the community in an institution-wide educational effort? How do you get the community interested in values issues? You can see why it was called "an ambitious dream." In an academic institution control of things curricular was firmly vested in the hands of the curriculum committee; we had to figure out a way to make things happen within that reality. We had only recently been through a major curricular battle over the core curriculum, and we did not want to fight that battle again. Somehow we would need a group with its own structure and organization and its own independence to experiment. The ordinary functions and responsibilities in the running of the institution with its various departments and offices were not going to go away. Yet the people who were involved in this group would also need to carry on with their routine tasks of teaching, research, and committee work while the values program evolved and functioned. So from the very beginning we walked the delicate and necessary balance required to be a force for change within the institution.

As I have mentioned, my plan was to invite key people among the faculty to wear two hats. My hope was that they would be involved in the work of the Working Group on Values and would become committed to it. In this way whatever resulted from the effort would not suddenly burst upon them or their colleagues. If it were seen as a counterinsurgent group or as a foreign invasion to be repulsed, the institution would reject it. My hope was that the WGV would eventually become the carrier of the vision to the wider institution.

Ours was to be another kind of educational effort initiated by a grassroots group of faculty and our highly respected colleague Edward Gorman, the director of college admissions. It would be quite different from the more tightly controlled operations under the daily tutelage of the college's administrative and committee framework. Instead, there would be another form of development and preparation going on that was free, grassroots, independent, unofficial. There was nothing about our activities that would be kept secret or invisible. We did not hesitate to share what we were doing with our colleagues in our normal daily exchanges in the hallways and in the faculty dining room. We were slow, however, in disclosing too much information until we had thought things through very carefully. Our colleagues could see that we were very interested in what we were doing and having a lot of fun doing it.

Even in its preparatory phase, the values project would have a scope that was institution-wide while also being open to the wider world beyond our campus. We labored to discover an effective way to signal to the faculty, staff, and administration that their input was wanted; we needed their help. Our desire was to carry the discussion, discovery, and implementation to everyone in the community and beyond. It was to be a grassroots movement; it would try to catch the spirit of the people within the community and tap its energy in this discovery process. The Values Program would grow out of a deeply felt need and approaches that could be empirically validated. We needed to discover a way to tap into the energy of the people around us.

Our values group would be "democratic," and it would reflect the collegial spirit of higher education. There would be careful and free discussion of controversial issues; each person brought his or her own personal and professional backgrounds to the table. We did not avoid controversial matters for fear of disedifying anyone, nor were we afraid to wash our linens out in the open. The age of "lay colleagueship" was in its beginning stages at our institution, and this group provided an opportunity to test its limits. Often during my weekly meetings with Professor Roger Shinn at Union Theological in New York City during my doctoral studies, we discussed education and the role of religion and the churches in the public forum and culture. I often remembered these sessions as discussions of the Working Group on Values developed.

The Students Coin a Word: ALIVE

As the momentum grew among the student body, some students coined a word or slogan to catch the sense behind the model's desire to bring the values and spiritual dimension to students and the community both "within the classroom" and "beyond the classroom" in a comprehensive manner. The word was ALIVE. Eventually printed on a popular T-shirt, it pointed to how students perceived the educational effort that was becoming more central to the institution. It pointed to images like the air we breathe, a life-giving source, a light and source of energy. In one word it catches our primary goal: "to assist students in developing for themselves a framework of values that is consistent, coherent, and defensible with the best of the philosophical, religious, and cultural traditions." It will do so by working toward our three institution-wide goals: to create an atmosphere that promotes the serious reflection of values and spiritual issues, to encourage faculty and staff to explore the relationship between teaching methods and the development of moral and spiritual sensitivity in students, and to involve students, faculty, and staff in an ongoing analysis and criticism of values.

ALIVE expresses our aim: to graduate students who are alive to the value and spiritual dimensions of reality, students whose minds and hearts have been ignited into a vision so they are able to see with new eyes, to understand the necessity and importance of the values and spiritual dimensions of issues, students so alive and on fire with commitment to this priority that they will spontaneously attend to the values dimension without any external prompting and will also have the skills and motivation to deal with it as a dimension at least as important as the technical dimensions of issues. All of this aim was underscored by the supposition articulated by the Jesuit John Courtney Murray that one cannot make an authentic act of faith unless one has freedom.

Connected by a Theme

The college was able to bring a variety of resources to bear on an annual values theme. The instrument through which it did so was the design, content, and interdependent function of each of the CAVE model's three components: the Values Institutes, the Academic Forums, and the Working Group on Values. Some themes we chose were "Peace and War" (1989–1990), "Families and Public Policy" (1990–1991), "Science, Technology, and Values" (1991–1992), "Values Education Across the Curriculum" (1993–1994), "Education and Public Policy" (1997–1999), and "Action for Justice in a Changing World" (2001–2002). (The dates here indicate the academic year during which the theme was discussed.) To illustrate the interconnections and interdependence of these themes, faculty from across the disciplines were encouraged to relate classroom material to issues of broad human import.

A Wide Variety of Perspectives

It is also important that an institution look at values questions from a wide variety of perspectives. The Values Program's mission and programmatic activities, in its pedagogy and learning, as well as its public lectures, Town Meetings, films, and student-initiated symposia, make this possible. Some wondered if this objective violated the mission of the founding religious vision of an institution of higher education. The program in no way violates Le Moyne's religious heritage. In fact, we took special care to ensure that Catholic perspectives were well represented. But as the media and the professional literature and talk shows make clear, when concrete matters are at issue—for instance, the war in Iraq, the Terri Schiavo case, stem-cell research—Catholic opinion is often divided, even among the hierarchy.

Speaking from his understanding of the Values Program's mission, academic vice president John Carlson remarked that the presupposition of this model and process is that "in the end our students, whether they are Catholic or not, must come to their 'own' views; they must also prepare to participate in modern pluralistic society" (1991, 13). As the chief academic officer in the institution, Carlson supported the program because he believed it helped to do these things.

Noting a criticism that programs such as ours "only muddle values and standards," the *Syracuse Herald American* asked the academic vice president of Le Moyne, "Does this approach merely instill the view that values are relative, rather than give a clear idea of right and wrong?" (13). At first glance the pluralistic approach taken by the Values Program could lead one to wonder the same thing. Carlson, a professional philosopher with expertise in bioethics and medical ethics, supported the mission of the Values Program effort and its programmatic aspects because he believed it "seeks to steer a middle course between relativism and its usual alternative, dogmatism." Carlson continued, "We believe that a key to avoiding these extremes is to work toward the clear articulation of issues, the search for consistent frameworks, attention to the best in the human traditions, and openness to new evidence as well as to the insights and arguments of others." He also noted that as long as it embodies these traits, the Values Program encourages "a deep respect for the opinions and perspectives of all—students, faculty and staff, and on-campus visitors. Such respect is quite compatible with commitment to one's own views" (13).

Carlson was convinced that the program did try "to help students achieve a 'clear idea' of right and wrong." But he cautioned, "Such clarity, however—especially regarding concrete issues—often comes only with great effort. Moreover, since the contours of values issues change with changing circumstances (e.g. recent developments in biotechnology), the search for clarity must be ongoing." He concluded his interview by asserting that in the end, "there is no substitute for the nurturance of individual habits of mind and heart" (13). How this nurturance happens is what this book works to describe.

Fitting into the Landscape of the College and University

The landscape then looks as follows: You have a college with its normal way of doing things—committees, departments, and administrative areas. The faculty do their thing, student affairs theirs, the administrators theirs. Into this scene comes a small, high-powered body dealing exclusively with the values and eventually the spiritual dimensions of issues. As we will see, there is something about this group, about the way they did things, and the plan and process that they proposed. Somehow all of it would come together and produce a product and model that would provide a catalyst and instrument with which an institution of higher learning would want to address a most awesome challenge. As a trained theologian and ethicist I cannot help but think of the move made by Pope John XXIII when he faced the monumental task of calling and implementing the Second Vatican Council. He appointed Augustin Cardinal Bea to create the Secretariat for Christian Unity. This small group functioned outside the normal workings of the Roman Curia, but its whole purpose was to keep within the forefront of the planning for the council the following question: "What do our Christian brothers and sisters in other churches think about what we are doing?" This single question helped to give a whole new nuance and tone to the planning process of the council. When thirty-five hundred bishops from around the world assembled for the council, a spark was lit that no one had ever anticipated. It set in place a deep personal and structural transformation throughout many parts of the world.

Without seeming to be triumphant, this is how I see the Working Group on Values. It always kept its "eye on the prize." It kept asking one question: "How do we engage the community in an institution-wide educational effort to discover and implement ways to increase the students' sensitivity to the value and spiritual dimensions of issues and their commitment to ethical decision making?" For all the years of the Values Program, the Working Group, even though the membership continued to evolve as interests and themes evolved, remained at the center of the planning process. Like the seat of the stool, it is part of the model and a catalyst for bringing the values and spiritual dimension into the institution in a whole new dynamic fashion.

One Last Question

But there is one last question that some raised about this small, high-powered body dealing exclusively with the values dimensions of higher education. It is a question that those readers who are part of religiously based institutions might also encounter: "Wasn't this area supposed to be the domain of the Jesuits? Wasn't this work what they do in the Theology, Religious Studies, and Philosophy Departments?" The very makeup of the Working Group made it clear that all the faculty, and eventually all those individuals institution-wide and beyond, were officially invited. It was everyone's responsibility to be sensitive and skilled in dealing with the values and spiritual dimensions of issues. In this group the emphasis was on the fact that the whole group was working together for a common good. We were not a committee. The emphasis would always be on both "working" and "group." Just as Pope John XXIII's ecumenical group had been able to bypass the Curia that was supposed to be planning the council, so too we would need to be very careful. Our opponents would say it was "only Kirby's thing" in an effort to try to minimize our effort.

For fifteen years the seed that was planted would silently continue to grow. For various historical reasons the Working Group and the emerging Center for the Advancement of Values Education often encountered difficult barriers. In spite of these difficulties, the group was able to make a significant and lasting contribution to discovering and implementing ways to help contemporary students deal with the moral and spiritual dimensions of their personal and professional lives. The model and process did work. It did and continues to work, holding within itself the power to once again make an institution and its students come ALIVE.

Let us now look at how the Values Institutes were designed and how they functioned.

The Values Institute

The Values Institute is the second of the CAVE model's three main components. I have already discussed the Working Group on Values and will discuss the Academic Forum. As we work to understand this component we need to keep as a backdrop certain realities. First, in our vision we were trying to create, implement, test, fine-tune, and reemploy all components at the same time. Just as the saddlebags on a horse packed for a long trip need to be carefully balanced and weighted, so too we worked to be ever mindful that each component was a separate entity with its own goals and aims while at the same time interdependent, interrelated parts of a whole that was greater than the sum of its parts. Second, the model and its programmatic aspects evolved slowly and gradually from the grassroots level, which meant we parceled out our limited staff, financial resources, and time in an almost triagelike manner, working first on one component and then on another, all the while trying to keep the three legs of the stool balanced and supportive of the whole stool. Initially, because of certain funding realities, the component that was most consistently allocated quality resources in terms of finances and personnel was the Values Institute. We never lost sight, however, of the fact that this element was only one of three components. As time progressed we gradually righted this initial imbalance, but our struggle for resources may have been one of the reasons we often needed to respond to our colleagues' incorrect perception that the Values Program and its process were concerned primarily with faculty development. I address the issue of acquiring resources and maintaining this balance in a later chapter more specifically.

Faculty Involvement

Because we had identified this critical need in both higher education and the wider society, our goal was to create a collegiate environment that enhanced students' values and spiritual sensitivity and also facilitated their commitment to ethical decision making. After much discussion we realized the best way to begin to accomplish this goal was to engage the faculty and get them to become involved and committed to the discovery process. Because the founding Working Group on Values was made up of faculty, we believed we were on strongest footing if we began with the faculty. If administrators or other aspects of the institution had made up the Working Group, then they might have discovered a better way to approach the task. For us, what better place to begin than with our own colleagues?

Beyond the Faculty

The Values Institute convenes faculty, staff, and administration from the college and beyond. Its makeup is mostly faculty. But we also became sensitive and aware that an institution of higher learning is not made up of faculty alone. It is good for faculty to remember this fact, which is why we always insisted that the goal of the center and its programmatic aspects was engagement in an institution-wide process. After fifteen years, nearly 75 percent of our institution's full-time professors have attended institutes. After the initial years we evolved to inviting faculty from other institutions for both creative cross-fertilization and so that they could take these ideas back to their own institutions and we could then learn from them. Eventually, many of the college's administrators participated, and personnel from all aspects of the institution, including admissions, continuous learning, faculty secretaries, coaches, and institutional development, joined them. Because the mission was to engage the community in an institution-wide educational effort, we were very careful to listen to and learn from all members of the institution. As Saint Benedict points out, one must listen carefully to everyone, even to the youngest, for one never knows through whom the Spirit will decide to speak.

The number of participants for an institute is twenty to twenty-five, a number we learned seemed best suited for this type of project. Participants applied to be included. When accepted to the institute they were appointed as CAPHE Fellows in recognition of the Consortium for the Advancement of Private Higher Education, the foundation providing the major funding for our first Institutes. (CAPHE later identified the grant that it had given Le Moyne College as one of its ten best projects.) Later the title evolved to "Values Fellows." This title helped us to impress upon the participants that they were assuming a professional commitment by agreeing to attend the institute. Also drafted for the institutes were two or three nationally recognized professors whom we called facilitators. They were very carefully chosen from among the best available in their respective fields.

The issue of legitimacy and competency is a major barrier that we worked hard to overcome among the faculty. The reputations of the outside professors brought with them both credibility and prestige. Our own faculty members in the beginning were honored to work with such esteemed colleagues from prestigious institutions. At first we arrived at legitimacy by bringing in visiting professors, but as we grew in confidence we turned to our own faculty to ask for facilitators. In Jewish religious understanding there is the same roots of the words *teach* and *disciple*. Behind the similarity in roots is the notion that only if you first have understood a process and mastered it can you then be qualified to teach others to do it. In our institutes we were communicating technique, legitimacy, and content (Kirby et al. 1990, chap. 9, esp. 176–77).

How Long?

The time length for an institute is something that each institution needs to discover, fine-tune, and study in a given educational or professional environment. A number of variables go into the decision of time length. In the first five years (1988–1992) the institute's participants met for three consecutive weeks in the summer, Monday through Friday, from nine to five. It was a big commitment. The fact that faculty kept applying year after year based on word-of-mouth endorsements and some more formal publication of our findings is a tribute to the quality and worth of the institutes. Eventually, we learned how to do the institutes in a one-week period; we also experimented with shorter periods of two to three days.

I find it quite compelling that so many faculty, staff, and administrators were willing to commit themselves to such an experience of three weeks. As members of the Working Group on Values it had taken us three years to go through our own personal, communal, and structural transformations. Looking back on the creative process, what we actually did was to design a Summer Institute that concentrated our three-year experience into a three-week institute. Our goal was to give our faculty colleagues the same kind of experience we had been through individually and as a group. The Values Institute functioned almost as a stone cast into a pond. As faculty learned from outside facilitators and from each other, their experience and their new ideas moved through the college community like ripples from a stone cast into the water. A seemingly small action began to have much larger effects. It was vitally important that we create an appropriate atmosphere conducive to values education. Our Values Institutes began this process of creating a favorable atmosphere. Because the atmosphere at the college had begun to be transformed, we were able to shorten our time period.

The participants were paid a stipend that was equal to what they would have been paid to teach a summer school course. It may be that given the quality of the institute the faculty may have come under any circumstances, but we had our reasons for paying the stipend. Most of our faculty had families with children and many other expenses, and it would have been too much to ask them to forgo other summer opportunities. Paying the stipend also signaled the professional importance and prestige of these events.

Funding

How was the institute funded? Who paid the facilitator and participants' stipends? Who paid for the coordinators of the institute, the research and assessment director, and the Academic Forum costs? Initially, the Working Group on Values learned to write grants and then encouraged others in the college interested in writing grants. The coordinators and directors of the Values Institute, the programmatic aspects and research and assessment, and various steering groups helped to write the grants. It is important to understand the impact of the fact that we ourselves did the lion's share of obtaining the funding.

What is the significance of the fact that it was we and not the administrators or the institutional development office that wrote the grants and paid for this program? It was we who visited and worked with the foundations such as the Consortium for the Advancement of Private Higher Education, National Endowment for the Humanities, National Science

Foundation (NSF), the Lilly Endowment, and many more small and medium-size grant-giving organizations. We learned from the foundations
and were able to take advantage of their expertise and ability to connect
us with other institutions working on similar or related projects. Over a
fifteen-year period, the Values Program carried out the only consistent
faculty-development program institution-wide. Because the faculty did
it we had a sense of ownership with the program; it was our program.
Finally, learning to write grants interconnected us with the office of institutional development within the institution. This relationship was a very
important connection for us to establish at the grassroots level.

In a later chapter I will develop more fully how we acquired resources
in terms of both funds and personnel by the approach of praxis—learning
by doing.

What Happened in the Values Institute?

The Values Institute centers on a carefully chosen values-laden theme. It is
this theme that will provide common substance and content for both the
institute and the educational efforts inside and beyond the classroom. A
critical discovery for us has been the use of the collegewide theme as the
basis of a common ground of experience and base of knowledge. In *About
Campus* (1998), I wrote that the collegewide theme presents the content as
a bridge between student affairs and academic affairs and provides the
community with an opportunity to gain knowledge and experience in
a central question of life. Because we worked with the supposition that
it was only through dialogue between individuals and the community
that an individual's true values are discovered, this theme proved to be
an important element. What this educational effort does is focus the dialogue and give participants a trusting, intelligent, and caring environment within which they can grasp tough issues from the world outside
the college community.

For reasons of preparation the theme is selected fifteen to twenty
months prior. Examples of themes are "Economic Justice," "Peace and
War," "Families and Public Policy," and "Science, Technology, and Values." An appropriate theme must mirror a significant educational and
societal need, it must be fundable, and there must be at least someone in

the institution who is willing to be the spear carrier to lead the process of creating and implementing the theme.

At least a year ahead of the institute, two to three facilitators are chosen to assist in the preparation of the institute. Choosing the best available facilitators with certain qualities must be done carefully.

Behind the praxis and what we ask participants to experience in the institutes is a supposition we make about learning and teaching. We believed that faculty would not be able to assist others in learning something like values education and development or spiritual growth until they themselves had gone through the experience. The Values Institute can be seen as a process whereby the faculty learn for themselves how to administer values education and development. In their interaction with the facilitators and with each other they are acquiring what could be a transforming experience.

First Stage

In the first stage of the Values Institute participants become familiar with the content and literature on the theme that will become the institution-wide focus for that particular two-year period. It might be "Science, Technology, and Values," "Action for Justice in a Changing World," or any selected theme. During the institute the faculty work together with the facilitators and begin to grow in understanding and experience of the theme. They share insights with each other and learn and experience the interrelationships and interdependence of ideas. "It's like going back to college and graduate school. I am remembering and appreciating anew what it is like to be a student," remarked one of the participants. The mixture of twenty to twenty-five participants, from all disciplines and positions, faculty, administration, and staff, sharing their unique connections with the college and wider community and their own individual communities provided a rich blend.

Second Stage

Once the participants have begun to better understand the content of the theme, the second level of the institute kicks in. The participants begin now to recognize, identify, and discuss the values dimensions of the theme. As they grow in sensitivity of the values and spiritual dimensions of the theme, they also begin to become more aware and to understand the importance of the values dimension in their own disciplines and teaching. This can be understood as acquiring legitimacy. For example, an economist, psychologist, biologist, philosopher, mathematician, and professor in literature and religious studies not only begin to become sensitive to and understand the values dimensions of the theme but also discover how the values dimensions of this theme are critical and important for understanding and working within their own disciplines. Once that connection happens it is as if a light has come on. The passions, the mind, the intellect, the heart, and the emotions have now become engaged in understanding the material. It is also at this point that the institute's facilitators hope that the knowledge and insight of the importance of the values dimension in one's own teaching and professional and personal work have touched such a deep personal chord that the participant begins to desire to become part of the discovery and implementation process of making an understanding of the importance and necessity of the values dimension a reality not only in themselves but also in their students.

The participants also learn technique so that they have the confidence to follow through with their insights. A major barrier that often causes faculty to resist change is they do not feel competent to make the change. Research data support the fact that if individuals do not learn how to do something, they will not attempt it. We understand that if faculty do not acquire techniques for values education and spiritual development and do so with competence, courage, and ability, then they will not be successful. The Values Institute also provided examples of teaching strategies and exercises. This point is one of the critical moments in the institute. To respond to this need, we made it our major goal in the institute to support participants as they formulated realistic plans for implementing what they had learned during the institute.

Faculty Commitment

One of the things that we try to make clear in the preparatory stages of every institute is that when faculty apply and are selected for that year's institute, they are making a commitment to developing a project while they participate in the institute. The agreement became that the faculty would work alone or with colleagues to develop a project and integrate it into the next academic year's teaching or extracurricular activities. How to hold participants to this agreement was something we had to learn by experience.

We have all been to conferences and institutes where there are many good ideas but little or nothing happens after the faculty return to their normal daily lives. So as part of the application process, we asked participants to bring in an idea for a project. During the conferences we worked with them and their colleagues about how their project might be implemented. We also instituted a regular mechanism of follow-up during the next academic year.

As we will see in a later chapter, there have been excellent examples of this follow-up in the areas of freshman orientation and in the force of having more than 85 of the faculty of 120, some two or three times, gradually being transformed by this experience and then gradually acting as catalysts to transform both the theoretical and the practical knowledge in their disciplines and departments. An immediate image that comes to mind is the Values Institute's impact on a department, part of a department, or a section of the college. Later I will discuss how the Political Science Department, for example, integrated service learning into its curriculum. There are also examples of the institutes being community builders among faculty and other groups. Finally, there are plenty of instances of the institutes functioning as renewable energy resources and catalysts for scholarship and renewed commitment to the students in terms of both scholarship and professional development of the faculty, staff, and administration.

Summary of Values Institutes

One way to understand the rationale behind the Values Institutes within a collegiate or university environment or in fact in any environment is to consider a truth that is all too common for any keen observer today. Because a person has a Ph.D. does not mean that person has good moral aspects to his or her psyche. Nor does it mean that he or she knows how to deal with the moral and spiritual aspects of problems and challenges. We believe that unless there is a catalyst or something that continually forces the institution to address and face up to the values and spiritual dimension, it will not happen. Within a number of years the soil will once again become dry, hardened, and nearly impossible to plant and cultivate.

For this reason we developed the Values Institutes. In these institutes we sought to help faculty and staff develop the necessary attitudes and skills and learn how to help students develop their own attitudes and skills.

The Academic Forum

This section provides an overview of the Academic Forum, the third component of the Values Program. It is the third leg of our stool, all interconnected and integrally related to the theme. Briefly stated, my goal here is twofold: to provide a preliminary understanding and appreciation of the fundamental insight behind the workings of the Academic Forum and to situate the forum within the Values Program's total design and function. I devote Chapter 5 to the Academic Forum. There I present its process and methodology, our approach and techniques, and reflections on our achievements gained through continual dialogue, discovery, and implementation. My hope is that this material will assist you in better evaluating the appropriateness of this approach.

Connections for Students

The Values Program constantly keeps in tension a careful balance between what goes on inside the classroom and what happens beyond it. Grounded in years of observations, practical experience, and the knowledge of many participants and their students, many people worked to fine-tune how to best make this connection so central to the CAVE model's design. The educational effort was designed to discover and implement ways to assist faculty and students inside the classroom in areas of pedagogy and the styles of interaction. It also engaged the community in efforts to discover and implement ways to assist students beyond the classroom. It did so through a wide variety of events and activities throughout the academic year that provided for an ongoing analysis and discussion of issues interrelated with the annual theme. The main function of these components is to help students discover connections between classroom material and the world outside the classroom.

Like the whole stool, however, its components inside and outside the classroom are interrelated and connected. They should be seen as part of a single piece. I have mentioned that the Wright brothers' goal was not just to develop an effective wing with necessary qualities but rather to create a wing completely and carefully integrated within the whole complex of an airplane. A similar situation exists with the CAVE model. Our goal is to discover and implement ways to engage the community in an institution-wide educational effort to create a comprehensive program of values education and development. The model must have the power to get this effort in the air, to stay in the air, have direction, maintain speed, be able to carry weight, and all the while be simple and light in design. It is a difficult image to grasp, but we must imagine all aspects of the institution working together to create this atmosphere and the strategies necessary to lift this educational effort off the ground.

In addition to assisting students in making connections between what they experience both inside and outside the classroom, it also seeks to provide professors with opportunities to develop and use their new-found skills acquired in the Values Institute. By focusing on both inside the classroom and beyond, these components provided faculty, students, and staff with venues for practice and a way to re-create real-life situations. The atmosphere within the institution helped students to realize that it was appropriate and necessary to attend to the values and spiritual dimensions of issues in their studies and in activities outside the classroom. They brought into classroom discussions questions generated by the events of an Academic Forum and other structured activities. The faculty was prepared for such questions, and allowed time in their lesson plans to accommodate them.

Events throughout the academic year provided an opportunity for ongoing analysis, criticism, and discussion of values issues related to the theme that unified the inquiry. Students were involved academically and through clubs, student affairs, and other aspects of student life. It also gave faculty and staff opportunities to explore the relationships between teaching methods and the development of moral sensitivity in students. These components thus furthered the primary goals of the center and its model and process.

Different images might prove helpful for understanding how the model is designed to bring about these connections. I see all aspects of the Academic Forum as instruments through which the energy, insight, and understanding acquired in the Values Institute are transmitted to the rest of the campus. You could think of it as an umbilical cord bringing life and nutrients to both individuals and the wider community. Or the function and impact of these components can be compared to the great spring of water at the base of Whiteface Mountain in the Adirondacks near Lake Placid, New York. The spring pours with such force into Lake Placid that a complete turnover of the lake's water takes place within only a few days. Or we can think of it in terms of the tradition of the Onondaga Indian Nation in central New York State. Its role within the Iroquois Federation was to transport the sacred fire from longhouse to longhouse. However you perceive it, the Academic Forum's function is to be the vehicle through which the faculty, administration, and staff discover how to communicate the energy and the deep insights of the Values Institutes to the students during the academic year both inside and beyond the classroom. Thus, one of the reasons it is sometimes called the "Academic" Forum is that it happens during the academic year.

Student-Centered Design

The CAVE model is designed to be student-centered. One of its objectives is to right the imbalance that often makes it so difficult to keep in focus that a major reason we build and run institutions of higher education is to educate the student. When all the nonessentials are scraped away, the determinant on our campus is always the same question: How do we engage the community in an institution-wide educational effort to enhance the values and spiritual sensitivity of students and their commitment to ethical decision making? Students are the primary intended audience of much of the energy of these components. The faculty, administration, and staff take the insights and the energy generated partially by the Values Institutes to the students both within and outside the classroom.

In a certain sense the university community becomes one big learning community focused on a particular values-laden theme. Within the course of a few years, different themes will have been chosen and will have brought out all sorts of creative efforts based on people's interests and concerns. When the community is engaged in an institution-wide effort—for example, to discover and implement ways to assist students with the values dimensions of science and technology—it is indeed a learning community. And it is hoped that all students, not just a select few, will be able to participate in this opportunity.

It is very possible that within a five-year period there could be as many as one hundred faculty who have participated in the Values Institutes and worked to integrate them into their classrooms and beyond. It is a significant number who have committed themselves to this process and does not count the staff and administrators who might have been involved. By doubling one's efforts there could be many more.

One Hundred Ways to Do Values Education

We do not think that there is only one way to administer values education and values development. If you have one hundred faculty who have been through the experience and understand the importance and the priority of this dimension to education, then there are now at least one hundred professors who have committed themselves to becoming part of the process of discovering how best to accomplish values education and development. There are at least one hundred ways to do values education. Each faculty member will discover how best to enact values education given her own, her discipline's, and her students' strengths and weaknesses. This element is another aspect of the grassroots and freedom inherent in the Values Program. It also means that as more professors, administrators, and staff understand and commit themselves to the discovery process, they will also touch more students. Our goal is that all students experience the impact of the institute, not just a small, elite core group.

The Method and Process

The main function of these components in the Values Forum is to help students discover connections between classroom material and the world outside the classroom. The specific format of programmatic activities both beyond the classroom and inside the classroom varies so that individual needs can be met and the program can continue to grow creatively to serve current interests and purposes. The programmatic aspects and activities of the Academic Forum and its related projects beyond the classroom and into the wider community are different each academic year because there are different people coming out of the Values Institute, there is a different theme every one to two years, the student body is constantly changing, and the world around us never stands still. But it still remains that an important source of all this energy is professors' desire to incorporate content learned in the Summer Institute into their classroom teaching.

Professor Patricia Schmidt, a professor of education, spoke for many of the faculty when she said, "I felt supported and mentored by the colleagueship generated by the program. It gave me confidence to go forward and attempt novel projects" (1997, n.p.). She worked to develop a course on diversity that was created for residential advisers. She also coordinated student retreats on diversity with Carl Thomas, director of the Higher Education Opportunity Program. We discovered that renewed energy from the institutes also stimulates the creative use of existing resources.

Katharine Rose Hanley, a professor of philosophy, caught the significance of the Academic Forum and the program: "The Program extends responsibility for initiative and leadership to all components of the college, including especially, alumni/alumnae and student leaders of residences and various campus organizations. . . . The program develops informed concern for values throughout one's life and service in the human community" (1996, n.p.).

In Chapter 5 I will provide a descriptive analysis, guidelines, and examples of the Academic Forum. At this time I need to clarify the word *evolving*, key to understanding the CAVE model.

The Key to an Evolving Model: Research and Assessment

The CAVE model is an evolving model, and it was evolving right from the very beginning. We know that all models evolve and that they do so in all sorts of different ways. But it is important for this study to understand where this model came from. I use the word *evolving* to characterize the nature of the CAVE model because it best describes its essence from its very birth. The model began to take shape because of our shared collective experience as educators. As we gathered for our first meetings we each brought to the table our own perspectives, disciplines, and approaches. We were specially trained in social science, humanities, business, and aspects of the natural sciences. But we soon came to a stark realization: if the critical need that we had discovered was correct—that graduates in higher education were unprepared to face the moral and spiritual challenges in their personal and professional lives—then we ourselves were faced with some very difficult challenges. Having a Ph.D. in history, philosophy, math, law, psychology, or religious studies does not mean that you have good moral aspects. Nor does it mean that you know how to deal with the moral and spiritual aspects of issues. Our years of study had guaranteed us neither the credentials, the legitimacy, nor the confidence to assist students in having a greater sensitivity to the moral and spiritual dimensions of issues. Nor did we know how to teach them so that they would learn to be more moral.

It was because of our deeply felt need that we wanted to get input from the students. Since its beginning, an underlying assumption of our model is that action should always be based on needs and approaches that can be validated empirically. Assessment results are regularly studied, evaluated, and then fed back into the fine-tuning of the programmatic aspects of the model in order to improve results. It is important to note, then, that assessment and research for us were not just conducted after the fact; they were a regular part of the feedback and reflection process.

An early challenge faced by the original developers of the assessment approach is the inherent difficulty of measuring perceptions, attitudes, valuing processes, and outcomes. Krystine Batcho Yaworsky and William Holmes developed a strategy of applying independent methods in a cross-verification paradigm (Kirby et al. 1990, chap. 9). For example, faculty self-reports of classroom behaviors have been compared to student reports of faculty behaviors. Pedagogical techniques, including lecturing, facilitating discussion, playing devil's advocate, functioning as a role model, and so on, were then correlated with values education outcomes. When possible, self-reporting measures of outcomes were compared to task performance and behavioral indexes. Special assessment instruments were designed by Batcho and Holmes to evaluate important aspects of valuing, such as sensitivity to values issues, perceived importance of the values dimensions of decisions, and the ability to make well-reasoned judgments on problems in different life contexts. A summary of the assessment strategy appears in the book *Ambitious Dreams* (Kirby et al. 1990) and in the book now being completed by Krystine Batcho detailing the method and findings.

A clear set of goals and means for assessing success keeps the program on track. Careful assessment ensures that the program is addressing current needs. Clearly articulated goals and an empirical evaluation process help us to develop effective strategies to effect change. We continue to refine our methods of evaluation and to use our findings to improve our efforts. We agree with anthropologist Mary Douglas's insight that an institution's healthy vigor is contingent on continually making explicit its understanding of itself to itself. The assessment process helps to deepen the understanding that comes from self-reflection.

The efforts of Krystine Batcho, professor of psychology and a psychologist, were crucial for getting the founding group to understand that research and assessment ought to be critical and important components of our model. At our very first meeting, she set the tone by saying that she "would have nothing to do with this project unless it was carefully researched and assessed from its very beginning."

That remark and decision on her part turned out to be one of the most significant moments in the history and the development of the design of the CAVE model and the Values Program. Its importance is felt in the words of a renowned major university president, who referred to the assessment operation as "the golden nugget" of the program's mission and activities. As he said, "I go to potential donors and ask them to give our institution $10 million dollars and all I can give them is a promise. In the Values Program you have something that has a tested and evaluated track record." Our research and assessment program gives us the ability to deal not only with anecdotal information but also with data and analysis. Our assessment program has also been one of the reasons we were able to win grants from major foundations. We received one of the first of the Lilly Endowment's grants on values and religion.

The report by the evaluation team representing the Commission on Higher Education of the Middle States Association in 1996 gave us high praise when it said, "The Program has very clearly defined goals and a very sophisticated approach to assessing them (1996, 18)." These points underline why research and assessment are so important in the educational effort to discover how to accomplish values education and bring students to moral sensitivity and courage. It is important not just for funding but also for the praise that it can bring to any institution.

Values Institutes

Digging and Discovery

In a more peaceful time, not that long ago, I worked on an archaeological dig in Israel. My assignment was the pits. The grid I worked to excavate had been an ancient Greco-Roman trash pit. It was strenuous work. The ground I was assigned had lain untouched for nearly two thousand years. My six enthusiastic college student colleagues and I worked daily under the hot sun with picks and shovels. Each day we uncovered hundreds of Roman, Greek, Philistine, Persian, and other ancient artifacts and shards. For our morning breakfast and water breaks we rested at the side of our deepening hole. We leaned our backs against a large dirt mound only a few feet from where we were digging.

One day a staff professional wondered what was within that mound. He asked us to make a few exploratory probes. Inside our mound of dirt stood a main gate to the ancient city. It was among the oldest well-preserved ancient gates to a city discovered in the Near East. Right before my eyes, but hidden by only a few feet of soil, was one of the major archaeological finds of the decade.

I left the excitement of the dig and after a side trip to Egypt I continued my sabbatical. One of the products of my efforts on that sabbatical was *Ambitious Dreams* (Kirby et al. 1990), a book recording the first findings of another journey of discovery. I did not fully realize it then, but that writing project described the beginnings of a discovery in its own right as exciting and probably more pertinent than the one I left behind in Ashqelon, Israel, beside the rich, blue Mediterranean. The fateful discovery was made not in an exotic place halfway across the world, but right in my own backyard—in the institution where I taught.

A paragraph in one of the chapters in *Ambitious Dreams* (Kirby et al. 1990) hints at what was behind the mound of soil in my own backyard. Thomas Curley recounts a moment in the first week of the Values Program's first Summer Institute on economic justice and values held in 1988. "Dr. Dolbeare introduced two significant changes during the first week. First, he reorganized the physical arrangement of the meeting room from chairs arranged in rows facing a lectern to tables and chairs arranged in a square. As a result, participants were able to interact with one another more effectively. Second, he shifted the responsibility for setting the agenda from the facilitators to the participants. As we shall see, these changes transformed the character of the Institute" (Curley 1990, 31).

By reorganizing the physical geography and giving the faculty participants the power to set the agenda, the facilitator of our summer symposium changed everything. It seems a small matter, arranging furniture. But instead it was a major breakthrough. We were no longer passive participants, ready to listen to an outside expert. Instead we were partners in this enterprise, expected to take responsibility for the direction of the seminar. It was a profound symbolic gesture. As people, and as educators, we immediately saw the power of example. Who we are and how we act do deeply impact our students.

This experience revolutionized the way I saw and understood teaching. On many deep levels the teacher and the student are equal in their humanity. One of the texts we studied that summer was *The Pedagogy of the Oppressed* (Friere 2000). One message of that text is that as an educator, the task is not to keep power in one location but instead to spread it around. As a college is traditionally structured, power to teach is centered in the faculty. But to be an educator means you must give the power to the students. This experience set the tone for our ambitious dream.

Purpose of the Chapter

This chapter discusses the Values Institute, its process and methodology, its approach and techniques, and offers reflections on our achievements gained through dialogue, discovery, and experimentation. In it I provide a descriptive analysis, guidelines, models, and examples grounded in years of observation, practical experience, and knowledge of the many participants and their students locally, nationally, and internationally. My hope is that this chapter will provide guidelines for those individuals interested in adapting and implementing the CAVE model to their own institution.

As we discuss the Values Institute it is important to recall from the last chapter that three major components constitute the CAVE model: the Working Group on Values, the Values Institute, and the Academic Forum. I have underlined that these components work not as the sum of separate parts but as interactive forces in an integrated, dynamic system. Each component serves a particular purpose and supports and strengthens the functions of each of the other components. Accordingly, to accurately appreciate the Values Institute within the totality of the CAVE model, you must comprehend both the Values Institute's particular purpose and function in itself and its function and purpose as part of a carefully designed series of interactive forces in an integrated, dynamic system. Therefore, in this chapter I will clarify both the institute (faculty and staff development) in itself and how it strengthens the functions of each of the other components.

As I discussed earlier, it is now recognized as quite normal to use the institute as a method for faculty development. Numerous successful approaches in higher education and the professional schools make excellent use of the institute approach. We need to keep in mind, however, that it is not only the methods one uses that will define a particular outcome of values education. For instance, just because one is using the techniques of an institute does not imply, require, or determine a particular result. These seemingly similar methods can have different goals and intentions. Each approach sponsors its own institute, and each will have its own goals, objectives, methods, intended target audiences, challenges, and intended outcomes. To be effective it needs to be able to fit the mission and purpose of both the program and the institution.

Throughout this chapter I will frequently stress that the outcomes of the Values Institute depend to a great extent both on the objectives and on the substance and matter, the stuff of the activities; we need to look carefully at both the content and the process of the Values Institute. My goal is to be very clear about what makes up this very stuff of the activities and what goes on. I will provide descriptive analysis, guidelines, models, and examples.

This material will include the substance of the activities and goings-on of what I classify as the three stages of the Values Institute: the preparatory stage, the institute itself, and what happens after the institute. This latter stage is covered in more depth in Chapter 5, "The Academic Forum." Stage 1 includes challenges such as choosing the institution-wide theme, the institute's facilitators, motivating the faculty to apply and attend the institute, and getting the commitment of key people in the institution. Stage 2 discusses the substance of the activities during the actual institute. I include a discussion of the mission and goals of the Values Institute and provide guidelines, models, and examples of bridging the gap between faculty, staff, and administrators. I close with some suppositions underlying the design and function of the Values Institute.

How the Values Institutes Came About

A Seminal Experience: The Working Group on Values

The Values Institutes were not part of the original dream but instead evolved as we proceeded along our path. At the beginning of our journey, six tenured faculty members in psychology, business law, history, political science, and religious studies met to discuss what I thought would be our general plan. I had recruited Edward Gorman, director of admissions at Le Moyne and the dean of admissions counselors in New York State, to accompany us on the journey; he was to become our scout, charged with keeping the "reality factor" alive in our discussions. Ed knew best where our students came from, geographically, emotionally, and educationally. My initial intention for this group was to create a senior seminar to help students integrate liberal arts and the Jesuit emphasis on socially responsible values into their major disciplinary fields.

After meeting twice monthly for two semesters, by the spring of 1986 this working group understood that attempts to address the need for values education would be ineffective if they were limited to isolated courses or programs. We unwittingly perceived an insight integral to our process. We would need to build some sort of umbrella-like structure to engage the entire institution. When we involved the entire college community, we would enable students to integrate their learning with their values. In retrospect this idea seems simple, even inevitable. But like the rearrangement of furniture that so stunned the faculty at the first Values Institute, this insight was revolutionary at the time. It felt as if we were venturing into deep and uncharted waters.

Three Seemingly Contradictory Realities

Our discussions and our trust for one another in the Working Group deepened and developed. At the same time we became aware of some tensions that refused to go away. As faculty we were a collection of diverse individuals. The different contexts of our personal and professional lives brought many shades and colors to our discussions. This fact was never more evident than when we tried to hold in tension three seemingly contradictory realities: encouraging academic freedom, impacting the culture of the institution, and responding to the changing needs of the students. We should not have been surprised that we experienced tension. Faculty at any academic institution are strong individuals, wary of being controlled, and careful to preserve their independence and autonomy. How could we reconcile our commitment to a process of serious inquiry with issues of academic freedom? We recognized that the academic freedom of the individual could and sometimes would conflict with the academic freedom of the whole institution. Faculty, after all, did not want to be instructed in how, or what, to teach. We needed to reach out to them without being condescending, or appearing to dictate their curriculum. Our commitment encouraged us to face, rather than to avoid, the toughest question: How do you maintain the delicate balance between academic freedom of individual professors and their individual rights while promoting the academic freedom of the institution as a whole and allowing the institution to assert its own identity?

These meetings were not just theoretical, academic discussions for us. As faculty members we were professors in one particular institution. If we were going to create a workable strategy, it would need to be thoroughly grounded in the reality of our situation. In the real world in which we journeyed, the challenge looked like as follows: How could Le Moyne

College be true to its mission and purpose (that is, be Jesuit and Catholic), stress serious values inquiry, and continue to respect the pluralism and diversity of its faculty, students, and administrative staff, all without yielding to empty relativism? It was, and remains, a tough question.

We resolved to live within this constant tension and to make it work for us. It reminded me of the tension in the strings of a violin. Too little tension, and no music happens, too much and they snap. In the hands of a master musician this tension makes possible the beauty of the music. But as any good orchestra conductor or musician knows, good music does not just happen. It is achieved only after a lot of practice and years of struggle and effort.

Being academics, we turned to the literature on values education and researched other institutions and programs. I was pretty sure that we would find a lot of help. But in 1986 there was not as much as I had hoped. The annual meeting of the American Association of Higher Education and the annual summer gatherings of the Society for Values in Higher Education proved very helpful. The work of Alverno College and the Pulse Program at Boston College also provided inspiration. We found that we were not the first to aim our sights at the entire institution. We may have been the first, though, to attempt to arrive there through a collegewide, interactive model.

As our discussions progressed, we became confirmed in our opposition to any educational practices designed to indoctrinate students into one particular set of theories or beliefs. We are not all Jesuits in mufti; neither are we relativists. Our aim was to create an institution that assists students both in becoming aware of values issues and in fashioning values frameworks that are consistent, defensible to themselves, and in keeping with the best of human traditions. Furthermore, when we had accomplished this aim, we wanted our students to have the moral courage to act on their principles.

Professor William Miller, of the Le Moyne College Mathematics Department, was a participant in the first Summer Institute. Dr. Miller agreed to participate but brought suspicion with him. "As an agnostic still in rebellion against the dogma of my Methodist upbringing, I was in no mood to be party to some camouflaged form of catechism" (Miller 1990, 101).

Miller was relieved to find the basic principles of the institute were "neither doctrinaire nor sectarian." He highlights certain points he assimilated from Richard Morrill's theories of values education:

> Indoctrination is not a tool of authentic values education; to the contrary, values education uses open inquiry to encourage self-reflection; it succeeds by gently and lovingly fomenting internal (that is, within a person's own value structure) dissonance. . . . Values education depends on dialogue; teachers must act as affirming mentors for human discovery, not as judging minions of sealed truths; they must be as skilled at listening as at talking, as prepared to learn from students as to share knowledge with them. (102)

We wholeheartedly committed to this mode of values education. We understood that anything other than an institution-wide effort would be doomed to failure. Everyone's experience verified that the institution would reject a one-shot program, such as bringing in an outside speaker, or involving only one or two faculty or administrative offices. We had all attended presentations by renowned speakers and seen the enthusiasm evaporate within days of the speaker's departure. We had all attended conferences and found our desire for change squelched when we had no fellow faculty members to share our vision. But where should we start? Within a year we decided to start with the faculty and the Summer Institutes.

An Educational Effort Designed to Discover
and to Implement a Values Institute

In 1988, we launched the first of a series of Values Institutes to help us fashion a collegiate environment designed to enhance students' values, moral sensitivity, and commitment to ethical decision making. We had recognized that all transformation begins at home. We could not speak of expertly working with our students until we had learned how to transform ourselves and then "trained the trainers."

From the beginning, an empirical research and assessment component in our Values Program contributed to a deeper understanding of moral development in colleges and universities and monitored the continuing effectiveness of the program. At critical junctures, quantitative and qualitative self-reporting and task-performance data enabled us to explore faculty and student perspectives on values outcomes. We investigated perceptions, attitudes, pedagogy, and abilities using social science methods and instruments developed for our purposes.

Within a few years of our beginning we began to take the first steps in expanding our ambitious dream. In 1990, we received a grant from the Lilly Endowment to support basic research to explore parallels between collegiate values and spiritual development. By 1994 we were convinced that the need for attention to spirituality is at least as great (if not more so) as the need for values education. The broadening of the mission of the program strengthened the significance of our work but more than doubled our need for programmatic, research, and assessment resources.

The Values Institute: Three Stages

The work of carrying out the Values Institute involves a series of actions that might seem familiar to anyone who has attended or organized an institute on the educational and corporate campuses in the United States or worldwide. We need to bear in mind, however, that it is not only the method one uses that determines an outcome of values education. Rather, the outcome depends on the goals and objectives and the substance and matter, the stuff of the activities. With this thought is mind these actions can be divided into three stages: the preparatory stage, the institute itself, and the follow-up. The first stage begins eighteen to twenty-four months prior to the institute, the second lasts the length of the institute, and the third lasts at least through the next academic year and, it is hoped, into the next years.

Stage 1: The Preparations

The preparatory stage is critical to the success of the Values Institute. Like the three-year preparatory stage when the Working Group on Values worked to "break up the hardened soil," the institute's preparatory phase functioned in the same manner to prepare the institution's soil to accept the seed when it was planted. A whole series of actions work their silent way through the institution like ripples in a pond. Slowly, almost imperceptibly over the months, the various carefully planned actions do their work. They make students and faculty conscious and aware that a new values theme is on the horizon. Then the audience begins to understand it and desires to do something about it.

This preparatory stage contains a systematic series of actions that if performed properly replicate the original experience of the Working Group on Values. Just as our Working Group became excited by the possibilities involved in values education, so we sought to excite the college community. We wanted to touch and enliven emotions and passions and help students and faculty to understand basic fundamental truths that are known only by doing. In theories of cognition, we are talking about insights that people arrive at only when they become actively engaged and involved in the learning process.

Working as a catalyst, the Working Group on Values is the "hub" of the wheel making up this series of actions. It is partially why the Working Group concept is now considered the third major component of the CAVE model. A core group of faculty and other constituents is in touch with the reality of the institution and qualified to identify a need that is resonating with others. It is also a group that has respect and legitimacy among the faculty.

One of its major responsibilities is to be partially responsible for initiating discussions concerning upcoming themes and possible topics. In various ways they begin discussions, surveys, and research to discover what theme needs to be discussed within the institution and beyond.

Choosing the Theme

The preparatory stage is already under way during the challenging effort to choose the next values-laden theme. Just as the Working Group on Values founders discovered an urgent need of our graduates that demanded to be addressed, so too this evolving new generation of students, educators, and wider constituencies has to go through that discovery experience themselves. They too have to go through the process of discovering a theme that has arisen from the grassroots level. The process of choosing the theme reflects in a microscopic manner the process of the entire Values Program methodology. The theme is not imposed from above; rather, it evolves from within the community.

Most important in this series of actions in stage 1 is the selection of a theme. Before any specifics about a Values Institute, choice of facilitators, funding, release time, invitations, or publicity can take place, the theme must be chosen. The important thing is that the grassroots nature of the values program is respected. The theme will be an effective instrument if it arises naturally from the needs and desires of the students and the institution. While all sorts of discussions are under way, surveys are sent out to students, faculty and staff, and administration. Slowly, a short list of possible themes begins to evolve; some of them will have been part of discussions in previous institutes and values-related meetings.

Sometimes you are lucky in your choice of themes. In 1989 the fall of the Berlin Wall and the emergence of the former Iron Curtain countries coincided exactly with the collegewide theme "Peace and War." At other times your hard work pays off. For instance, the theme "The Spiritual Dimensions of Higher Education: Attending to the Sacred in Our Midst" worked its way through the community for five years before it finally surfaced as a theme whose time had arrived. The time seemed ripe, as the college was approaching the fiftieth anniversary of its founding. Sometimes you are forced to work with a totally unexpected situation, as when the Values Institute in 2001 focused on the theme "Action for Justice in the Contemporary World," with an emphasis on Service Learning. Three months later the tragedy of September 11 forced us totally to revamp and rethink our Academic Forum events and needs. The theme needs to be a big theme, large enough to give the *Queen Mary* enough room to turn around.

The Search for Personnel

Often a steering group will be asked to develop the outlines of the selected theme and a possible two-year program. The membership of this group will usually be at least two Working Group members but usually two or three new people who have real interests in the topics. They in term will consult and bring in various interested faculty and others within and beyond the campus to advise them.

The search for resources, both personnel and financial, is also an important part of preparing the soil and breaking up the hardened ground.

We found it necessary to prepare and submit grant proposals to many different foundations, associations, and individuals. As anyone who has written grants knows, this process involves real commitment to research and development of the topic. An attempt to sell the product successfully further lights the fire and keeps things alive.

Phase 1 is a series of exercises that begin to accomplish for the faculty and other members of the corporate institution the three goals of the Values Program: awareness and consciousness, the establishing of a framework of values, and the beginnings of a commitment to act on what we see as the priorities. By this time a core group of faculty will have surfaced with a special interest and commitment to make the theme happen. From among these members we hope to find faculty who volunteer to act as director of the Values Institute and director of the Academic Forum. These faculty members must work together with the Working Group on Values, future facilitators, participants of the institute, academic deans, faculty senate, student-life personnel, development office, and grant-writing offices. Gerard Manley Hopkins's poem "Our Blessed Lady Compared to the Air We Breathe" speaks of grace as beginning to permeate all aspects of reality, much like the air we breathe. So too the ripples of the Values Program begin to infiltrate all aspects of the institution.

As the theme begins to emerge it becomes time to begin to search out possible facilitators. We found it best to have selected the facilitators up to at least eighteen months ahead of time. These people are usually in high demand, and advance warning is necessary in order to get on their schedules. This lead time also allows for the writing of grant proposals, selection of institute participants, and brochure preparation.

The facilitators are the guides who lead the participants to their own self-discovery and creative imaginings of ways to assist students. Facilitators will perform this task for the faculty and participants, who will in turn learn how to do the same thing for their students and others. It is a long process of winnowing out who we want. The selection process involves discussions with the ad hoc group working to prepare the theme and the institute, and the Working Group on Values. It might also entail all sorts of phone calls with various people in the field. This general preparation demands that the WGV, the ad hoc group, and others involved are clear and focused on the Values Institute's goals and purposes. In order to recruit the proper facilitators, one needs to be able to explain what the institute is and how it is different from other institutes on other campuses, corporations, and societal situations. When we decide on a short list of whom we would like to invite, we have to be sure we have the money to pay them. We also need the authority to arrange dates and times for preliminary discussion and planning, dates of the institute, and the many other things. One of the reasons we worked to get an endowment was the critical need to have funding so that planning for the future could take place.

Once the theme has been decided, the coordinators chosen, and the funding ensured (you need about fifty to one hundred thousand dollars), it is now time to advertise the institute. A brochure now needs to be designed and sent out with the invitation explaining the upcoming Summer Institute. This involves input from the communications and graphics offices in the institution. The WGV, ad hoc group, coordinator, and staff all work hard to create a clear brochure giving in an attractive way the important aspects of the upcoming Values Institute and its theme.

Meanwhile, the Values Institute coordinator is working with the Academic Forum coordinator and the Values Program clerical staff. They work together to set up schedules, classrooms, office space, room-and-board arrangements for facilitators, audiovisual provisions (all Values Institutes were videotaped), arrangements with the food service, scheduling the Villa (a facility for extended retreats) for a day of discussion, and dinner for the participants.

Motivating Faculty: Breaking Down Barriers

One of the biggest issues for all groups is motivating the faculty to participate. To recruit the best of the faculty, the promise of success needs to be in the air. The fact they are being paid to attend the institute reinforces its professional and academic aspect. Payment also signals that this educational effort is a priority in the institution, that the "search for meaning and value" is central to the mission and identity statement of the institution. At our institution this centrality was reflected in the preamble to the criteria for eligibility for tenure and promotion.

For more than eighteen months before the opening bell on the Values Institute, all sorts of connections have been made and barriers have fallen. By December, six months before the June institute, the advertising has gone out, and faculty are planning their summer and academic research with the realization that one of their options will be the Value Institute. Many threads have come together to get this far. Tension and electricity are in the air.

What distinguishes these institutes, before, during, and after the institute, are the goals and objectives and substance and matter, what I call the stuff of all these activities. The faculty and staff invited to participate in the Values Institute are not just participants. Our goal is to help them understand the importance of addressing the values and the spiritual and moral dimensions in their own professional and personal lives. Once they have understood this aim, we work to help them begin to want to commit to this goal.

Everything I have said highlights the need for being connected to the larger institution. Requests for released time for coordinators and other major positions need to be heard and accepted. This campaign involves selling the institute and the entire Values Program and its theme and goal to the administration and the departments who will have to sacrifice a department member for at least one course as they coordinate a component. Usually, there is also a stipend for the coordinator and the director and the facilitators.

What distinguishes the Values Program from other approaches is its institution-wide, interactive CAVE model that is designed to engage the entire institution over a long period of time. One wonders sometimes how one deals with this program when it is so unpredictable. You begin with a theme about which people care very much—all sorts of people care very much. All people are invited to be part of this institution-wide educational effort to discover and implement ways to assist students with the values dimension. I would normally think this plan is a most terrifying thing to do, to let all of these people from all sorts of situations be part of a process that is so central and critical to the academic enterprise. What surprised me was how well it worked.

Now that the preliminary stage is completed, all of these elements will begin to come together. We now arrive at stage 2, participation in the institute.

Stage 2: Experiencing the Institute

As a professor I am used to people saying, "You teach fifteen hours a week and you have your summers off. That is the kind of job I'd like." I have given up trying to explain that my work is much more time-consuming and demanding than it may look on the surface. What some do understand is the comparison of being a professor to being part of a wedding day. The wedding ceremony and the reception are over within eight to ten hours. Planning for the wedding, however, usually takes far more than a year; it is months filled with decisions made on a million details. Fulfilling what is involved in the marriage commitment takes years and perhaps a lifetime. I like to think of the Values Institute in the same way, like a wedding. It is a brief event. But if the parties and the institution are well prepared, the brief exchange of promises symbolizes the commitment to future action.

On the evening before the institute, or sometimes a few days earlier, a dinner and reception are held for the participants, and we invite faculty and participants from past institutes. A keynote address is given to focus the event; for example, Thomas F. Green, author of *Voices: The Educational Formation of Conscience* (1999), spoke at one institute, and Richard Morrill, author of *Teaching Values in College* (1980), spoke in 1988.

Like the wedding ceremony's rehearsal and rehearsal party, the opening day of the institute sets the tone for the institute. The tone directly addresses the biggest barriers to institutional change. The president of the college or the academic vice president attends and welcomes the participants. The director of the Values Program also welcomes participants and puts the mission and aims of the Values Program within the context of what they will be doing for the next one to three weeks. Next, the director of research and assessment explains once again the research element of the Values Program. She then distributes the research instrument that will provide the baseline for the research and assessment for the group. They will be assessed again immediately at the end of the institute and one year later. This aspect of our program is highlighted by Krystine Batcho in her forthcoming book, in which she describes the methodology and features certain findings.

On the first morning it is important to introduce the faculty to the goals and objectives of the Values Institute and of the Values Program.

Faculty are introduced to each other, to talk about why each person is there and what they hope to accomplish, to meet the facilitators, and to hear the details of the institute from the coordinator of the Values Institute.

Three Phases Within the Institute Itself

During the actual institute itself the participants experience three interconnected phases. In the first, participants work to understand the theme's material content and to identify and discuss the values dimensions of the issues. During the critical second phase, participants discussions' move to discovering how the values dimension relates to their own professional and personal lives. They also move into the new territory of how this values awareness is related to teaching in their discipline and in this particular institution. The third phase is dedicated to the task of supporting each other as they work to discover and implement practical ways to integrate the program into their teaching and professional work.

Phase 1. Each participant is like an explorer becoming acclimated to this new terrain. The goal is that participants acquire reasonable competence and confidence with the theme's content. Every workshop I have ever been in goes through this stage. In graduate school I took an interdisciplinary course in bioethics and the life sciences open to students at the Columbia University Law School, Union Theological Seminary, and other graduate schools. The classes were at Columbia University in New York City. During the early stages we listened as the physicians, scientists, and biologists worked the content. It took those of us in the humanities and social scientists time to learn the terms. It was also important to our experience that there were many different disciplines in the room and that they all participated in trying to understand the content. That same dynamic functions in the Values Institutes. For instance, during our institute on the theme "Science, Technology, and Values," participants actively engaged each other in an effort to understand important but difficult terms and their content. They struggled to clarify the distinctions between science and technology as looked at from the different disciplines of engineering, biology, chemistry, psychology, physics, and religious studies. This desire to master difficult content also occurred during the institute dedicated to the theme "Values Education Across the Curriculum." It needs to happen in every Values Institute.

Lunch is provided each day, an integral part of the institute. It gives the participants time to relax with each other. Over a leisurely lunch the participants have time to talk, think, and let ideas develop. As in the WGV, a period of relaxation time was critical.

At the end of the day we discuss where we have been and where we will go tomorrow. The discussion is open, and participants have opportunities for input. The important thing is for the participants to keep ownership of the institute.

Once the participants have become confident and competent about the topic, then the facilitators can move them to the next step: identifying and then discussing the values dimensions of the theme. Now the institute is moving toward one of the goals of the Values Program itself: to raise the consciousness and awareness of people about the values dimensions of issues. This moment is where issues such as legitimacy begin to evolve. In the early days it was a major hurdle. But we had worked hard to foresee all of the obstacles.

As the trainers-to-be are being led through a series of exercises, they begin to learn a whole series of skills and techniques. They are not just learning about the techniques and skills, however. The goal is that these experiences provide them with a number of arrows in their quiver. They then have to experiment with what arrow will be best in this situation. It is an educational effort designed to discover and to implement ways to assist students. The participants actually practice. They suggest and experiment with other ideas and techniques that come to them only out of the interconnection of the situation. As my colleagues and I had experienced with the WGV, we were able to know and discover things that we had never thought possible for us. We also found that we had somehow given each other the courage to try things. Being a member of this type of group had given us courage.

In the institutes, as I first explained in Chapter 3, we hope to give participants TLC: technique, legitimacy, and content. In the first phase of the Values Institute, participants gain knowledge of the theme's content, and they also begin to discover how to identify and distinguish the values dimensions of the theme. The participants are now able to move to stage 2.

Phase 2. Having become more sensitive and aware of the content's values dimensions, the participants now begin to reflect on how the values dimension is pertinent in their professional and personal lives, their courses, discipline, and the institution itself. Now the question of *legitimacy* begins to be a concern. Both those individuals training the trainers and the trainers themselves find this moment critical. In the institute on economic justice, this moment arrived when a faculty member in the Economics Department had great difficulty discerning whether there was a value dimension in economics. It was a memorable moment as she moved her attention away from the facilitators to the arguments of her faculty colleagues. All who participated in that institute have vivid memories of the exchange as she and her colleagues coaxed and persuaded each other to try to shed light on this issue. Her emotions and passions and those sentiments of the people in the room with her were being touched in this process. Why? It happens because of the emotional component of values.

Phase 3. This phase develops as the participants work to formulate realistic plans to implement the insights and energy of the institute. They have the help of the expert outside facilitators and the deep sense of community. They are now empowered to go out and tackle the tough values issues. Gradually, the trainers begin to grow in confidence and competency. They can master and understand the content of the theme. You do not have to be a high-level expert on a topic to have the permission to speak about and reflect on aspects of the content of an issue. After all, how many items in our lives will we have complete mastery over?

After much experience with these institutes, I see that there is an ever deepening personalization of the issues happening during the institute. It is not easy for faculty and their colleagues to become more conscious and aware of the values and spiritual dimensions of issues. The 1991 Values Institute, focused on the theme "Science, Technology, and Values," provides a good example. By design, the institute's different phases combined to do two things: first, to create an experience that made it possible for the participants to recognize that there are values and spiritual and moral dimensions in all issues of science and technology and, second, to come to a deep personal realization that these issues are my issues both personally and professionally.

The institute's facilitators included Beatrice Robinson of the Biology Department of Le Moyne College, Taft M. Broome Jr. of the Engineering

Department at Howard University, and Langdon Winner of the Political Science Department of Rensselaer Polytechnic Institute.

Participants engaged first in a discussion of the scientist as portrayed in cinema. From this beginning, facilitators branched out into discussions of the images of the scientist in society at large, the foundations of ethics as applied to engineering, science, and technology; and the role of choice. As the breadth of understanding of science and technology grew in the participants, so did their awareness of the values dimension.

I have said that one characteristic that distinguishes the Values Institutes is its ability to "Keep your eyes on the prize." When you study the two questions that structured the work of this institute, it becomes clear how the values dimension was kept in the forefront during the institute. The questions were: How are individual and social values influenced by scientific discoveries and technological changes? What impact can and should values have on the conduct of scientific research and the development and application of new technologies?

Topics of discussion included birth and death, reproductive technologies, life extension, genetic engineering, and biomedical technologies. Issues of privacy were included, as were computers and artificial intelligence. Global society, multiculturalism, technology transfer, and developing nations and subordinate cultures generated comment as did the environment, nature, time, water, land, air, space, and resources.

Personalizing the Experience

Our aim is that participants recognize not just that there are values issues related to the theme's content but also that values issues are intrinsic to everything they do in their professional and personal lives, which is also true for everyone else. The task of the institute then becomes discovering ways to assist the faculty in recognizing that there are values dimensions in their own professional and personal lives. Having understood that concept, the next insight that follows should be that faculty and staff ought to be attending to the importance of those values issues. This goal is accomplished partially as the institute's participants struggle to identify and discuss the values dimensions of issues. Involving faculty in this exploratory process will require acquiring certain skills and techniques, just as learning the content of an issue involves certain skills and techniques. This work then is what goes on during the Values Institutes. The faculty and some staff experience the process of discovering effective techniques and skills and then work their way through the difficult process of discerning which of these methods are going to actually work in relationship to the institute's theme. Then the next step is explored: how the techniques are related to them personally and professionally. Now for the participants the lights are coming; they begin to understand that they themselves face values and moral and spiritual challenges. They find that they usually do know how to handle these challenges. As a group they work together to explore and discover ways to assist students in facing these very same challenges that they have now found in their own lives.

The Mission and Goals of the Values Institute

Three components and a theme combine to create the Values Program. One of the components is the Values Institute. The purpose of the Values Institute is to help educators fashion a collegiate environment designed to enhance students' values, morality, ethical sensitivity, and commitment to ethical decision making. The primary target is the faculty, but we also open it up to administrators, staff, student-life professionals, trustees, and coaches. Given the vital role the faculty plays in values education, we recognized the importance of beginning the program with them.

The Values Institute is organized around a particular values-laden theme. Through consideration of the theme, participants seek to understand the role of values education across the curriculum and gain experience in pedagogical techniques that encourage students to reflect on their values. Participants must include administrators as well as faculty since both groups must work together to create an environment that nurtures values education.

The payoff of the Values Institute is twofold. First, the group creates a clear road map for the work ahead. Second, each participant gains a sense of empowerment by the collegial experience of the Values Institute itself. The result is a cadre of professionals from every part of the college who are deeply committed to assisting each student through a process of personal discovery.

The Values Program's institute brings together about twenty selected faculty, staff, and administrators for one to three weeks. Participants explore a values-laden theme and develop plans for bringing what they learn back to students in vital ways. The theme is foundational to the integrative nature of the overall program. Beginning in 1988, themes have been:

1988: "Economic Justice"

1989: "Peace and War"

1990: "Families and Public Policy"

1991: "Science, Technology, and Values"

1992: "Values Education Across the Curriculum"

1993: "Values and Diversity"

1994, 1995, 1996: "The Spiritual Dimensions in Higher Education: Attending to the Sacred in Our Midst"

1997, 1998: "Education and Public Policy"

1999: "The Student Connection: Values Connection"

2001: "Action for Justice in a Changing World"

Each theme was introduced at a summer Values Institute in the years listed above. The theme then carried over into the following academic year or years.

The institute's participants become familiar with selected relevant literature and focus on identification and discussion of pertinent values issues. Participants are actively engaged in addressing values questions and exploring how these questions apply to their own professional and personal lives.

The institute's primary purpose is to support participants as they formulate realistic action plans for implementing the fruits of the institute. Support takes place in the form of resources, such as expert outside facilitators and the deep sense of community that develops among participants. The collegial experience fostered by the institute empowers participants to return to the college community with renewed vigor, ready to tackle the tough task of values education.

Patricia Schmidt, Ph.D., a professor of education at Le Moyne, comments about the impact of the Values Institute and its aftermath: "Because of the Values Program, I am confident to go forward and attempt novel projects. I have been supported and mentored as I tried new ideas, ideas which I believe have helped me and others grow spiritually" (1997, n.p.). Dr. Schmidt's work with the Values Program grew directly into her highly regarded work edited with Ann Watts Pailliotet, *Exploring Values Through Literature, Multimedia, and Literary Events: Making Connections* (2001).

William Miller, mentioned earlier as a skeptical institute participant, commented on his experience at the 1988 Values Institute:

> Master values educator Ken Dolbeare guided us as we built a fully functioning scale model of a values-centered class. We used real materials—readings about economic justice and concomitant topics; real tools—small groups, role playing, round-table discussions (held around a square table), varied physical settings, and mock hearings; and real blood, sweat, toil, and tears (the first and last, as far as I know, only figurative!). . . .
>
> For me, the power and beauty of the Summer Institute lay in the fact that it was not merely *about* values education—it *was* values education. We learned primarily from direct experience, and experiential learning has a potency unrivaled by other forms of learning. (1990, 102–3, 105–6)

Detailed essays describing the first two summer institutes, 1988 and 1989, can be found in our book *Ambitious Dreams: The Values Program at Le Moyne College* (Kirby et al. 1990). They will only briefly be described here.

The Institute's Inclusive Nature: The Facilitators and Participants

Choosing the facilitators. The facilitators are key to the Values Institute. To understand what makes an institute work, it is critical to understand who makes the best facilitators, how they are chosen, and what the facilitator's purpose and function are within the institute and the wider framework of the Values Program.

You get only one opportunity to make a first impression. Since the first institute in 1988 would establish many precedents, we worked carefully to choose the facilitators. For that first Values Institute, three outside facilitators were chosen. We needed to establish credibility, legitimacy, and prestige in values education at Le Moyne, so we choose facilitators with national reputations, people you would want to spend three weeks with in the summer.

We also knew that we as a Working Group had ourselves been through a powerfully transforming process as we struggled together within the reality of our institution and the world to first understand the problem before us, and then to create strategies and processes to address those problems. We wanted the faculty to go through the same experience that we had. We wanted to create a systematic series of exercises and reflective situations that would give them the opportunity to re-create our experience. It would also need to be an experience that would appeal to their emotions and passions and thus give them the motivation to act. And, finally, it was to convey to them deep truths and insights that would light a fire within them to go out and do for others as had been done for them.

The first person we lined up was Richard Morrill, at the time the president of Centre College in Kentucky. He later became president of the University of Richmond. He is the author of *Teaching Values in College* (1980). I had attended a workshop he gave at the American Association for Higher Education annual meeting on his book and thought he would be a good person to kick off the first institute. He was invited to give the inaugural values lecture in the spring of 1988, two months before the Values Institute on economic justice began. The faculty who had been selected to attend the institute attended with many of the students and some of the administration. His presentation was excellent and prepared the way for the institute in terms of expectations. He was expected to provide content.

Kenneth Dolbeare, professor of political science at Evergreen State College, is the author of *Democracy at Risk: The Politics of Economic Renewal and American Public Policy, a Citizen's Guide* (1986). Ken Dolbeare's role, as initially envisioned, was to provide guidance on the process of the institute. These two nationally known figures were contacted some twenty months before the dates of the institute.

Because the Working Group initially adopted a traditional process-content distinction in the Values Institute, we saw the need for two facilitators: one whose strength matched the theme of the institute, and the other whose strength was tied to the process of educating. In the actual working out of the Values Institute, this distinction blurred. We began to understand that because both facilitators were educators, they would therefore be concerned with both process and content.

As the institute approached, a scheduling conflict arose. Richard Morrill was planning his move from Centre College to the University of Richmond and could give only two days to the institute. As a result, we decided to seek a third facilitator. John Langan, S.J., Rose Kennedy Professor of Christian Ethics at Georgetown University, agreed to attend the second and third weeks of the three-week institute. Langan was chosen partly because he had familiarity with the evolution of the U.S. bishops' pastoral letter on economic justice, which had inspired the choice of topic for that first Values Institute. As a Jesuit, he would also have an understanding of our institution's roots and basic educational philosophy.

As the Values Institute process evolved within the larger framework of the vision of the entire Values Program, we modified the approach we took in 1988. In 1989, facilitators included Barron Boyd, a Le Moyne faculty member in political science who had attended the 1988 institute. We had earlier made the decision that we would work to wean ourselves away from dependence on outside well-known names; our goal was to establish in the minds and hearts of own faculty that we had the legitimacy and the wherewithal to do values education with competency ourselves. The other facilitators selected were the Most Reverend Thomas Costello, the auxiliary bishop of the Diocese of Syracuse; David O'Brien of Holy Cross College; and Roger Shinn, professor emeritus at Union Theological Seminary. If we recall the imagery of the ripple effect of the stone in the pond, you can see what we were doing. We were spreading out to give the faculty more empowerment as values educators. We were touching key administrators in the Roman Catholic Diocese of Syracuse who impacted education in grades K–12 and in religious education, and we were reaching out to other Jesuit colleges and universities and to other nondenominational schools of theology and seminary training.

Beginning in 1989 all Values Institutes followed this evolving, flexible process: from now on, facilitators would be both outside experts and members of our own faculty. We also worked to choose facilitators from among diverse faculty groups so that facilitator duty rotated among faculty and included members of the Sociology, History, Biology, Philosophy, and

Psychology Departments and administrators. By 1997 the "Education and Public Policy" institute facilitators included three Le Moyne faculty and four external facilitators, including two local school superintendents and the vice president of Henneberry Hill Consultants.

Choosing the participants: Motivate the best to attend. Persuading the best faculty to attend is a major challenge to anything of this type. How do you engage the faculty to take on this extra work during their valuable summer hours? If we keep in mind the ripple effect, we see it in action with the selection of the participants for the Values Institute.

Working to get the faculty on board involved a whole series of carefully thought-out techniques. In 1988, the Working Group on Values decided to ask faculty to apply for the institute's places. Remember that this enterprise was a grassroots initiative by a group of faculty; it was being conducted using no coercion or force by the administration. The Working Group created and mailed a simple one-page application form to all full-time faculty members. The group hoped initially to attract senior faculty, a diverse representation of departments, and motivated and enthusiastic participants. In 1988, the first year, nineteen participants representing thirteen departments were chosen. The participants were all full-time tenured or tenure-track faculty. They would meet together for three weeks of intensive work.

The ripples began to spread across the pond of the institution in terms of participants by the second summer. Gradually, we worked to include not only the faculty but also key administrative posts. In 1989 Barbara Blaszak, the associate academic dean, was chosen as a participant. With her selection we now had an important dean who would bring back to her daily duties and her meetings with other administrators the insights of the institute. This trend of including administrators in Values Institutes continued. In 1990 Daphne Stephens, a counselor in continuous learning, was invited to participate. We had now reached out to the adult nontraditional sections and offices for students. By 1991 the program decided to reach beyond the campus for participants. Two professors from Wheeling College, one in social science and one in chemistry, and a member of the Department of Philosophy from King's College joined the Le Moyne faculty and administrators in the 1991 institute.

The ripple effect was broadening even more as we sought to reach other institutions in the Northeast. The work was slow and deliberate. The mix of disciplines and of participants from within and outside of Le Moyne College encouraged fresh insights and reflected the dynamic, ever changing character of the Values Program.

Participation Expands

From the very beginning the WGV had felt frustrated with our inability to connect with student-life professionals and the whole area of student affairs in the institution. We had to wait until 1992 to experience what would be two of my most satisfying breakthroughs. The first happened when the associate dean for student life, Barbara Maylone Karper, applied for and was accepted to the institute on the theme "Values Education Across the Curriculum." For the first time a key force in the student-affairs section of the institution would sit together with the faculty as an equal in discussions about the values dimensions across the curriculum.

It had taken five years of careful, slow work and influence to bring the environment to the point where this important connection was made. Her status within the institution and her personal connections among many of the participants opened up all sorts of issues in the larger curriculum beyond the classroom. As we had noted in 1987, of all the hours in a week, only fifteen are spent in the classroom. What about the other types of classrooms where values education is continuing—the cafeteria, the dorm room, the all-night talk sessions? The dam had been broken. From then on, the connection with student affairs had been cemented.

The second breakthrough occurred when we accepted international participants to join the Le Moyne participants in the institute for the first time. These international participants came from Nanzan University in Japan and the Ateneo De Manila in the Philippines. They were joined by participants from Wheaton College in Illinois, DePaul University in Chicago, and Keene State in New Hampshire. The participants from Japan and Asia together with the diversity of backgrounds from the other participants helped us to understand the values dimensions and the wider curriculum in new ways.

In 1993, for the first time, students were participants. The eleven students included one recent graduate, one senior, six juniors, and three sophomores. This experience taught us that for a formal institute, the mix of faculty and students did not work. The roles of faculty and students are too different. Students are in the institutions for a short period, whereas the faculty is thinking more long-term.

Nine participants from the staff or the administration, including a special assistant to the college president, joined the fourteen faculty who took part in the 1994 institute. Six administrators, four external participants, and ten faculty made up the mix for the 1997 institute. In that year the external participants included the executive director of the New York State Catholic Conference, a representative from the New York State United Teachers Office, the district director for Congressman James Walsh's office, and the associate superintendent of the Diocese of Syracuse Catholic schools.

The shortest Values Institute ran for only three days, in 1999. Its theme was "The Student Connection: Values Connection," and it was scheduled for May 17–19. Participants included three students (one graduating senior and two juniors), thirteen faculty, and ten administrators, including the head basketball coach and the head men's lacrosse coach, as well as the dean for campus activities and programs and the director and associate directors of continuous learning.

The inclusive nature of the Values Institutes builds on the sense of community mentioned by the first participants in the Working Group on Values. It is designed to heal the division in a college community that has been commented on by Parker Palmer: "If we want to develop and deepen the capacity for connectedness at the heart of good teaching, we must understand—and resist—the perverse but powerful draw of the 'disconnected' life" (1998, 35).

The liberal arts curriculum tends to reinforce a disconnection between science and technology and everyday life. Many students have no choice but to view science and technology as esoteric curiosities. Students in science-related departments are also poorly served when they are encouraged to master specialized content and techniques without sensing the social and ethical dimensions of scientific research and new technologies. The 1991 Values Institute was charged with building bridges across those gaps and finding means to address the related problems of science illiteracy and values illiteracy. As Palmer states, "We are distanced by a grading system that separates teachers from students, by departments that fragment fields of knowledge, by competition that makes students and teachers wary of their peers, and by a bureaucracy that puts faculty and administration at odds" (35–36).

The inclusive nature of the Values Program at Le Moyne seeks to bridge these gaps between sciences and the humanities, between faculty and students, between faculty and administration, and between educational institution and the local and larger global community.

Let's look first at how a perceived gap between mathematics and values education was bridged. At first glance, it would seem most difficult for a mathematician to include any discussion of values education in his curriculum. However, Professor William Miller, after his experience at the 1988 Values Institute, disagrees:

> Various stereotypes to the contrary, mathematicians are people. As people, mathematicians face the same moral dilemmas as others. The dilemmas range from the splashy—like whether to accept Star Wars money for research . . . and how to provide equal opportunity in mathematics to women and people of color—to the mundane—like how to treat a student who has missed a test. In addition, as people, mathematicians suffer the consequences of living in a world where *incredible* numbers of decisions are made upon the recommendations of mathematical models and consultants. . . . My conclusion is that those taught to use mathematical tools *must* be encouraged to consider how the tools *ought* (in the moral, not mathematical, sense) to be used. It sounds a bit melodramatic, but to my way of thinking, blind obedience to mathematical authority is no more allowable as a defense for making imprudent decisions than blind obedience to military authority was for making immoral ones at Nuremburg. (1990, 114)

Next, let's look at how a potential gap between faculty, staff, and students was bridged. Chapter 3, which describes the CAVE model, begins with a story about a group of upper-class students gathered together for a mock late-night dorm rap session discussing the gaps between "what the college had promised and what it had delivered." What was unusual about this discussion was that the faculty, administration, and key student-life professionals were listening in. This faculty convocation had grown out of a two-year theme and effort trying to specifically emphasize the "student connection" aspect of values education. The Values Program with this theme had wanted to explicitly focus on better ways to make the student connection with values education. In this case the students themselves had conceived, implemented, and produced *Let's Talk,* an opportunity for students to speak with faculty about issues and concerns that were of importance to them, not just those matters of importance to the faculty or administration.

As early as 1989, the Values Institute faculty and staff worked together to enhance the freshmen-orientation experience. Prior to their arrival, incoming students were required to read an assigned text related to the search for values for the new millennium. During the early weeks of the freshmen's first academic year, faculty, administrators, and staff led small-group discussions on the texts. Discussion leaders were recruited from the Values Institute. This orientation activity, directly related to the values theme, brought many members of the campus community together. Students, personnel staff, the academic dean's office, and a number of faculty made a coordinated effort. The gap between what had been traditionally viewed as academic and nonacademic realms was bridged. Influencing students during their first steps on campus, we set the expectation that values concerns are a priority at Le Moyne. From the beginning, students anticipated that developing their valuing skills would be an important component of their undergraduate experience, and, we hoped, would continue into their entire life. Katherine Corrice, a Le Moyne graduate in the class of 1997, said, "The Values Program has had one of the greatest impacts on me here at Le Moyne. It has benefited my college experience, my human experience. [The program] has been an inspirational source of determining, instilling, and preserving a sense of ethical humanity in my everyday life" ("Values Program" 1998, n.p.).

Katherine Corrice's comments speak to the observation by Gerhard Casper, president of Stanford University from 1992 to 1999. In an interview with the *New York Times,* published on September 22, 1999, Casper commented on changes in the curriculum at American universities:

I deeply agree with Harold Bloom of Yale, when he says nobody has become a better person for reading Plato. What we really need in universities, from the first year onward, is a very vigorous and particularly a very rigorous discussion about the human condition, its elements, its values. I don't so much care whether a student reads Plato or reads Confucius, as long as they *read* the author, and as long as they have intense discussions about the implications of what they are reading.

The single most important aspect of Western civilization in universities is that universities, American universities, Western universities, are pursuing the truth. That openness, that is what, to me, Western civilization is all about. (Wilgoren 1999, B11)

The Values Program has committed itself to promoting, on a collegewide level, the vigorous and rigorous discussion about the human condition that Gerhard Casper recommends.

Stage 3: After the Institute

After the Values Institute, as faculty return to classrooms with their sharpened teaching tools, students are encouraged to ask questions about their own experience and to be actively involved in their own educational process. In an institution where values education is legitimate, students want to make connections between their values and deep faith priorities. The faculty are trained to respond to students who are concerned about these issues and are better prepared to understand their students' values questions. Krystine Batcho's forthcoming volume will describe what happens in the classrooms and highlight our findings. In the next chapter I will describe the Academic Forum and what happens beyond the classroom.

Conclusion

There are six suppositions underlying the design and function of the Values Institute. First, the Values Institutes are *inclusive.* Invitations are sent out to *all* faculty members from all disciplines institution-wide. Initially, only full-time faculty were asked to apply, but later we added invitations to some part-time adjuncts. There was no coercion. No one was required to attend. Participation is freely chosen. People attend of their own free will; we hope they are attracted by the reputation of the institute and the quality of the institute. They receive a small stipend equal to teaching a summer school course.

Second, the institute participants by intention cross barriers and boundaries within the institution. Like the process of the total Values Program, the institutes bridge gaps within the academic experience of faculty and students. We hope purposely to convey the message that no one group, discipline, or person owns the values education process. The institute is intentionally designed to help heal the divisions and the disconnectedness within the institution.

Third, the institutes are inherently, intrinsically academic. Faculty and others experience the institutes as being at the core of the academic enterprise. It is not marginal, nor is it peripheral. It is integrated into the mission and identity of the institution, related to rank and tenure criteria and norms and recognized by the reward structure within the institution.

Fourth, the Values Program makes a commitment to the participants, and the participants themselves make a commitment to follow up the institute experience. The Values Program promises it will begin to present participants with the necessary content, technique, and legitimacy to become sophisticated and competent values educators. This ambition will occur not only during the institute but also afterward. One of the criteria by which those individuals applying to participate in an institute are selected is the quality of their commitment to develop and implement a project growing out of the institutes during the next academic year. The commitment thus includes both the institute and the follow-up during the next year.

Fifth, it presents a collegewide, rigorous, and vigorous dialogue and discovery about the values dimension of a theme and its ramifications for the faculty and staff as individuals and professionals.

And finally, the participants take ownership of the institute from the beginning. Neither the facilitators, the Values Program, nor the institution owns it. The experience empowers the individuals and the group with technique, legitimacy, and content. They will not need outside permission to be values educators. They grow in competence and confidence to do the job. Fear, the major barrier to personal and institutional change, is overcome.

The Academic Forum

One spring day, I purchased a bike at the Bicycle Loft in North Syracuse. The young woman who sold me the bike owned the shop with her husband. She was very bright and mysteriously different from other salespeople I had talked to about bikes. She paid real attention to the needs of her customer; in fact, I am pretty sure the needs of the customer were her first priority. I sensed her goal was not to sell the bike but to help me discover what was best for me. Once I understood my options, it was my decision whether to spend the money and devote my energies to being a bicyclist. I did not feel I was being pushed; I was freely making a decision. I walked out of the store with the bicycle, and I remain a very happy man to this day. As I looked around the "loft" it was clear this business was more than just a job for her and her husband. They were committed to working with others to improve the environment and to work toward providing healthy recreational paths and safety rules. They were on fire to assist others to share in a truth they themselves had experienced.

As I was paying for the bike, we got into a discussion about writing. She mentioned she graduated from Le Moyne as a biology major and had especially loved her fine arts and psychology courses. After graduation she went on to earn a graduate degree at the State University of New York (SUNY) School of Environmental Science and Forestry. She mentioned that her favorite teacher was Bea Robinson, a professor in the Biology Department. Dr. Beatrice Robinson had died of cancer at an early age a few years before our conversation.

When she asked me what I did, I told her I was also a professor at Le Moyne and involved as the director of the Values Program. I explained that Bea Robinson had been deeply involved in the program; in fact, she had been one of the facilitators at its Values Institute on the theme "Science, Technology, and Values." Dr. Robinson once told me that her experience and engagement with the people involved in the Values Program's educational efforts had been the most important transformative experience of her professional life since her doctoral studies. She said it freed her "from the tyranny of the curriculum and the content" so that she was able to focus more clearly on the students that she was teaching. The bike shop owner expressed regrets that she had graduated from the college just before the Values Program had begun to function.

Her remark caused me to wonder how her education might have been different if she had gone through this same college a couple of years later. She would have had many of the same professors, lived in the same dorms, and done a lot of the same things the other students did. She would have worked just as hard and would probably still have missed the annual student spring holiday, called "Dolphy Day," to finish her sculpture for her fine arts project. But the nagging question still remains: what sort of difference would the Values Program have made?

The Academic Forum Within the Context of the Total Values Program

A way to begin to get at that question is to look carefully at the Academic Forum, the third leg of the CAVE model and then to situate it within its larger context. As I have explained, the Values Program consists of three major components working together as interactive forces in an integrated, dynamic system. One leg is the Values Institute, dealing with faculty and staff development; another is the Working Group on Values; and the third, called the Academic Forum, pertains primarily to the educational efforts to make connections "beyond the classroom." Each of these components serves a particular purpose and supports and strengthens the function of the other components.

In this chapter I will describe the Academic Forum, its objectives, methods, challenges, outcomes, and variety of intended audiences. I will also explain how it is structured and how it functions both in itself and as a part of a larger dynamic system. My hope is that with a better understanding of this component, you will be able to better evaluate the importance and necessity of this model of discovery and inquiry.

One way to grasp the substance and content of this chapter is to envision it being like computer software that can be picked up and used in a wide variety of institutions. I am reminded of the story of how Paychecks Corporation got started. Paychecks Corporation has created a computer system for institutional payrolls that is adaptable to places as diverse as Saks Fifth Avenue, Radio Shack, St. Joseph's Hospital, the local newspaper, and a national grocery chain. When the company was getting going, the founder's father said to a friend, "You know what my son has got me doing? He's got me going around to companies and picking up their payroll data so we can issue all of their paychecks. Have you ever heard of such a thing?" No one ever had. Paychecks Corporation is now considered one of the best companies to work for in the United States. My hope is that this book is written in such a way that someone else can buy into this computer program; if they do it properly, the result will be something that is very unique and very much needed. In the future our program can be used and adapted at institutions such as the SUNY School of Environmental Science and Forestry, Siena College, the University of Oregon, or Fontys University in the Netherlands. Just as someone once asked what the Paychecks system does, so too we ask what the Academic Forum does. What is this computer program to be used for?

It will help to be clear about what the Academic Forum is not. It is not just a series of events. Often, a college or university will hold a high-powered event, such as sponsoring a senator, for example, Hillary Clinton, to speak on a New York State issue. This kind of high-profile event will be looked forward to, will draw a large crowd, and will spark discussion. However, the Academic Forum has a different purpose.

Influenced by one Academic Forum, a faculty member completely transformed the way he taught genetics. This outcome is not the normal result of a visit to a campus by a celebrity, however well known. Instead, they point to the possibility that the Academic Forums could be influential in changing people's thinking over the long term. The forum's programmatic aspects ought to be seen as interconnected to a much larger educational effort designed to discover and to implement ways to assist students in establishing for themselves comprehensive frameworks for making values decisions.

What then does the Academic Forum do? The forum interacts and coordinates with the Values Institute around a common theme each year. It provides both form and content for the transference of energy, to sustain the energy over the course of the academic year. It focuses extracurricular activities in a significant year-round theme. Together the Values Institute and the Academic Forum enable students and faculty to bring newly acquired knowledge, material, and enthusiasm to the classroom. The Academic Forum dovetails nicely with the faculty's lessons from the Values Institute and their competency for using new materials and approaches on the same coordinating theme. Based on the integrating theme each year, the Academic Forum focuses the attention of the college community on issues to which liberal education speaks with profundity and wisdom.

A supposition of the Academic Forum is that students learn outside the classroom as well as inside the classroom. The challenge is to find ways of encouraging and supplementing the process of self-education that has always gone on.

As Bruce Shefrin wrote in *Ambitious Dreams,* when describing the forum in relationship to the whole Values Program, the goal of the Values Program is not explicitly to modify the curriculum. Instead, through the Values Institute the faculty freely, of their own choice, modify their courses and improve their teaching skills. A values program will work only if people understand the importance and the necessity of doing something and then learn the skills to go with their newfound commitment. Shefrin writes, "The Academic Forum would be a series of learning experiences throughout the academic year designed to introduce values education into all aspects of student life. . . . [T]he Forum would complement, integrate, and reinforce the values-laden issues and ethical concepts raised and developed in the classroom" (1990, 63).

How the Academic Forum Is Structured

By examining how the Academic Forum is structured one gets a clearer understanding of its essence and nature. One dictionary definition of *forum* is "an assembly for the discussion of questions of public interest." In that sense, the Academic Forum is well named, since it consists of diverse assemblies discussing questions of inherent public interest. Missing from the denotative label, however, is the active dimension of the forum that facilitates the implementation of ideas. As contemporary interests and purposes change, the specific format of activities varies so that individual needs are met and creative growth continues.

Early on in our process we realized that faculty development was only one-half of the learning equation. The Academic Forum must affect the other half, by providing the college with a supportive program of student development, thus giving faculty and students a common framework and a shared enthusiasm. The goal we wished to reach was to integrate the students, faculty, and administration into a socially conscious learning community.

Our model had to be interactive. Key to its success would be the variety of interdisciplinary events covered by the forum umbrella. The diversity of formats—debates, panels, first-year student orientation, films, student art and essay contests, student-faculty dinner-discussions, and others—became a curricular innovation whose aim was to weave a strong connection between in-class and out-of-class education.

The Academic Forum helps students discover connections between classroom material and the world outside the classroom. Professors incorporate content learned in the Values Institute into their classroom teaching, and students find points of connection in forums outside the classroom.

As professors weave theme-related issues into their lesson plans, and as the broad variety of forum activities plays out across the academic year, the entire campus community becomes actively engaged and confronted with fundamental questions. Absent the dynamism of the CAVE model and its three components, these questions might not be encountered through traditional course work.

The Academic Forum established itself as a vital extracurricular activity at the college. It has included many events over the fifteen years of its history; some highlights will be given here.

Examples of Past Forums

In order to give a more concrete and practical sense of these forums, I have highlighted certain examples, beginning with the first Academic Forum, in 1988–1989. The faculty's reaction to the first Values Institute in the summer of 1988 was extremely positive; the most unexpected outcome was the deep sense of collegiality that emerged among the participants. During the institute the participants had made plans for carrying the theme of "Economic Justice" into the following academic year. The nineteen faculty members from fourteen disciplines who had participated in the Values Institute in 1988 were moving into new and unfamiliar territory. They were feeling their way.

The Academic Forum was inaugurated by four planned events and activities sponsored by four different campus groups and one statewide group (largely generated by the faculty) and took place in the fall of 1988 and the early winter of 1989. The function of the forum's programmatic efforts that year was to spark a deepened awareness and consciousness of issues of economic justice raised in the previous summer's Values Institute and to begin to discover and to implement ways to build bridges among different constituencies within and outside the college. In the beginning it was slow moving, but the faculty found they had a community of support among their fellow institute participants and colleagues as they crossed discipline boundaries and often ventured beyond the classroom. The following sample of Academic Forum events in the first year describes some of the plans that were developed and executed by groups of faculty.

El Norte

In November 1988, the film *El Norte* was shown on campus and introduced with a talk by a professor from SUNY-Cortland. This Argentine film dramatizes Western Hemisphere issues of economic justice. It depicts two Guatemalans, a brother and sister, whose parents have been killed in a civil war. The pair flee the dangers and despair of their homeland to seek a new life in the United States. They make the arduous journey from Central America through Mexico to the U.S. border. Their border crossing is dangerous and difficult, but both characters are relieved to find a safe haven and work in the illegal alien community of San Diego. Their escape is blighted, however, when the sister develops a fever from a rat bite she never even noticed in the hazard of their border crossing. There is nothing her brother can do for her, and she dies of blood poisoning. Students were moved by many of the vivid scenes in the film—for example, when the young woman, approximately their own age, cannot figure out how to work the clothes dryer in the upscale household where she has been hired as a laundress. As an alternative solution, she spreads the clean laundry carefully on the lawn and hedges, just as she would have done at home.

Faculty Education

In December 1988, the Syracuse Consortium for the Cultural Foundations of Medicine sponsored a panel discussion by faculty who had been part of the Values Institute. The title of this panel discussion was "The Values Institute on Economic Justice: An Alternate Model for Faculty Education." The goal of this panel was to report back to the college community on the thoughts and processes experienced by the faculty during the institute. It took the novel and powerful dramatic direction of presenting faculty as learners, sharing their knowledge. Because students saw that the faculty were brave enough to take on the role of student once again, this presentation became an important bridge-building exercise between faculty and students.

Economic Justice in Central New York

On January 23, 1989, a panel of local welfare specialists presented a symposium titled "The State of Economic Justice in Central New York: Housing, Nutrition, and Health Care for the Poor." This event had two on-campus sponsors, the Biology Society and the Human Services Association. Audience members were electrified by unscripted interruptions to the presentation by members of the local community who had attended the event.

An Artist's Perspective

The fourth event in this series was a slide presentation on January 25, 1989, by Professor William West, of the Fine Arts Department. He called his talk "What Injustice Looks Like from an the Artist's Point of View." This presentation was an example of the bridge building that occurred at the first Values Institute and brought the Fine Arts Department into the collegewide discussion of economic justice. This discussion might have otherwise been limited to the Political Science or Sociology Departments.

South Africa–Le Moyne

A significant outcome of the 1988 Values Institute was the faculty discovery of the importance of their involvement and ownership of the institute. Could the faculty stand back and let students take and run with an idea? It appeared that they could, and the first large-scale success of the Academic Forum was South Africa–Le Moyne, a weeklong event generated and developed by students. This dramatic event generated news coverage by the local media. Undergraduate student David McCallum Jr. described it in the book *Ambitious Dreams* (Kirby et al. 1990). I will briefly recapitulate his remarks here.

David McCallum was a member of the student senate and through that activity became involved in the first Academic Forum in the fall of 1988. One of the plans growing out of the Values Institute had been to discover a way to involve an influential student group such as the student senate. The student senate leadership desired to become part of the educational effort to assist students in deepening their consciousness and understanding of the issues.

His senate committee was charged with designing events to illustrate the theme of "Economic Justice." McCallum described his committee as being "in a sort of limbo," unable to come up with ideas for programs, until it was approached by the minority group on campus, POWER (Pride in Our Work, Ethnicity, and Race). The result of one brainstorming session between these two groups was a list of events long enough to fill up a week, called "South Africa–Le Moyne."

> The idea of passing out armbands early in the week with an informational package about South Africa was adopted. By using armbands of two different colors, red and green, we separated the campus into an oppressed majority and a privileged minority. The campus was divided so that the reds could use only the back entrances to the buildings and inconvenient bathrooms. The reds were even segregated in the cafeteria and prohibited by the greens from having ice cream. . . . After a few days, the reds were even conspiring to revolt. The most effective part of the simulation came later in the week when we broke into classrooms and abducted students; we then "imprisoned" them in mock stockades

located in the hallways of the academic buildings. With coverage from several television stations and newspapers, the event was as exciting as it was effective.

One of the other events that had a great influence on the impact of the week was a Donahue-style discussion, hosted by Barron Boyd, a professor of Political Science and an expert in South African politics. The discussion focused on the experiences of two South African students who attend Le Moyne. They recalled, for the audience, the many cruelties and injustices inflicted upon them and their families by the government. As one student told of her brother's abduction and the long trial of her family, she brought tears to the eyes of many in the audience. It struck me, then, that the most effective bridge in our values education stems from our emotional responses and from our instincts. We could be lectured at for hours about an issue taking place on the other side of the globe, but real emotional contact with that issue makes the most impact upon our values formation. (1990, 124–25)

A dramatic and emotional march around the campus ended the weeklong program. More than 150 students, faculty, and administrators carried banners, flags, and candles. At a bonfire in the quad, the crowd burned all the armbands, and the college president said a prayer for the end of racial tension and injustice at home and abroad. "Looking at the faces around the fire," McCallum writes, "I felt that we had accomplished something significant. There is no way that such an event could have succeeded without the cooperation of student groups and collaboration with the faculty. . . . We received no academic credit or stipend for our efforts, but that didn't matter. The satisfaction we felt in helping raise awareness of an issue of such importance was overwhelming" (125–26).

Looking Ahead to the Values Institute, 1989

It is important to lay the groundwork and prepare the soil for each new Values Institute and new institution-wide values-laden theme. In an almost imperceptible way year by year, like ripples in the pond, each new theme brings a whole new community of interests into the learning environment of the campus and beyond into the wider community. The first-year theme was "Economic Justice," followed by "Peace and War," "Families and Public

Policy," and "Science, Technology, and Values." Year after year, the ripples quietly impacted the various shorelines of the institution.

One of the keys to the effectiveness of the program is the long-range planning. In the fall semester, as early as seven months before the new theme and the new Values Institute are to begin, the faculty, staff, and students need to begin to be exposed to some of the issues and challenges associated with the next annual theme. Already by this time the Working Group on Values will have scheduled the next Values Institute for the summer. About twenty faculty from diverse disciplines will have been selected by January, and preliminary preparatory planning sessions have been held with the facilitators, the Working Group, and other offices on campus.

As preparation for the new Values Institute and theme in 1989, three films were shown during a weekend of war and peace movies in April 1989. These films included *Platoon*, the *Biography of Martin Luther King Jr.* and *The Killing Fields*. *Platoon* tells a story set in the Vietnam War, and *The Killing Fields* tells of the genocidal regime of Pol Pot in Cambodia. Each of these films sparked discussions related to issues of war and peace.

Do The Right Thing

An Academic Forum event brought the issue of violence and peace home to students in a heartfelt manner during the fall semester of 1989. Among the planned activities that sparked significant student interest was the showing of the Spike Lee film *Do the Right Thing*. A three-day program was created around this controversial film that portrays a love relationship between an African American man and an Italian woman. Spike Lee was enjoying a spate of media attention at that time, and students were eager to meet an actor who had worked with him.

Actor Giancarlo Esposito, who played the character Buggin' Out, addressed an overflow crowd in Shanahan Chapel as he discussed his life as an actor, his work on the film, and his views on racism in the United States. Esposito was born in Copenhagen, Denmark, of an Italian father and an African the American mother. He came to the United States at the age of six and a half and learned English. The electrifying moment in his talk came when he revealed that because of the role of a drug dealer that he had played on the TV show *Miami Vice*, young people had assumed he was a drug dealer in real life. At that moment he resolved not to play roles like that one in the future.

In a heated question-and-answer period with students who had confused Esposito the private person and actor with the character he portrayed in Spike Lee's film, Esposito defended a policy of moderation and closed with the remark, surprising to some students, "Our message must have more love in it."

Here was a real-life instance of values creation and values education happening beyond the classroom. It connected economics with issues of justice and peace and brought them clearly into focus for the students, faculty, and administration who attended the event.

Town Meetings

A key characteristic of the Values Program is that it does not seek to reinvent the wheel; instead, it works with what is already present in the institution and seeks to breathe new life into it. The Town Meetings provide a good example of the catalytic factor at work. The Values Program and the Academic Forum did not originate the idea of using a Town Meeting format in our institution. The concept of the Town Meeting drew on an event that had first been held on campus in 1987, but experiences from the Values Institutes breathed new life into the concept, and it has become a vital annual program. (The first Town Meeting was held in 1987, the second in 1988. No meeting was held in 1989, and the Town Meetings began an uninterrupted annual schedule, sponsored by the Values Program, beginning in 1990.) The Academic Forum was able to provide a vehicle for the Town Meetings to be even more interconnected to the educational enterprise and the wider community. The basic notion underlying the event is the traditional town meeting of New England, where a community was called together to discuss a topic critical to the well-being of the group.

Because the Town Meetings at this particular institution of higher education grew out of collaboration between the college's Division of Continuous Learning and our local Public Broadcasting System affiliate, WCNY, this event was seen as not only a town meeting but also an educational device that reached out to the wider central New York community. Professor Robert Flower, the project designer, mixed the "genre" of the town meeting with the concept of theater-in-the-round. A mixture of dramatics and academics, the format combines dramatic dialogues, academic presentations, and open discussion. Persons from all walks of life are invited to participate: community leaders, "ordinary" citizens, professionals, faculty, and students. The evening is an unpredictable mix of a formally scheduled and scripted program and spontaneous "happenings."

A Town Meeting as part of the Academic Forum, held in April 1991, was called "Songs of the Hearth: Sacred and Profane" and focused on the issues of family and public policy discussed at the 1990 Values Institute. Invited speakers included a judge for the Syracuse Family Court, the executive director of a local children's center, a professor of pediatrics from SUNY Health Science Center at Syracuse, and a representative from the Catholic Diocese, among others.

Values are themselves a unique blend of "head and heart" or thoughts and feelings. In the setting of the Town Meeting, the actual "feel" of the values in question is present as persons are asked to reflect on them. In some cases, the dramatic presentation of the evening allows participants to hear and feel great passion, anger, or bitterness, but in a manner somewhat distanced by the format.

The title of the evening was meant to suggest the tribal fire of the Inuit Indians, a monthly gathering to which the men of the tribe came to "sing their song." The family, or "hearth," is suggested as a temple. That which lies outside of the hearth represents the profane. The songs were of both the sacred or the private (which are connected to the family) and the profane (which have an alien sound, or a public nature).

Another metaphor considered during the event's planning came from Plato's concept of *metadzu ti* or, in English, "something-in-between." It is mankind that lives "in between": above the beasts and below the gods. This theme can also be applied to the family, as it often straddles issues of private versus public and finds itself "in-between." As Dr. Flower stated,

> Unmistakably, the subject matter of family and public policy embraces a myriad of issues and concerns. Our evening will reflect this panoply. One of our speakers, a physician, will share stories arising out of the practice of geriatric medicine. Another, a family court judge, will take

us into the legal labyrinth of family and public policy. Another, a pediatric physician, will speak of the difficulties he has experienced between public policies and his practice. Yet another, the director of a home for "wayward" children will address the institutional problems in caring for children from failed homes. And yet another will address the problems for families brought about by poverty in America. And these represent only those who speak to us with a special invitation. (Flower 1991, n.p.)

Professor Flower encouraged spontaneous presentations and found that after the invited speakers took their turns, the flexible format of the evening allowed lively audience participation and debate. It was obviously not a one-man show. Its planning and production brought together students, faculty, staff, and people from the wider community who worked for many weeks to bring this production to completion.

Academic Forum, 1991–1992

In an effort to explicitly bring the science disciplines into the Values Program's educational efforts, a group of faculty, members of the Working Group on Values, and some interested alumni with science backgrounds began to plan for a theme dealing with values and the sciences. In 1991, the theme of the Values Institute was "Science, Technology, and Values." The facilitators included Dr. Beatrice Robinson of the Biology Department of Le Moyne College, Dr. Taft M. Broome Jr. of the Engineering Department at Howard University, and Dr. Langdon Winner of the Political Science Department of Rensselaer Polytechnic Institute. Each of these participants came to the institute with a reputation as a superior teacher. One was a "pure" scientist, one came from the field of applied science, and one was a social scientist. This careful selection meant that the facilitators' views on foundational issues were often at odds and provoked spontaneous and stimulating debate.

For anyone interested in implementing a program in their own institution it is helpful to note that within only a few years' time, our faculty had all known colleagues who had participated in past Values Institutes and word of mouth had begun to make it easier to recruit faculty from all the disciplines into the institute. Not only had the faculty at the institution begun to take ownership of the institutes and forum events more readily, but faculty and others in the institution were also growing in confidence that they themselves had the legitimacy and the competency to struggle with the values dimensions of issues.

We experimented in the "Science, Technology, and Values" institute with inviting three participants from other campuses. We had begun to wonder what might be the effect of bringing in a few participants who would have a different perspective from our own. Outside participants included two faculty members from Wheeling Jesuit College and a professor from King's College in Wilkes-Barre, Pennsylvania. We discovered our visiting participants to be an important complement to the institute membership. We wanted the focus to remain on the home institution, but the visiting participants broadened our vision both theoretically and practically. The experience of the institute for the visitors caused them to wonder whether this educational effort could be adopted within their own institutions. It also gave us renewed confidence that the CAVE model was adaptable to a much wider audience.

Slowly, the ripple effect was beginning to spread not just inside our classrooms and beyond the classroom. Our faculty were now making vital and long-lasting connections with faculty from other institutions. We had already initiated exchanges between our students and faculty with Wheaton College in Illinois. Wheaton had sent faculty and students to experience certain aspects of Le Moyne, and a fruitful exchange began between certain members of these institutions, including Professor Paul de Vries who wrote a chapter in *Ambitious Dreams*, giving an outsider's perspective on the program's strengths and applicability (1990, chap. 10). At that time Wheaton began to publish a newsletter called *Discernment* that had been partially inspired by visits to the Values Program activities.

The three-week institute on the theme "Science, Technology, and Values" began with a discussion of the scientist in cinema. From this beginning, facilitators branched out into discussions of the images of the scientist in society at large; the foundations of ethics as applied to engineering, science, and technology; and the role of choice.

The institute included a laboratory exercise. A Le Moyne College biology professor who is well published in chick embryology fertilized seven chicken eggs as a way to promote hands-on appreciation of an experimental scientist at work. For professors of English literature, fine arts, or accounting, this may have been their first excursion into a laboratory since their high school days. In addition, discussions, case studies, pen-and-paper exercises, and videotapes were used to help participants explore the theme in various ways.

Two questions structured the work of this institute: How are individual and social values influenced by scientific discoveries and technological changes? What impact can and should values have on the conduct of scientific research and the development and application of new technologies?

By the last day of the institute, a number of projects were already in place. As well as examining a carefully selected reading list and engaging in discussion of these issues, participants in the institute made plans for carrying these themes over into the following academic year. This partial list shows how the barriers between disciplines and boundaries were beginning to fall. An outside grant was sought and provided by GTE for a yearlong speakers program on life-extending medical technology, which included participation by Dr. Daniel Callahan, president of the Hastings Institute. The Sociology Department agreed to sponsor a film series on science and technology. The Student Life Office planned a series of student-faculty dinner-discussions focused on current events relating to the institute's theme. A member of the Philosophy Department committed to organizing a Town Meeting on the theme. The president of the student senate agreed to sponsor and promote one event on this theme each semester for a year.

Finally, as well as reaching out to college administrators and students, the institute extended an invitation to the wider community as well. Three teachers and one principal from area high schools interested in the Values Program were invited to observe. Two Le Moyne professors, one secretary, and two outside speakers agreed to address the group on their specialties.

The four lectures funded by a grant from the GTE Foundation were presented free of charge in October 1991 and January, February, and March 1992. Robert M. Daly, M.D., a professor of medical humanities at the State University of New York Health Science Center gave a speech titled "Medical Care Near the End of Life: Values, Practices, and Limits." Daniel Callahan, Ph.D., director of the Hastings Center, presented "Ethics and the Technological Imperative: Can We Know When to Stop?" Dr. Callahan is the author of *Setting Limits: Medical Goals in an Aging Society (with an Answer to My Critics)* (1995), a study about allocating public resources for health care with regard to the elderly population. Dr. Callahan's work with the Hastings Center has been instrumental in putting the issues of bioethics on the national agenda. Carl J. Schramm, Ph.D., J.D., president of the Health Insurance Association of America, gave a talk entitled "Life Supports at Birth and Death: How Much Can We Afford?" And the Reverend Richard McCormick, S.J., a professor of moral theology at Notre Dame University, presented "Physician-Assisted Suicide: Compassion or Collapse?"

The audiences for this series of talks included members of both the college community and the broader Syracuse community. Press coverage came from the student newspaper, the *Dolphin;* a local newspaper, the *Syracuse Herald American;* and *The Catholic Sun.* Faculty were now engaging their students about these issues in their classrooms, and students were bringing their interests back to classrooms and dorms.

1992 Town Meeting

The 1992 Town Meeting took as its theme "Science, Society, and the Sacred: The Possibility of Dialogue." It was designed to cap the yearlong sequence of lectures on themes in biomedical ethics mentioned earlier. Five Le Moyne faculty—Professors Susan Behuniak-Long (political science); Edward F. Cunningham, S.J., (psychology); Robert Flower (philosophy); Beatrice B. Robinson (biology); and William Morris (director of theatre)—collaborated on the evening, which included attention to some of the following questions:

• What exactly is a conflict of values?

• Is it possible to create a bridge of dialogue across silence or the chasm of anger?

• What is the role of modern medical science and technology in the creation of value conflict?

• How does our sense of the sacred affect our values and our participation in the value conflicts of our society?

After the meeting, John Carlson, academic vice president and dean, wrote in a memo to the organizers: "Your bringing to bear of various perspectives on science and technology testified to the success of Le Moyne's Values Program; it also served as an example of liberal and interdisciplinary education at its best."

1993 Town Meeting

The April 1993 Town Meeting was titled "The Limits of Diversity: A Question of Toleration, the Spectre of the Intolerable." Again moderated by Dr. Flower, this meeting was tied into the Values Program theme of diversity for the 1992–1993 academic year. Panel members included representatives from the Libertarian Party, the minister of a Baptist church, a gay- and lesbian-rights activist, the chairperson of the local chapter of the American Civil Liberties Union, and others. Several of the audience of two hundred jumped into the lively debate, applauding some speakers for their views and taking others to task.

Essay Contest

Tied into the Academic Forum was the continued sponsorship of the Le Moyne College Essay Contest for Values Scholarship. The purpose of this contest is to foster among area high school students thoughtful investigation, reflection, and commentary on issues and questions concerning human values. This contest is predicated on the belief that by means of such engagement with the values issues of our day, the youth in this community will be better prepared for the struggle toward maturity and citizenship. Another goal for this essay contest is to enliven decency and respect for human dignity within our own community.

Each year a topic is chosen, and information on the contest is sent to area high schools, including a call for typed essays of 250 to 500 words. First prize is one hundred dollars, second prize is seventy-five dollars, and third prize is fifty dollars. These awards are presented at the annual Town Meeting, and the winning essays are published as part of the meeting program.

Academic Forum, 1994

The Academic Forum in 1994, titled "The Spiritual Dimensions in Higher Education: Attending to the Sacred in Our Midst," was so successful and sparked such keen interest that this topic became the theme for two subsequent years, 1995 and 1996. That the use of this theme was extended over three years again illustrates the grassroots, evolving nature of the Values Program. The structure is flexible and allows for depth of exploration when participants feel that it is needed. Although the format had called for a new theme each summer, at the end of the institute in 1994, this format was redesigned, at least temporarily. One issue you will need to think about is whether your theme will last one or two years. The advantage of the longer time is that the theme has a longer time to percolate within the institution, and it also gives people more time to plan and make necessary connections.

The ways the institute on spiritual dimensions was introduced into the institution offer some valuable lessons for anyone interested in applying this model both to the values and to the spiritual dimensions of issues. Planning for this institute began in March 1993, sixteen months before the institute was actually held. Information was distributed throughout the campus to alert the community about the new theme for the Values Institute in 1994. A process of exploration began among various constituencies institution-wide. Preliminary exploratory meetings were held with faculty, athletic teams, physical-plant workers, staff, and secretaries. The Working Group and other members of the faculty, staff, and administration began to realize that more and more people wanted to be part of this educational effort.

As the groups worked to discover ways to assist students with issues of spirituality, they worked with two assumptions: one, that education seeks to enable a person to be fully human and, two, that to be fully human involves recognition that each individual has a spiritual and religious dimension. Conventional ways to conceptualize this relationship are: a doctrinal or confessional approach or both that emphasizes spiritual, religious, and value systems at the expense of others, or a secularized approach that relativizes all spiritual, religious, and value questions.

The Center for the Advancement of Values Education at Le Moyne College hoped to frame a third option by exploring two new questions. One, can we create a college community that values the diversity of "varieties of religious experience" and respects the spiritual dimension of each person as a central and unifying "way of knowing" and acting within the college? And two, can we conceptualize such a community as an innovative reinterpretation and refinement of the college's foundational identity as Catholic and Jesuit? These questions were distributed to the college community as focus questions in March 1993. They were revised a month later to include revisions suggested by students and questions about transforming the institution itself.

At the same time that Le Moyne was exploring these themes, a similar project began at Wellesley College in Massachusetts. This project, called the Education as Transformation Project, was founded in 1996. Diana Chapman Walsh, president of Wellesley College, told a national gathering at Wellesley: "Our task together is to envision a whole new place, a whole new space and role for spirituality in higher education, not as an isolated enterprise on the margins of the academy, nor as a new form of institutional social control, but as an essential element of the larger task of reorienting our institution of higher learning to respond more adequately to the challenges the world presents to us now: challenges to our teaching, to our learning, to our leading, to our lives" (quoted in Laurence 1999, 6).

In December 1998 a three-day program at Skidmore College in Saratoga Springs, New York, included sessions titled "Common Ground: A Walking Meditation," "Knowing and Being: Spirituality in Higher Education," and "Finding a Common Ground: Science and Spirituality" (5).

In bringing questions of spirituality before the college community in 1994, 1995, and 1996, the Values Program was leading a groundswell of interest in these ideas among college communities nationwide. In 1999, Parker Palmer wrote, "I reject the imposition of any form of religion in public education, including so-called 'school prayer.' But I advocate any way we can find to explore the spiritual dimension of teaching, learning, and living" (quoted in ibid., 4).

The principal goal of the "spirituality" values events was to involve the entire Le Moyne community in a vital exploration of paths for attending to the sacred in our lives. Philosophy Professor Katharine Rose Hanley explained: "The program extends responsibility for initiative and leadership to all components of the College including especially alumni/ae and student leaders of residences and various campus organizations.... The Program develops informed concern for values through one's life and service in the human community" (1996, n.p.).

Academic Forum, 1995

A major event in 1995 was the "Spring Spirit Fair," modeled after a Renaissance fair. The fair was the brainchild of a faculty member who, following the Values Institute in 1994 on the theme "The Spiritual Dimensions in Higher Education: Attending to the Sacred in Our Midst," wanted to celebrate the lived forms of spirituality within the college and wider community. The Spring Spirit Fair celebrated diversity, pluralism, and freedom. It offered all members of the community an opportunity to sample some twenty activities that nourished the spirits of people at the college at that particular time. Each event lasted about one hour. The fair extended from morning through late evening and involved every sector of the college. The events included the following:

• "Ignatian Spirituality," a presentation by scholastic Steven Spahn, S.J., of some of the distinctive features and highlights of life centered in Christ incarnate in the tradition of St. Ignatius of Loyola

• "Tae Kwon Do: Exploring the Mental, Spiritual, and Physical Aspects of Tae Kwon Do," which included demonstrations of board breaking

• "Journeying Together: Reflections on the Process of Spiritual Direction," presented by Sister Joan Kerley

• a presentation on weaving and using net bags as an image of the creativity of person, culture, and cosmos, given by religious studies professor Mary MacDonald

• "Meditation Practice," an introduction to the benefits of meditation followed by a mindfulness meditation, a guided-healing meditation, reflection, and discussion, delineated by philosophy and education professor Tom Curley

• "Gospel Spirit," a presentation by the college group Voices of Power, praising God in song; reflecting on aspects of the history, style, and spirit of gospel music; and providing the community with an opportunity to sing together

• other events dealing with praying with Christian scriptures, gospel music, and elements of the Ignatian spiritual exercises, with such participatory events making the sacred visible in ways that had not been evident before

Just as ripples spread when a stone is tossed into a pond, so too energy for the techniques and newfound legitimacy spread throughout the entire campus—both inside and outside of the classroom. It spreads to dormitories, nontraditional students, student life, campus ministry, and all aspects of the institution's culture. The Spring Spirit Fair was one way we answered the question we asked ourselves in 1986: How can we weave the fabric we desire? Because we committed ourselves to a process of discussion and discovery, we began to find our way.

Academic Forum, 1997

The theme for 1997–1998 was "Education and Public Policy." This theme and all its educational efforts and activities with its Values Institute, Academic Forum events, and preparatory efforts by the Working Group on Values provide a snapshot of deepening awareness and sense of responsibility within the institution for the quality of public and private education in grades K–12. This Values Institute and the forum events were designed to undertake the study of the social cross-weave between education and public policy. The very diversity and quality of the institute's participants and facilitators speak to the credibility and legitimacy the Values Program had earned both on campus and in the wider community. The institute ran for one week, June 2 through June 6, and included a total of twenty-six participants, including sixteen members of the college community: ten faculty and administrators and representatives from multicultural affairs, academic affairs, academic support, and student life.

Off-campus participants were a labor relations specialist from the New York State United Teachers Office, the district director from Congressman James Walsh's office, the associate superintendent of the Diocese of Syracuse Catholic Schools office, and the former executive secretary for the New York State Council of Catholic Schools Superintendents.

Facilitators from on campus were Dr. Robert Flower from the Philosophy Department, Dr. Cynthia DeCorse from the Education Department, and Professor Edwin Baumgartner from the Mathematics Department. Dr. DeCorse had made a presentation in 1996 to the Association of Teacher Educators Conference in St. Louis, "Teachers in Dilemma: Understanding School Violence and Teaching Moral Values."

Off-campus facilitators were Robert DeFlorio, the retired superintendent of Syracuse City Schools; Jerome Melvin, the retired superintendent of the Cicero–North Syracuse Central Schools; and Ned Deuel, a vice president of Henneberry Hill Consultants, Inc.

Look at this list of participants and facilitators from on and off campus, and you get a sense of how the interest and commitment to the values and spiritual dimensions of issues had spread within the institution and into the many levels of the wider community.

The keynote speaker was Thomas F. Green, author of *Voices: The Educational Formation of Conscience* (1999). The basic theme of the institute was divided into several components. The plan was to define a baseline for education, that is, to seek to discover what constitutes "a good education." The content for the institute and the following year's activities focused on money issues, the home environment, societal and legal issues, and corporate influence.

Money Issues

Most public schooling in grades K–12 is financed through property taxes, which means that schools in poor areas have small budgets, whereas schools in wealthy areas have larger budgets. Is this process fair? Also, should fixed-income retirees have to foot the bill for schools if it means they will be at risk of losing their homes?

Home Environment

Classroom success depends in large part on parental involvement. The presence or absence of parents, books, and computers in the home has a beneficial or a detrimental effect on each child.

Societal and Legal Issues

Discrimination continues to exist. What impact does it have on education? What values underlie legal approaches to this factor?

Corporate Influence

Indirectly, education is affected by corporate demands for specific skills. Also, corporate gifts and grants have a direct effect on the institutions that receive them. For example, the Biology Department might have a strong tie to a Bristol-Myers Squibb, Inc., facility. This setup is beneficial to the college in that excellent laboratory equipment has been donated. But are there strings attached to this gift? The master in business administration program at Le Moyne benefited from a close relationship to the Niagara Mohawk Power Corporation, for whom special classes and programs have been developed. Does this relationship mean an untoward influence is exerted by industry? Another effect of corporations on education in our country is a growing movement toward "privatization" of education. Should for-profit companies develop educational curricula for children? What values underlie such development?

How far does public policy go in addressing the factors identified above? How far can it go? How far should it go? What possibilities for action are there? Is it possible to legislate solutions? What are the underlying values to these questions? These questions were especially pertinent. Because of its status in central New York State, the college has a serious commitment to educating educators. With a graduate program in education in place since 1994, its Education Department has always produced a significant number of teachers, especially for the greater central New York area. This theme would be very applicable anywhere.

Finally, it is important to recall that renewed energy from the Values Institutes also stimulates creative use of existing resources. For example, in 1996, the Values Program took a fresh look at the already established leadership/scholar program. Each year, the Admissions Office provides approximately ninety incoming freshmen with "Leadership/Scholar Awards." Students are chosen for past academic achievement and promise as leaders. These awards present an excellent opportunity to build connections from academics to leadership outside the classroom.

In 1996, a position was created within the Values Program for a graduate assistant who would work specifically on the leadership/scholar project. This step was an important advance for the Values Program and for the institution itself in a number of ways. First, the college agreed to generously fund the position in terms of graduate tuition and a stipend. Second, because the graduate student was selected after a careful competitive process involving the Graduate Education Program, financial aid, admissions, student affairs, and the Values Program, it meant that these groups were now talking and working together in a new way. Equally important, it meant that there was now a qualified graduate student in education whose first responsibility was to work to discover how to build bridges between the admissions and financial aid offices that granted the scholarships, the student affairs office that helped to administer the program, and the various groups of students who won the scholarships. The presence of the Values Program in this effort provided a bridge between academic affairs and these different constituencies that is not usually present.

More specifically, this concern for the "leadership/scholar" students worked its way into the classroom. This effort soon began to bear fruit. In the fall of 1997, some of the previous year's sophomore leadership group elected to take a required junior-year core course in ethics offered by Professor Robert Flower. The course explores human dignity as understood by Aristotle through Kant. Owing to the participation of so many leadership/scholar award winners, Professor Flower modified the course content to focus on characteristics that make for good leadership. Some students in the class "already had a chemistry of community that was exciting," said Flower (Kirby 1998, 19). He believed that this community of learners was a result of the Values Program effort to reach students. For him, it was a quality example of values study and values education.

Distinguishing the Academic Forum
from Other Similar Efforts

The examples and programmatic aspects described in this chapter highlight how our program aids students in making connections across courses and to problems in life beyond the classroom. I have tried to explain how intensive Academic Forum and Values Institute experiences empower faculty to design courses and staff and students to design student-life activities to help students shape socially responsible attitudes and values.

As you evaluate and come to understand the CAVE model, a number of questions might arise. One remark I sometimes hear is that at first glance, the Academic Forum and the Values Program look a lot like what is being done in the other programs on other campuses. It is true that the Values Program and Academic Forum share many of the same goals and methods of the other initiatives. With Learning Communities these methods include working to create an intensified learning environment and a sense of community, striving for curricular coherence, making connections with courses and ideas, and teaching skills in a meaningful context. It also shares the hope for creating an academically and socially reinforced experience that enhances the confidence and independence of learners. With Service Learning it shares the concern to add an experiential component to learning, to create partnerships with the larger community and to facilitate the opportunity to get students to think about the role of responsible citizenship. Like Ethics Across the Curriculum it works to instill and promote ethical thinking and decision making, helping students recognize ethical issues, develop critical skills, and work to elicit a sense of moral obligation and a personal code of ethics.

So I ask the question again, if you have these other things, why do you need the Values Program and the Academic Forum?

An Analogy from Sports

I will try to clarify this point by making a comparison. It is true that some of the goals and methods are similar to what other programs and initiatives do. This same sort of thing happens in sports and other fields involving great skill and talent. Someone may be a good hitter, but so are a lot of people. Someone is a good fielder, but so are a lot of people; someone is a good base runner, but so are a lot of people; someone is good in a clutch situation and a power hitter, but so are a lot of people. You can use any sport or any skill-related field.

I remember watching Chris Evert, one of the founders with Billie Jean King of modern women's tennis, being interviewed. She was reflecting twenty-five years later about her impact on the sport and her relationships with the other players, both men and women. She talked about a cover story that appeared about her in *Sports Illustrated*. She was intrigued by the story because it struggled to get to what was the mystery behind her success and influence. The article described how every once in a while a player or a musician will come along that may not be the best at certain aspects of her craft, but when it is all put together it comes together in a special way. Whatever it is, in some way the skills come together in the final dynamic process in a quantitative leap beyond the next player. It's a mystery.

So it is with the Values Program and its components. It's not only the faculty-staff development of the Values Institute or the programmatic events of the Academic Forum or the grassroots grounding of the Working Group on Values; rather, it is the combination of these components that makes the real difference. But the real difference becomes apparent only when an entire institution decides to choose this model, becomes involved, and then makes it happen. Then the real mystery and joy of discovery manifest themselves.

I believe that engagement with the Values Program and its Academic Forum is a lot like Chris Everett playing tennis. She used all her senses of touch, seeing, hearing, feeling, and even smell as she engaged her tennis partner. The magic came together only when she brought it all together in just the right way. At that moment the sport of tennis came alive. The simplest of things can become classic. The rest is history.

The Academic Forum needs to be integrated into the totality of the Values Program very carefully. It is important that you have the right persons and the right ingredients, that they be put together in a particular way. The objective is to engage the entire institution in a process of discovery and implementation that is right for these students and faculty and right for this institution.

The Values Program is properly understood and experienced only when all the parts are working together, strengthening and reinforcing each other. Many of the faculty who has been through this educational effort have been transformed. They have had an experience that helps them to envision and practice their craft and profession in a new way. It can happen because there has been a concerted effort to train the faculty and staff, to give them credibility, competency, and confidence. The faculty can now bring new ideas and content from the Values Institutes into the classroom. Because of the forum, students and members of the community both within and beyond the campus will now have an opportunity to participate in and shape their expedience. The Academic Forum provides the form and content that enables the energy from the Values Institute to reemerge into the campus and beyond during the academic year.

Six Characteristics of the Academic Forum

Keeping in mind that the Academic Forum has its own objectives and methods and is also integrally connected to the total design of the Values Program, I will highlight six characteristics that help describe the Academic Forum.

First, it is more than just a series of events. Instead, it is like a catalyst that permeates and infiltrates even the most mundane of events. Like yeast, it subtly infiltrates the dough with a new ingredient and a new quality. Every campus has and would like more plays, lectures, workshops, and extracurricular events. Schools such as Dartmouth, Georgetown, Harvard, and Duke are the envy of us all for their endowment monies that bring in all the high-priced talent. We miss the function and purpose of the Academic Forum if we concentrate only on these high-profile extracurricular events. Instead, the Academic Forum is a dynamic, umbrella-like structure that provides the form and content to transfer the energy of the Values Institute to the academic year. Remembering "to keep our eye on the prize," the whole point of the Values Program and its three components is to help students create for themselves a framework of values that are consistent, coherent, and defensible with the best of the religious, cultural, and philosophical traditions.

What does this concept mean in the concrete? It means the prize for us is to work with your daughter and son so that he and she begin to better understand the importance, necessity, and urgency of the moral and spiritual dimension in their personal, social, and professional lives. Just to understand what the values dimension is, to become aware and conscious of it, demands a consistent, pervasive, subtle, yet forceful effort in all aspects of one's personal and professional life. This belief is why we think all professors should be sophisticated and committed to this process, to discovering how best to reach and to touch both the mind and the heart of your child. But as I have said, your daughter moves from biology to literature, engineering, her dormitory, her job off campus, and her social life. We want to help her bridge the gaps, to make the connections, to see the whole picture, not just part of the picture. Juggling all of these elements is much like the function of the leader of a jazz band. You need to keep the group together, but you also need to allow for the individual skills, creativity, and inspiration of the musicians and somehow manage to put all of it together. The Academic Forum is the vehicle for transferring the energy of the Values Institute to the academic year.

Second, The Academic Forum's umbrella-like structure is dynamic, flexible, and evolving. Since the Values Program is so dependent on its grassroots motivation and energy, it needs to be careful that what it is proposing to do is actually based on the felt needs of the students. From professor to professor, student to student, course to course, year to year, and constituency to constituency, contemporary interests and purposes change. Much like the design of a bicycle, the design of the program and its components needs to be dynamic, have balance and sturdiness, yet be flexible. The Academic Forum is one of the factors that hold all these things in the balance.

The impact of the September 11, 2001, terrorist attack on the United States provides a good example of why colleges, universities, and professional schools will profit from something like the Academic Forum. It provides the form and content to get to questions such as, "What happened? What does this event reveal about our world? What is it saying to us?" It happened that the values theme for the institution for 2001–2002 was "Action for Justice in a Changing World." This theme had been selected through a careful process in the year 2000.

On September 11, 2001, the destruction of the World Trade Center, the attack on the Pentagon, and the flight that was downed by the passengers in a field in Pennsylvania forced us to change many of the things that we had originally intended to do. We did not need to convince the students that this issue was important. This event provided us with a golden opportunity to go from interest to understanding, choice, and ultimately action. It is only one example of the need to remain flexible and to adjust and evolve as needs and interests change and world events occur.

Third, the forum's primary function is to make connections between classroom materials and the out-of-class world in which students live. The Academic Forum is the bridge builder, the connecting link between the diverse constituencies and issues within the institution. An important East Coast railroad, the Delaware and Hudson, was called "the bridge line."

It crossed many rivers, valleys, and mountains to make communication and transportation possible. As the railroad stopped in Albany, New York City, Baltimore, and Richmond, it picked up local people and their products; it was the form and content for much of the stimulation and growth of the East Coast. Today, the Internet and the search engines of the World Wide Web are the bridge builders.

Why is it important that an academic institution have a bridge builder and connecting link? If we go back to your daughter in college, we can ask why she needs something like the Academic Forum in her educational environment. She is perhaps already in a learning community and the integral honors program. Aren't connections and bridges already being built within this educational environment?

The Values Program is subtly different. The notion of weaving a new fabric of experience might be compared to the understanding of life issues under the categories of "seamless garment," a "consistent ethic of life," or "the bridge to compassion." Behind these categories is the need for consistency, defensibility, and coherence of a position on the issues of life. Any life issue needs to be understood not by itself but in relationship to other life issues such as capital punishment, abortion, violence and death, war, poverty and nutrition, and welfare issues. Your position on one aspect of the issue needs to be consistent, coherent, and defensible with how you understand other issues of life. The structure of the Academic Forum works to keep this balance.

Fourth, The Academic Forum's goal is to impact all of the students. The forum's primary intended audience is the student body, the whole student body. It is not focused on one small core group, honors program, a learning community, or a particular freshman or senior learning experience. Why is this element necessary? Why not deal with just a few students? Why keep our eye on the prize as the whole student body? It is a bit like stopping smoking cigarettes. It only works if the environment around you is also smoke free. If you do not smoke but your friends and family smoke, you live in an environment that is toxic to your health. The same thing is true with clear water. Everything is interdependent and interrelated. You cannot have one clear river by itself; the other tributaries are just too interconnected to make it possible.

So we set as the prize the total environment. This goal reflects the mission of the Values Program, which is to engage the institution in an educational process to discover and to implement ways to help students grow in awareness of values issues, to establish a comprehensive framework, and to learn the courage to act on what they understand to be necessary.

Fifth, the Academic Forum fills a need for a space that is trusting, welcoming, and challenging. Even though faculty are central to the purpose and function of a college, university, and professional school, they are not the only part of the educational institution. The students, staff, administration, and other constituencies are also very necessary. Every research confirms that education goes on throughout the institution in significant ways. It does not happen only in the classroom. This fact gives rise to another insight: the educational community must work together as a whole. Each part must be allowed to contribute to this enterprise because they all have something to give. There is a need to make a bridge, to make the connections between different aspects of the enterprise. It is this need to make connections that is so important. It is this need that gave rise to the idea of the Academic Forum. There has to be some place in the institution where people can come together in trust and participate in this endeavor. The Academic Forum, which is institution-wide, provides that space and place.

Finally, the Academic Forum makes it clear that we all have many miles to go. Every teacher and parent meets the child and student who thinks this time now is when I must learn everything. Slowly, the recognition arrives that acquiring knowledge and insight is a long-term process, a never-ending process. The Academic Forum is that process in action. No single course, one year of college, or two or four is enough to complete a student's moral and spiritual growth. When they leave you, they still have many things to learn and much development still in progress. The teacher, the textbooks, and this particular group of peers will not be around to prod and assist the individual.

The supposition of the Academic Forum is that this spirit and fire that are often present in the classroom can still be present and manifest their truth outside the classroom as well. The fire will still be present and continue into today and tomorrow to reveal the truth and to instruct us.

After the professor leaves, the ability to grasp and participate in the values dimensions of issues must remain. That intense feeling of tender affection and compassion, that something that elicits deep interest and enthusiasm in somebody, needs to be continually revealed. It can never be reduced to matters of doctrine; it is ALIVE. In theological terms we would say, "Ultimately we need to go beyond knowledge about God and encounter God in ourselves and our lives." In the secular sense we would say we need to go beyond knowledge about truth, morality, spirituality, and love and we encounter this love in ourselves and in our lives. This process is never-ending; it is not something we do on our own. We need to understand that the force that the values dimension is trying to get at, the Holy Spirit, is eager to teach not just our minds but also our hearts about the way we need to live. All we need to do is open our hearts.

Conclusion

This chapter's sampling of Academic Forums and some of the wide variety of their programmatic events represents the fruit of practical lived experience and reflection by many colleagues and committed participants over the past nearly twenty years. With these examples I have tried to give a sense of the struggle that is involved in being part of an educational effort to discover and implement ways to assist students in making connections between classroom material and the world outside the classroom. These examples for the most part reflect some of the successful attempts at making the connections. For every success there were many that did not succeed. It requires patience and perseverance for the faculty to work to incorporate the content and techniques learned in the Values Institutes into their classroom teaching. It also requires commitment by the administrators and staff to coordinate their efforts under the umbrella-like design of the Academic Forum. In the end the Academic Forum worked. It provided the structure and the context to assist students in finding points of connection between their studies in the classroom and the forum events beyond the classroom.

By describing the various forums and some of their programmatic aspects, I hope to have provided an understanding and a sense of the design and the dynamism of all the parts of the CAVE model working together.

I have tried to show how the efforts of the professors, administrators, and staff worked to weave theme-related issues into their lesson plans and to discover and implement ways to bring them together in a broad variety of forum activities. My aim was to show how these efforts played out across the academic year.

My hope is that this chapter has given you material to think about. I suggest that the Academic Forum and the CAVE model are worth considering for your institution. The Academic Forum has demonstrated its power to grab and keep the attention of an entire campus community. It has proven that it can actively engage and confront the entire community with fundamental questions. And it can do so while maintaining its reputation as a process of serious and open inquiry. One of our objectives was to design this model so that it would be applicable to other institutions and situations. I ask you to think about it.

Engaging the College Community
in the Quest for Resources
Human and Financial

The quest for resources can be described by two metaphors. On one hand, it can be a lot like tossing a pebble into a pond and trying to capture the energy of the ripples as they spread. On the other, it can be a series of unplanned and unpredictable challenges, more akin to what President Abraham Lincoln described when asked to explain his course on Reconstruction after the Civil War: "The pilots on our Western rivers steer from point to point as they call it—setting the course of the boat no farther than they can see, and that is all I propose to myself in this great problem."

It is that simple; it is also that difficult. First, you need the right people with the right pebble in the right pond and just the right moment. Then you must figure out how to harness the energy of the ripples. Be prepared also, at the same time, for every conceivable eventuality as your journey takes you to the next bend in the river.

As director of the Center for the Advancement of Values Education, which administered the Values Program, I depended on the skills and insights of all sorts of colleagues as we progressed along our journey. The Values Program engaged the college community in a campuswide educational effort designed to discover and implement ways to assist students in heightening their awareness of values issues, developing a comprehensive framework for addressing these issues, and strengthening their moral courage to act on their principles. I had to continually learn anew how to capture those human and financial ripples and harness their energy so that we might have momentum to navigate and reach each successive point in the river.

In this chapter I describe the process and challenges of acquiring resources. In the words of one successful administrator, it means "people, time, and money." I have designed this chapter almost as a case study that others can use to derive guidelines and suggestions as they struggle to discover and implement ways to engage various constituencies and resources within their own institution. The greatest resource of every institution is its people. For an idea, however, to become an effective program, it needs both adequate resources and personal commitment. Another intention of this chapter is to highlight how something like the CAVE model in action, such as the Values Program, can actually become a valuable catalyst for attracting such resources. If you get the right people and the right vision, then it becomes more likely that you will acquire the financial and other required resources.

Since most educational institutions struggle to find the necessary resources, this chapter will be of interest. In spite of these challenges, or maybe because of them, efforts to acquire human and financial resources for the Values Program exceeded our original "ambitious dreams." For example:

• The Le Moyne College Board of Trustees selected the Values Program and CAVE as a recipient of a one million–dollar endowment in the college's 1996 twenty-five million–dollar capital campaign.

• The report of the Middle States Accreditation Team during their visit in 1995 singled out the Values Program for special recognition, calling it a model of teaching and learning that brought eminent distinction to the college. The report recommended that the college find ways to support the personnel, programs, and research of CAVE. It also recommended that resources be found to support dissemination of the program's findings to the wider educational community.

• Kurt Geisenger, then vice president for academic affairs, reflected the current attitude: "This is the signature program of Le Moyne College. It tells the world what we value and what we expect our students to be." We also had the president, the Board of Trustees, and the Jesuits, the founding religious order of the college, behind the program.

• The program earned the strong support of the faculty as reflected in the fact that more than 85 percent of the 127 full-time faculty had participated in the program's Summer Institutes. A critical mass of students, faculty, administration, staff, alumni, and others, with no connection to Le Moyne, stood behind the program.

In this chapter I will refer interchangeably to both the Values Program and CAVE. Because the Values Program and its process have proved transferable to many different types of institutions, CAVE was actively involved in disseminating our process and research findings not only to colleges and universities but also to the wider educational community at the K–12 levels, postsecondary levels, and the wider community.

To hope to implement a collegewide interactive model that actually engages the entire community in an institution-wide mission of values education is indeed an ambitious dream. Of course, it was more common-place during past centuries in the colleges and universities of Europe and the United States. Our changing culture and institutions, however, have made that reality much more of a challenge. The purpose of this chapter differs from the ones that have gone before. Now I wish even more ex-plicitly to face up to the challenge of engaging an entire institution in the mission of values education. How do you involve many elements of the institution in such an institution-wide educational effort designed to ac-complish this mission?

One of the themes that I will outline is the process our fund-raising followed. It is not possible to describe this procedure in isolation, however, because intertwined within all elements of the program is the process of continually attracting and engaging new faculty, students, and staff in the values process. I will need, then, to maintain a double focus: attracting both human talent and funding resources.

Always in the back of my mind as director was the conviction that in order to engage the entire community it would be necessary to get their at-tention on a regular basis. How does one keep an idea consistently before the community but do so in a way that is not overkill? A Working Group member phrased our dilemma this way: "How do you keep values in the forefront of the student's consciousness but do so in such a way that it pre-cludes a student complaining, 'If I ever hear the word *values* again, I will get sick'?" Once we had resolved that issue, we would need to engage them in such a way that they would eventually recognize that this process was also something that deeply touched them personally and professionally.

In order to bridge the gap between vision and reality, we needed to eventually convince and win over certain constituencies beyond the faculty and their colleagues. Because the institution is made up of many different levels and many divergent realities, the soil would need to be prepared very carefully. The design of the CAVE model proved to be just such an instrument. This chapter gives the highlights of that journey.

I take you from the grassroots beginnings when we had little more than the right people, an awareness of a critical need, and a strong desire to commit ourselves to doing something to meet that need. Using the image of a pebble tossed into that pond, I will lead you through the journey all the way to the college's capital campaign. These steps are unique to our institution. I believe the insights here are valid in many situations.

Our program scored three significant success stories in terms of human and financial resources: First, the Values Program was designated in 1996 to receive one million dollars of the twenty-five million–dollar capital campaign. Second, the college's new chief academic officer called the Values Program the "signature program" at Le Moyne. Third, many talented, already overworked individuals were motivated by a great desire to make this program succeed, even against staggering odds.

How did it happen? I will try to show that the quest for resources is much more than finding someone to give money to your center or your program. It involves a living, dynamic process that demands constant effort. But it is worth every minute of it.

The Beginnings: The Right People with the Right Idea in the Right Time and Place

My story starts with a real stroke of luck. I happened to find the right colleagues, and together we found the right pebble and the right pond at the right moment. The right pebble was what we created: the CAVE model. The right pond was Le Moyne College in Syracuse, New York, in the mid-1980s.

Our history and process are described earlier in this book. As far as fund-raising, we began with a "do-it-yourself" approach of applying for small seed grants. In these beginnings of our grassroots movement, all the essential elements required by foundations and donors for successful grant proposals were present:

• We identified and articulated a critical need (values education) and presented the evidence that supported the need for the project both in educational institutions and in the wider society

• We were able to present innovative strategies that met those needs and demonstrate that they were adaptable to different types of educational institutions

• We were clear about our objectives and goals, our methods, who would do what, and how our progress would be assessed.

I have stressed the importance of finding the right people. An underlying question throughout this chapter is how you create a strong desire in people that motivates them to work against formidable odds. It is now obvious to me that financial resources are not the first or even the second most critical requirement. If you do not have people who are motivated to work on your program, who want to be part of it, then you have nothing. You need a good idea, a big vision, and a big dream. Your project needs to be something worthy of the energies and hearts of talented people. Long before you seek financial resources, you have to develop your number-one resource: your people. As one of my most wealthy and talented associates said, "You couldn't get me to work on this for money. I don't need it. But the program is so important that I am willing to give of my time and my talents to this."

The Grassroots Stage, 1987–1992

In the grassroots stage, from 1987 to 1992, we kept the process and program alive by writing grants. The first were seed grants, ranging from five thousand to one hundred thousand dollars, providing resources to identify and articulate the problem. No one at this time thought about the need for an endowment. For us, these seed grants were critical. During the first five years, we cobbled together many small to medium-size grants to create and implement the process and the program's three components. We were also able to get special prestigious grants for the assessment and research aspects of the program. Among the funding agencies were the Lilly Endowment, Raskob Foundation, National Science Foundation, and Consortium for the Advancement of Private Higher Education.

Since, as faculty members, we had no experience with writing major grants, we found cash to pay an experienced grant writer from another institution to help us craft our first proposals. We raised most of the funds needed over the next four years from these master proposals. But more important, the grant writing forced us to focus on the assessment aspect of our program, because prestigious foundations required assessment. This process also encouraged us to think beyond the boundaries of our own institution to a wider constituency, since many foundations will fund only programs that are significant for other institutions. This foundation requirement gave us access to expertise we did not have, people with a more national perspective. The Consortium for the Advancement of Private Higher Education made us part of a national consortium, and we attended national meetings. This experience helped us build valuable connections. It opened our horizons to the world of the foundations, a major source of help and assistance. Finally, it acted as a catalyst for the college to hire a grant writer, because we had shown the college the value of this office.

As early as 1989, it began to dawn on us that it would become more difficult to get start-up grants because we were no longer a start-up organization. We turned more to the college for resources, and soon learned that this process would be difficult for many reasons.

Foundations gave us visibility and the leverage to get started. For our educational effort to be successful, however, it would have to learn to stand on its own two feet.

A Soul-Searching Period, 1991–1992: Had We Become Too Successful?

The summer of 1991 was a critical moment. At that time, after being together and doing our process for five years, we embarked on a process of strategic planning. If ever an event was to have a major rippling effect, it was this one. If ever we needed a river pilot to guide us to the next point, it was at this moment.

It would take a long list to describe the pressures that had built up to force us to do a "vision plan" in 1991. In the end, it all came down to the fact that we were exhausted; we had reached the end of our rope.

The grassroots organizational structures and resources initiated six years earlier in our first grant proposals and deliberations were no longer able to bear the weight of the demands being made on them both within and beyond our institution. The Values Program's limited staff and resources were about to buckle. It was like adding more and more weight onto a two-wheeled, single-axle wagon. We knew the axle was about to break. We needed a new wagon, and we needed help.

Since our beginnings in 1986, the ripple effect of our "ambitious dream" had expanded:

• At an annual cost of seventy thousand dollars, this grassroots movement had created, implemented, funded, and maintained an institution-wide effort, whereas those individuals running the program were faculty members also fully involved in teaching and regular department duties

• Each year we planned, funded, and ran a three-week summer values institute for at least twenty faculty and coordinated a series of academic forum events during the following academic year

• We created and used sophisticated instruments for assessing our goals, which was demanding and time-consuming

• We completed the award-winning book *Ambitious Dreams* (Kirby et al. 1990), authored other seminal articles, and presented papers at many national and international conferences

• We had adapted our innovative strategies to meet the need of different types of educational institutions, and we were in demand to make presentations locally, nationally, and internationally.

By the summer of 1991, our habit of continually reflecting on our practical lived experience prepared and enabled us to ask questions such as, What could and ought we to be doing? There were a million possibilities, and we knew we could not do everything. Through a contact our group was introduced to Jack and Carol Lawyer, cofounders of Henneberry Hill Consultants, an organizational development consultancy group. Jack was the right person at the right time. Together we began a process of revisiting and reshaping our purposes and aims. Their efforts would provide critical resources to help us navigate to the next point. During the next twelve months, the Working Group on Values and others worked on drafting our beliefs, mission, objectives, and strategies. The final event involved 35 colleagues in a two-day strategic planning session on January 9–10, 1992. For anyone weighing the possibility of implementing or adapting this model, it is very important to recognize what had changed and how it had changed. To pay attention to the results of our combined practical lived experience and reflection during 1987 and 1992 provides a vivid example of what it means in the concrete to engage the members of the community in an institution-wide educational effort.

The milieu within the college in 1992 was quite different from the milieu in which the Values Program was begun in 1987. Then the ground was hard and barren, and it was difficult to plant any seeds that would last and bear fruit. But, five years later, the situation was very different. We had discovered and implemented ways to apply the CAVE model for four years. We had many committed colleagues. Nearly 70 of the 127 full-time faculty in our college had participated in the three-week Summer Institutes on the themes "Economic Justice" (1988), "Peace and War" (1989), "Families and Public Policy" (1990), and "Science, Technology, and Values" (1991). Other faculty, administrators, and staff had worked in the Academic Forum and its spin-offs to begin to transform the culture of the college and reinvigorate undergraduate education by permeating the culture of the institution through the Academic Forum. The college community was like soil that had been worked and reworked. It was being brought back to its fruitfulness. It was becoming alive in a new way. After five years, it was time to rethink, reevaluate, and adjust our vision and our plan.

Each year since 1987 we worked to define our CAVE model and process. By 1991 we knew what we stood for, what was negotiable, and what was not. We needed to pull it together in a systematic manner. Our "ambitious dream" had evolved into a reality. We needed to reexamine that dream, understand our vision, and create a plan to get us to that ever expanding vision and dream.

After much discussion, the Working Group came up with a list of 35 people from our own faculty, administration, and staff whom we would invite to this process. It was a bold move. We wanted to engage a large part of the community in our planning and vision process. As a mixed group, these participants struggled with their various professional and personal language and concepts for two full days to nail down a vision and strategic plan. The fact that this group was a mixed and diverse crowd gave us the freedom to create a language of our own. We had to create a language that was accessible to everyone and did not alienate any groups.

A Vision Plan (1992–1997)

The ripples from the stone in the water were expanding. The product of this effort was *A Vision Plan (1992–1997)* distributed in attractively designed pamphlet form to all the faculty, staff, and administrators and published and reprinted in the college newspaper. Various people were invited to become part of the various focus groups. The response was heartening. The second phase was well under way. We now had the attention of the college. We were engaging the entire college community in a process of discovery and implementation. We had a very attractive vision, a planning piece that told people where we were going, all done in an inclusive, welcoming manner that invited participation. We also had a renewed sense of energy and enthusiasm in recapturing the vision and working through the strategies of getting from the vision to the concrete goal and all the steps in between.

In many ways we were once again casting our pebble into the pond. This time, however, the pebble was more carefully fashioned by the Working Group on Values and by others who had joined with us. The pebble that we were now throwing, our CAVE model, had not only the promise but also the power to cast transforming ripples through our collegiate community and beyond. Also very changed was the quality of the water in the pond. Like the pilots on the western rivers, we were steering from point to point by reflecting on our practical lived experience. Praxis was our compass. The vision plan provided a much-needed map for the next five years. With this map, we would engage an ever widening community in our effort to discover and implement ways to assist students toward our goal of values education.

A New Point in the River: A New College Administration

The ink was hardly dry on the vision plan when we met our next serious challenge. Within a year, in 1994, the college's president resigned and an interim president assumed office. New administrators who did not know a lot about the Values Program now governed the college. The problem was exacerbated by the fact that it was an interim administration. How long would it last? How do you get the new administration's attention? How do you get new people to be understanding and committed to the program and the process?

Many things happened during this time, but I will mention only two: our report to the college and the creation of the Board of Directors of the Values Program.

The Report to the College

As so often happened in our story, the next critical move could not have been planned or predicted. The newly appointed special assistant to the interim president suggested that we prepare an executive summary document, one that was brief, succinct, and to the point, covering basic information. It turned out to be a critical communications document. Because we had already written our strategic plan, *A Vision Plan (1992–1997),* we were prepared to negotiate this hurdle.

A coordinator was assigned to manage the task and to help facilitate creation of the document. Working together with Henneberry Hill Consultants, many of the same people who had created the vision plan, with the addition of people such as Andrew J. Brady, S.J. (a founder of the college), the Working Group on Values, and some administrators and faculty, we finished our product on July 1, 1994. It took seven months. We titled it *The Values Program at Le Moyne: An Ambitious Dream Evolving—a Report to the College (1985–1994).*

The report proved to be a powerful instrument for raising resources, both human and financial. It is an executive summary of the Values Program, fewer than twenty pages in length, in concise language, attractively prepared. It gives the program's mission, overview, description of the three components, staff, past accomplishments, future goals (five-year plan), and in two appendixes the history of the program and a list of the more than 150 Values Institute participants and their offices and academic departments. It is the kind of document you can give to all sorts of people. It gets their attention, builds understanding, and is a bridge between constituencies. For us, it quickly demonstrated to others how the Values Program was connected to the college's larger institutional vision.

The document provided the college community with an informational report describing our effort to enhance Le Moyne's values education tradition. It was an instrument for introducing the program to those individuals who were not familiar with it (including the interim president); for those individuals who had worked with us in Values Institutes and Academic Forum events and programs, the report served as an update. It was still another step in soliciting the support, cooperation, and commitment to this process of the entire community.

What the report did was force us to state our mission and our aims in a language and format that were accessible to a busy executive or board member. This document would be put in the hands of the president's cabinet. For the first time, we had a very accessible document that got the attention of busy executives.

Getting the Program on the Institutional Agenda

By 1995, the president's interim status was changed to permanent. As stability returned to the college, the challenges continued to come fast, one after another. The administration announced that it was planning to create a strategic master plan for the next ten years that would determine the budget. Our challenge was now clear: unless the Values Program was included in the strategic plan, there would be no place and no funding for the program and it would be cut away from the life of the institution.

We were once again in a process of engaging a whole new element of the institution in this process of discovery and implementation. This time we would have to stretch ourselves to reach into the highest administration, the Board of Trustees, the president's cabinet, the faculty senate, and all the aspects that go into policy making in the institution.

Creating a Board of Directors

As in other critical moments, this crisis moved us to the creation of our next critical resource: the Board of Directors. Like other elements of the program, the board grew out of necessity. We had again reached a point on our journey where we needed new pilots to steer us through the unfamiliar channel. By early 1991, the program had grown very complex. In addition to creating new structures to organize programs and personnel, there were also complicated issues of financial policy that involved the institution, the community, issues of law, and the program itself. The issues sometimes were too complex for internal college people and ourselves. Like colleges, universities, and nonprofits everywhere, we needed to seek advice from outside.

The first glimmerings of the need for an outside board came from a local businessman whose foundation had been the first and most consistent benefactor to the fledgling Values Program. On numerous occasions he raised with me the need to think about having a board. He got me to see the importance of having such a board. His name was John Amos, and his foundation was the Amos Foundation.

Encouraged by our conversations, I began to surface the idea of creating a Board of Directors with the Working Group on Values. It took nearly three years for the ideas to gel. We were ready to go, but the institution was not ready to go with us.

The Board and the Case Presentation
to the Capital Campaign Committee

I can give a vivid example of the importance of the board in raising revenues. It involves what we called the Case Presentation, the process and final documentation by which we made our case before the institution's Capital Campaign Committee as to why the Values Program and CAVE ought to be included in the 1996 capital campaign for at least a one million–dollar endowment.

When a college plans a capital campaign, there is always a fierce struggle among the various constituencies to have their programs and projects listed among the items in the capital campaign. The Values Program board provided a large part of the energy necessary for getting the Values Program on the capital campaign list. As the college administration and the college Board of Trustees struggled to work through its capital campaign strategy, the Board of Directors of the Values Program worked with my staff, the Working Group on Values, and many others in the college community and beyond to create and articulate our Case Presentation.

For many weeks the Values Program Board of Directors met to hammer out how best to make a presentation before the college and its potential donors. I think the preparation of this case is where the Board of Directors began to find its voice.

Our major effort was the Case Presentation, but the effort took many other forms. The college president invited me, as director of the Values Program, to accompany him to Washington, D.C., to meet with key alumni and to talk about the Values Program. We also gave presentations, as we had since 1988, at the college's Board of Trustees meeting, on alumni weekends and family weekends, and before parents and interested prospective students at admissions gatherings. My office also began to work closely with the administrators of the capital campaign.

Many things happened in this process to help us make our case. We worked closely with the administration officers to integrate the Values Program's mission and purpose with the goals of the college. We clarified in writing the relationship between the Values Program, CAVE, and the college. With our new Board of Directors, we struggled to get the attention of the institution, to discover a language and an alignment of the facts that would attract and engage key decision makers. This effort probably did more for the board than anything else because it completely engaged the members in the process.

We found that our Board of Directors added a vital dimension to our fund-raising process. The board is a source of advice and expertise. It brings an outside perspective, and its members can ask intelligent questions. Board members understand strategy. They are respected and can get the attention of the institution.

With a Board of Directors, our Values Program acquired a powerful voice. The choice of whom to serve as chair of the board is critical. The chair will symbolize the seriousness and the soberness of the board and the program. He or she will personify what the Values Program stands for. The chair will deal as an equal with the college president, the Board of Trustees, and the vice presidents of the college. This person needs to be an equal among equals. An appropriate choice will attract and be a leader among other very strong board members. The chair needs to be a person you can deal comfortably with, someone who understands you, but also someone whose experience and background enables him or her to give adequate judgment about what you are proposing.

The board members will take on certain responsibilities and duties. The board engages the entire community, especially outside the college, but also inside. It can raise questions of accountability toward the program to key groups such as the president, the college Board of Trustees, the vice presidents, and the alumni. It can also hold the Values Program accountable in terms of budgeting, programming, the job description of the director, and other aspects of the program.

Conclusion

As I began this chapter I was intrigued by three questions:

• In an age of scarce resources, what had happened so that the Values Program was singled out for a one million–dollar endowment in the 1996 Le Moyne College capital campaign?

• How do you create a strong desire in people that motivates them to work on a project even against the most difficult odds?

• How do you get a clear signal from your institution that being engaged in values education is a top priority, one that is going to be rewarded?

We began our journey down the river with grassroots fund-raising and fulfilled our budgetary needs by securing small start-up grants. As our program grew, we put together documentation to describe it to outsiders. We made key players in the administration aware of our efforts, and we created a Board of Directors, drawn from outside the college community. We already had the right people, the right idea, the right place, and the right time. Now these other elements came together to make our program a "signature program" at Le Moyne, and to fund it even beyond our ambitious dreams.

No initiative in learning and teaching can long survive unless it is able to attract the best human resources to the endeavor and to also persuade the institution's policy makers that in this time of limited resources, the project is worth attracting resources. In higher education and elsewhere, everyone knows that the success and priority of any endeavor are signaled by the adequacy of the people, places, time, and money allocated to it.

In this chapter I have stressed the importance of finding the right people. Who these right people might be can change as the journey unfolds. Necessary also is that they be caught by a vision worthy of their commitment. Eventually, they will need to see the importance of that vision for their own and others' personal and professional lives. If they do not make this connection, it will be very difficult to expect the type of long-term commitment necessary to discover and implement ways to assist students in this process. Thus, the resources needed are: the right people, a vision to meet a critical need, a personal understanding of the critical need and its necessity and importance of resolution, and a model that can be implemented that has reasonable hopes of completion.

In other chapters I have discussed how we began to meet those requirements. In this chapter I focused more on how the journey of serious inquiry and the search for the right people and their commitment spread out across the campus and the wider society. As the demand for increased resources of people, time, space, and funding expanded, the CAVE model proved its ability to spread the ripples to further boundaries; critical to the process is the continual renewal of resources. In this chapter I have tried to show that as the environment became more ALIVE, resources generally did become more available.

Implementing the CAVE Model
in Diverse Contexts
Why the CAVE Model?

This chapter begins by describing why and how the CAVE model and process can be an asset to any institution of higher learning. It then turns its focus to the advantages and challenges involved in the process of implementing the CAVE model in professional schools, and particularly in three types of professional institutions: medical, law, and business schools. Since these schools are usually part of a much larger university system, I also include some brief remarks pertinent to the larger university situation. I have already described the history and origins of the CAVE model and have discussed in greater depth its programmatic and structural aspects, its interrelated components, and other elements such as the theme, Working Group, Values Institute, and Academic Forum.

I believe it is important to highlight these types of institutions. One reason is that my perspective up to this point has pertained mostly to colleges and universities dedicated to the liberal arts and sciences or the more comprehensive institutions of learning with their great variety of disciplines and programs. First, many of my examples, guidelines, and suggestions were articulated in the language of the college or university dedicated to the learning and scholarship in the humanities, social sciences, natural sciences, communications, and computer science. Since much of my primary source material for this book is the lived experience, reflection, and praxis of many people associated with various stages of the CAVE model and the development and fine-tuning of its components, it was only natural that I use these types of schools for my examples. Second, I hope to spark the imagination of the reader to consider different types of environments and possibilities. Thinking about how the CAVE model might work in one of these schools, or in an engineering or communications school or a college of agriculture and technology, forces us to consider even more possibilities for our journey of discovery.

What gives me the confidence to think in these categories is the fact that the CAVE model has already been applied at several institutions and associations of colleges. For example, administrators and staff at Georgetown University invited us to discuss with them how this model and process might be helpful in integrating values education into their emphasis on service learning; within the Pennsylvania State University system, ideas developed by the CAVE model were essential in its effort to produce an integrated program across Pennsylvania, making values a priority in the university system. For the Fayetteville-Manlius, New York, school district we were part of the inspiration for its involvement with concern for values and character at the secondary and primary levels. More specifically to the point of professional schools, Fontys University in the Netherlands have made a major commitment to use, adapt, and implement the CAVE model. Spread throughout the country, each of the Fontys Colleges is devoted to a particular profession such as communications and media, pharmacy, engineering, and physical fitness. They began to implement their vision in 2004.

We have introduced this model as a "process of discovery" and a "process of serious inquiry," which means no one can give you or your institution all the answers. You will need to discover an appropriate approach to many of them for yourself. We also understand that many colleges, universities, and professional schools already have centers, institutes, and departments to discuss practical and professional ethics and their applicability to materials studied. We are not in any way denigrating or suggesting replacing aspects of institutional life already in place. We are instead suggesting an alternative model, which may be appropriate for your institution or can enrich an already existing program. In this chapter, I provide some guidelines, both general and specific.

Colleges and universities face an ever increasing competitive world in which they must set themselves apart in order to attract the best and the brightest of students. A brief glance at Web sites for various colleges and universities will show that some stand out because of exceptional offerings. Brown University profiles its "Resumed Undergraduate Education Program" for students at least twenty-five years of age who have been away from formal study for five years. On its Web site, the University of Notre Dame gives pride of place to its Reilly Center for Science, Technology, and Values. Penn State University reminds visitors to its Web site that it is a leader in distance learning. Yale University's Web site showcases a 2002 photograph of its president standing next to Kofi Annan, secretary-general of the United Nations, in order to emphasize its focus on "Yale and the World."

Families are increasingly concerned, justifiably so, that their children be prepared to meet the challenges of modern society. Students desire more than narrow technical training. They wish instead for education for the whole person. It can be provided by the CAVE model at your institution. Among its other benefits, the CAVE model has the potential to have a positive effect on admissions.

A vigorous CAVE model can also work as a catalyst to aid fund-raising in the eyes of both institutions and alumni. For many years, directors of development have been aware that large companies and foundations have shifted their support from the general to the specific, from the speculative to the proven. The CAVE model has a fifteen-year track record of success, and it can show potential donors that your institution is serious about creating something new, something successful, something important, and something that works.

High-quality faculty may also be attracted. The Center for the Advancement of Values Education on your campus has the potential to become a research center that will be the site of inquiry and a source for answers about values education. These attributes could attract precisely the kind of faculty you value.

Employers may also look differently at your graduates. Applicants to your institution will know that they are more valuable to employers because of the education they have received in values. Employers in every field are hungry for employees who know themselves and have the courage of their convictions. Such employees tend to be highly motivated.

They are more confident of their goals. Also, they are more likely to make valuable contributions to the workplace sooner than young employees who are still searching for, wondering about, or even wholly ignorant of fundamental values issues.

Finally, in addition to attracting students, faculty, and dollars, a properly implemented CAVE model can provide your institution with a significant faculty-development benefit at a low cost. This particular economic advantage of the CAVE model is not incidental; rather, it is fundamental to the program's success. In our case, over a seven-year period, more than 80 percent of the faculty and much of the staff participated in one way or another with some form of training, orientation, or cross-disciplinary research that sprang directly from the CAVE model. The program breathed new life into existing aspects of the college and gave birth to new and important projects such as the Town Meetings and the South Africa–Le Moyne week. When the value of the CAVE model is judged, its contribution to faculty development cannot be discounted, particularly in this era of cost cutting.

Implementing the CAVE Model

Some practical questions you will face as you begin to implement the CAVE model at your college or institution are the following:

• How do you engage and commit a whole institution to the mission of values education?

• How do you get the faculty involved, and how do you keep them involved? How do you provide faculty with the legitimacy, technique, and content necessary for values education?

• How do you manage to impact nearly every student in your institution? Does this activity enhance or diminish students' values and moral sensitivity? How do you assist students in making connections, in achieving integration? How do you engage students in real-life experiences?

• How do you cross discipline boundaries, and, when you do, how do you intertwine content, pedagogy, and learning and create a community of learners with both faculty and students coming together? How do you get the administration, staff, and different constituencies to buy into this idea?

• How do you keep this program at the center of the academic enterprise and avoid the danger that it becomes marginal?

Given these questions I experience a tension as I consider how best to proceed. On the one hand, I do not want to repeat the model in detail as I go through each of the different types of institutions that may want to use the CAVE model. There are certain commonalities for every situation, and their application should be somewhat clear. But having struggled to create the program, I also know how difficult it is to go from a theoretical or practical question to discovering an adequate response.

Since I have already given a lot of focus to colleges and universities, I will offer discussions of the applicability of the CAVE model in the following cases: medical schools, law schools, and business schools. I will then end with some general conclusions.

A Personal Story

Before we begin our discussion of the applicability of the CAVE model to your specific institution, I would like to share a personal anecdote that sowed the seeds of my belief in the importance of the study of values issues and showed me how and why discussing such issues could engage and unite individuals across a broad spectrum of backgrounds and philosophies.

As I have mentioned, when I was a graduate student, I participated in what was among the first interdisciplinary seminars in the then "new" field of bioethics and the life sciences. My fellow students, all in their final years of school, were selected from the New York metropolitan-area medical schools, law schools, and doctoral programs in the liberal arts and sciences. I had not known previously any of the students or professors with whom I was working. Our meetings were held at Columbia University. We dealt with the cutting-edge bioethical life issues beginning to surface in 1971 in the hopes of defining and understanding them. My semester-long responsibility, shared with two law students and a medical student, was to prepare legislation for the New York State legislature that would address the medical, legal, ethical, economic, moral, and religious issues surrounding surrogate motherhood.

What struck me forcibly was that these young men and women, from divergent professional orientations, were questioning basic issues that confronted their personal and professional lives. Even though we represented a broad diversity of race, creed, nationality, and culture, I understood that we all shared a common human nature. Whether we were in training to become a lawyer, physician, college professor, or priest, we all faced the same difficult questions and worked hard to grapple with these issues, new at the time, raised by the concept of surrogate motherhood. If a child can be conceived in a test tube, what then does motherhood mean? What does fatherhood mean? Will such institutions as "sperm banks" be necessary, or even wanted? In 1971 these considerations were new and shocking questions.

In discussing these questions, and the implications of "test tube" babies, all the members of our seminar experienced certain emotions. We attempted to apply logic to a situation that had been impossible only twenty years before and still seemed to us illogical. We needed to think: Because this new technology was man-made, was it "unnatural"? Was it somehow "wrong"? Should it be regulated by state law? If so, how? Could we be logical about a question that had emotional resonance for us all in different ways? Perhaps some of us at the seminar had a friend or family member who had experienced infertility. Would this background shape our thinking about this new technology? Is there, or should there be, a religious or theological aspect to the issue of human reproduction? We each were dealing with the basic questions of when life begins. These considerations are values questions that transcend professional orientations and merely technical education but have profound and immediate resonance when a medical technician, doctor, nurse, or researcher is working in the field.

We needed to access the best in traditional thinking and balance it against our own thoughts, experiences, and emotions in order to make new judgments and decisions about an innovative technology that we could previously not imagine. Were we not engaged in applying the skills that so much later the CAVE model would create a viable system to develop?

The CAVE Model Applied to Medical School

Let us look at how the CAVE model may be applied to a medical school. Doctors and medical school students face ethical issues all the time. These individuals are on the front lines of societal change. It is they who deal first with technology that affects us all. We have already seen how in 1971 the idea of a "test tube" baby created a ripple effect of change in concepts of motherhood, fatherhood, and parenthood, and introduced many procedures in the field of infertility treatment.

The field of medical ethics or bioethics is not new. Its first phase began in the fourth century with the Hippocratic oath and lasted until 1962. Its second phase began in 1962 with the explosion of technology in the health field, specifically the development of an artificial kidney and the availability of hemodialysis to treat patients with kidney failure. This new technology was first available at the University of Washington in Seattle and could benefit only a handful of patients, whereas tens of thousands of patients in renal failure across the country would be denied access because of a lack of hemodialysis machines. The first bioethics committee was convened in Seattle to decide how to ration out this lifesaving technology. One result of the study of this issue was that end-stage renal disease is now the only disease for which treatment is totally funded by the federal government.

Ethical questions also surround both beginning-of-life issues and end-of-life issues. Does life begin at conception? If so, should birth control pills that result in the sloughing off of a fertilized ovum be prescribed? Should the nation or the states enact laws to control the medical procedure of abortion? Since the age at which women can conceive can now be extended artificially, should a doctor prescribe fertility drugs to a forty-nine-year-old patient? Should a fifty-nine-year-old woman reverse the process of menopause and seek to bear a child by the implantation of a fertilized embryo in her womb? Is there an age past which a woman or a man cannot or should not become a parent? Who should decide these issues—the individual, the doctor, the state?

Ethical issues also surround the end of life. If a heart is to remain viable for transplant to a patient who needs a new heart, it cannot stop beating. What then constitutes "death"? A criterion for "brain death" was needed before harvesting organs for transplantation could be undertaken. This question was obviously one for the field of bioethics.

Also, is the United States a "death-defying culture"? Is there such a thing as a "good death"? When does one begin, withhold, or withdraw life-prolonging medical treatment? Where can a medical professional receive guidance for decision making? Do different minorities in the United States hold beliefs that may be unfamiliar or troubling to a physician from the mainstream culture? How does a physician deal with a patient whose religious beliefs demand that he refuse, or refuse for a member of his family, a needed blood transfusion?

The 1990s saw an expansion of bioethics committees, either freestanding or ad hoc, that became involved in hospital procedures and decision making. Acute health care institutions across the county established mechanisms to address these issues. Strategies ranged from multidisciplinary monthly committee meetings, ad hoc committees, and ethics teaching rounds, to name a few. These structured forums provided the legitimacy, content, and technique for dealing with questions of biomedical ethics as they arise in practice. All these questions and their answers demand careful consideration by those individuals trained to deal with values issues and the impact of beliefs and values on our actions.

Dr. Belding H. Scribner, a physician who pioneered at the University of Washington in the use of hemodialysis machines, writes, "We have never had a national or international forum in which to discuss the issues of allocation of scarce medical resources. . . . Our improved treatments do not address the questions of who should be treated when the resources are inadequate or the question of when treatment should be stopped. Such moral and ethical issues must be decided primarily by society, and not by us alone, the medical caregivers. But the issues must be addressed squarely and openly" (2002, 1066–67). Ethical issues surrounding medical treatment are realities in the experience of any medical professional. There is far more to medicine than mere technology. A solely technical education in medicine will surely fail the serious, committed student. Although committees and programs of bioethics are now part of the hospital fabric, a medical school is an ideal setting for the development of a CAVE model.

Dr. M. Catherine Hough, a professor of nursing at the University of North Florida, has created an applied nursing ethics course, which she presents every semester. This course has now become a core course and an essential part of the nursing curriculum at the University of North

Florida. After assessing the Values Program as described in this book, Dr. Hough comments, "The Values Institute would be an ideal component for incorporating into a medical school setting. Much of what I do is to 'train the trainers.' The Values Program would be an ideal add-on to a medical school already engaged in the study of bioethics" (2006, n.p.).

Themes for a CAVE Model Based in a Medical School

Let us return to an earlier question: how do you engage and commit the whole institution to the mission of values education? Let us recall the major components of the CAVE model. The backbone of the program is the theme discussed at the Values Institutes and expanded upon during the follow-up forums. There are many ways in which a theme can resonate within a medical school setting.

Whatever theme you choose, it should be a strong values-laden theme that is broad enough to engage and encompass many different disciplines and to transcend boundaries within the school. It should provide an opportunity to reflect on the values dimension while at the same time undertaking what needs to be done: the medical, technical, theoretical, and skill learning necessary in medicine.

We suggest that you begin with the themes that worked for us in the past, which we have already discussed. The theme "Economic Justice" is both broad and deep. It is a natural for adaptation to a medical school setting. Let us look at some ideas that spring to mind when this topic is applied to medical issues.

More money is spent in the United States on drugs for problems such as impotence and obesity than on drugs that might serve individuals in the global South. HIV/AIDS patients in Africa often lack drugs that might be helpful to them because the cost is beyond their ability to pay. So too do malaria patients in Africa. Clearly, individuals in the United States can and will buy drugs to treat problems that concern them immediately. Can and should they, or anyone, think about drug treatments for problems that do not exist in the United States? Should there be financial incentives in research and industry that might provide products not useful to customers in the developed North, but of great need in the less developed global South? If so, how could they be created and applied?

Another idea worthy of discussion might be the intersection of drug manufacturers and practicing physicians. Any visitor to a doctor's office has noticed a sign on the door directing pharmaceutical representatives to plan for appointments on certain days of the week so that they do not interfere with days when the doctors are busiest with patients. Do drug companies "target" doctors, or do they "serve" doctors? How should a physician think about the financial incentives to prescribe or not to prescribe certain medicines? What values issues come into play here, over and above questions of having access to "cutting-edge" treatment?

One of the costs of practicing medicine in the United States is malpractice insurance. Do medical schools bear some responsibility in educating emerging doctors about their legal responsibilities and obligations? Can or should medical schools offer education on medicine and the law? What values issues come into play if a doctor sees a patient as not merely an individual who is ill but rather as a potential opponent in court?

Another monetary problem in the United States is the proportion of our citizens who are uninsured or underinsured. The uninsured poor and indigent have access to local, state, and federal aid programs. However, the working poor, the low-income wage earners who cannot afford the insurance programs supplemented by their employers, are always at risk. How does a middle-aged diabetic woman, earning eleven thousand dollars per year as a sales associate in a department store, who is the sole support for a family of three, pay for health insurance for herself or for her family? The answer is: she can't. Instead, she puts off treatment for herself and for family members until a crisis forces her or a family member into lengthy hospitalization that then may lead to bankruptcy for the family. Recent studies have shown that the majority of personal bankruptcies are tied to the problem of overwhelming medical bills.

Here you have an issue that is clearly tied to the theme "Economic Justice." How does the richest nation in the world pay for health care? Who makes decisions about treatment—doctors, federal or local governments, insurance companies? How do we begin to deal with these values issues of money and medicine? Here again, future leaders need to have a basic vocabulary for dealing with values issues. Here again, the CAVE approach, applied to medical schools, can assist students who will be dealing with these and similar issues for decades to come.

Medical schools need to make time for discussion of these issues. Of course, doctors need to be experts in technique. No one wants to think that his or her doctor failed the practicum where hernia repair was taught. But doctors need a larger vision of their place in society. It is during medical school that time should be devoted to creating a time and a space, a platform, for discussion and consideration of these issues. The CAVE model, applied to a medical school, will provide the needed structure, a proven technique, and a forum for values education.

At a medical school, you may find that your faculty uses many different formats: lectures, labs, practicums, tests, readings, examinations, evaluations, floor experience, one-on-one interaction, and tutorials. Some instructors are primary-care practitioners who also teach. How do you deal with the different groups such as surgeons, internists, and family medicine providers? You will also need to consider the different needs of emergency medicine, dermatology, dentistry, neurology, oncology, and medical researchers.

How would a Values Institute and Academic Forum adjust to this diversity of environment? How can an Academic Forum be added to the schedule of an already overburdened medical student? We have found that the CAVE model breaks down boundaries and discipline barriers and brings in new sources of energy and knowledge. Once the institution makes a commitment to sponsoring the theme-laden Summer Institute and the faculty adds a values component to its teaching, this program will build bridges and be a catalyst to developing and expanding discussion of ideas and issues. Our experience has been that certain disparate groups can be connected, including admissions, missions and identity, grants writing, corporate and private philanthropy, community relations, relations with hospitals and other health and community services, and international awareness. Consider also involving rank and tenure, promotion, and the critical hiring and reward structure. The CAVE model will also involve questions internal to the medical school and external to the medical school. How will it relate, if at all, to membership in or the requirements of the American Medical Association?

Examples of Bridges to Be Built

The following are some examples of the kinds of bridges that might be built: a lecture series on HIV/AIDS and the costs of retroviral drugs, values, and possible connections with other educational institutions in the community. Another topic might be medicine and public policy, town-gown connections, community medicine, or medical care for the uninsured. You might also bridge a number of courses together and ask what kinds of service and health clinics can be integrated. Can you use television, media, film, theater? Is there a possibility of international discussion or comparison of treatments in various nations? Can you connect to your university's office of international affairs?

Barriers You May Face in Medical School

There are some barriers that you might face in medical school. One is the issue of legitimacy: students may be fearful because they do not have confidence. The student may doubt his or her technique, thinking, "I am a doctor or nurse. I am not an ethicist." There may be problems with perception of content: "I don't have the training to deal with values and spiritual dimensions."

The CAVE model provides answers to these questions and asserts that the questions of values can no longer be delegated or relegated to only philosophers and theologians. Just as churches have embraced the laity and given them a sense of their own dignity, so too must medical technicians open their minds and hearts to questions of values. The priority here is always the student. Other benefits will flow from making the student your first and most important priority. To overcome these barriers, commit yourself and the institution to a big vision beyond yourself and commit yourself even to the larger world community.

You will find that once your program is up and running, the CAVE model will allow you to cross discipline barriers and to create a community of learners with students and faculty working together.

The CAVE Model Applied to Law School

Now let us look at how the CAVE model might be applied in a law school setting. In 1980, Chief Justice Warren Burger wrote, "My thesis is simple and straightforward. Every law school has a profound duty—and a unique opportunity—to inculcate principles of professional ethics and standards in its students. This duty should permeate the entire educational experience beginning with the first hour of the first day of law school" (377). The CAVE model is an excellent and adaptable tool with which to achieve this end. Do law schools currently have such a model? Let us look at how law schools handle ethical questions and the regulation of the profession.

Lawyers by necessity are detail oriented and conscious of the needs for regulation. The American Bar Association (ABA) maintains a Center for Professional Responsibility and provides regularly updated Model Rules for Professional Conduct. Ample numbers of regulations govern the practice of law.

Currently on the Internet there are many legal ethics forums. Issues discussed on these sites include legal malpractice, attorney disqualification proceedings, professional standards of care, alleged unethical conduct, the unauthorized practice of law, and many other fine points. State bar associations sponsor many disciplinary hearings, and one has the sense that the profession is highly regulated. There is no shortage of scrutiny and discussion of ethics in the legal profession. On the other hand, an ABA survey found that only 14 percent of Americans have confidence in lawyers. Who of us has not heard an acid joke made about attorneys? As Supreme Court justice Louis D. Brandeis remarked, "If we desire respect for the law, we must first make the law respectable" (1993, 244). We contend that the insertion of a Values Program model into a law school curriculum will go a long way toward meeting this goal. Let us look at how that might work.

Law is the primary means by which public policy is put into effect in people's lives. Law is intimately concerned therefore with civil and human rights and inextricably tied to what we value. Lawyers deal routinely with criminal law, health law, family law, even animal law and ethics. Laws govern where and how we drive our cars. Laws govern freedom of information and individual privacy. Law concerns interactions with money in a thousand ways, of which only two are bankruptcy law and estate law. Laws govern family life, including when and how a divorced parent may see children who live in the custody of the other parent. As we have seen earlier in this chapter, laws also govern scientific research and intimate human issues such as reproduction. There is literally no way to separate values from the study of law.

Some will argue that by the time a student gets to law school, it is too late to have an effect on his or her ethics, that beliefs are already formed. But at what age does one set ethical boundaries—at three, when one learns that a toy belongs to a sibling and that sharing is a virtue; at five, when one starts school; or at thirteen, when puberty arrives? Are we not always learning and growing throughout our lives? If we say that it is impossible to teach ethics at any age past eighteen, then why do we offer postsecondary education? Professors who ask students of any age, eighteen-year-old freshman in college or adults returning to school, to write a personal code of conduct will find that the assignment is challenging and revelatory regardless of the age of the student.

During their practice of law, lawyers will face certain specific ethical questions. Among them may be questions regarding warning a client of limitations on representation. A lawyer may face a question of identifying to whom he owes duties. Is there a disciplinary standard of competence? Is there a difference between "diligence" and "zeal"? Does a lawyer have liability to certain nonclients? What duty does the lawyer have to communicate with her clients? What is prohibited assistance? These questions will come up in real-life legal practice. Law school is the logical time to begin to teach the young attorney what to expect and how to create a code of conduct and values that will stand the test of time and practice.

As in a medical school, you might face objections: that faculty and students are not specialists in ethics, not interested in questions of philosophy. The point is to open the floor for dialogue and exploration. That purpose is why the CAVE model is structured as it is, with an institute to break down barriers between the faculty and a forum to include the students in the creation of programming. The payment of a stipend can be an incentive for faculty, and the sense of creating and being part of wide-ranging and stimulating discussion will attract students.

In his monthly column in the *Corporate Legal Times*, Bruce D. Collins wrote that CAVE offers the "best bet yet to change some of the worst traits of individual lawyers." Collins had a unique perspective on CAVE as a board member, as he reveals in his article. Commenting on the ABA survey (already cited) that found that only 14 percent of Americans have "strong confidence in lawyers," Collins draws the conclusion that if 86 percent of Americans do not think highly of lawyers, then it is "a pretty strong signal the profession might be moving in the wrong direction. . . . My experience with CAVE's model (as a member of its board) tells me it can be effectively applied to law school without undermining the instruction of pure reasoning upon which the profession so famously relies." He assures his readers that "a value based legal education would leave legal analysis intact" and at the same time be "fostering civilizing approaches to problem solving that might otherwise go unnoticed and thereby unlearned" (1999, 7). He believes that the frequent lack of such civilized approaches is responsible for part of the bad opinion Americans hold of the legal profession.

Themes for a CAVE Model Based in a Law School

Those individuals wishing to create a CAVE model at a law school might use a theme that we have tested and tried. "Families and Public Policy" is a theme that has special interest and applicability to the law. Laws governing divorce, separation, and child support impact many families in the United States. Workplace law touches on any person who is employed. Punishments that assign a family member to a prison term have a definite effect on any family.

Another theme that might be used in a CAVE model at a law school might be the nature of crime and punishment. Does punishment in the United States disproportionately affect African Americans and Hispanics? Have any of your law students ever visited a family court, a county jail, a federal prison? Have any of your students met the family of a man or woman who is incarcerated? What is the thinking of those individuals who oppose the death penalty? What is the thinking of those who support it? Can a compelling argument be made for each side? "Criminal Punishment" might be a potent theme for a CAVE model at a law school.

Our experience showed us that the curriculum was enriched by a variety of different pedagogical techniques and topics. Faculty learned to integrate values concerns with their specific disciplines. For example, a psychology professor developed a module on homelessness for inclusion in his Abnormal Psychology class. Similar modules on the experienced nature of prison sentences in our society would enrich the law school curriculum and add depth to the student experience.

Another topic for generating a theme might be the nature and structure of corporations. Do corporations have a responsibility other than generating profit? Should corporations voluntarily give back a percentage of profits to their local area, as does the Target Corporation? Is that policy a good one or a bad one? What would society look like if the government mandated a set percentage of corporate profit to be set aside for public education in the state where the corporation does business? Also, in the area of wages and compensation, what is the differential in pay between the average American worker and the chief executive officer of a corporation? Has this difference in pay scale changed over time? Is it anyone's business beyond the stockholders of the company? Is it an area that should be governed by law or by the market?

For another, consider laws that govern minimum wage. Where does the U.S. minimum wage stand in relation to other developed nations? Is it higher or lower than the minimum wage in, for example, Ireland? What effect would an increase or decrease in the minimum wage be for a particular local area? Can and should the state set wage levels?

Questions of economic justice can lead to fruitful discussion on a number of topics. Supreme Court justice Thurgood Marshall once remarked, "A child born to a Black mother in a state like Mississippi . . . has exactly the same rights as a white baby born to the wealthiest person in the United States. It's not true, but I challenge anyone to say it is not a goal worth working for" (2007, n.p.). Can we change our society so that this goal can be realized? What can the law do in this case?

Lawyers influence the society we live in, both nationally and internationally, because individuals with legal training both create and enact public policy on a national and an international level. Shouldn't your law school devote at least part of its resources to an education in ethics and values for your students? Again quoting Justice Brandeis: "The greatest dangers to liberty lurk in insidious encroachment by men of zeal, well-meaning but without understanding" (1928, 438). The inclusion of a Values Program at a law school, to work alongside an existing program in legal ethics, can help build students, and lawyers, who have genuine understanding.

The CAVE Model Applied to Business School

At least two challenges face the introduction of a CAVE model in a business school. The first is the attitude of "caveat emptor." This Latin phrase, which translates as "buyer beware," encapsulates the potential adversarial nature of any business transaction: I sell, you buy; once the item is yours, I have no more responsibility. Does this attitude mean that an education in values has no place in a business environment?

The same challenge that faces the administrators of a graduate school of law also faces the administration of a graduate school of business. Its students are already adult and are self-selected as business majors. Can one change the opinions of students who are already of legal age? Can one make them interested in values issues? Are not their characters already formed? It can be argued that students in law school have some implied interest in justice, jurisprudence, fairness, and issues of right and wrong. By contrast, is not business a cut-throat operation? Is not the "bottom line" the most important line on the balance sheet? If in business economic considerations are supreme, can there be any discussion of values at all? We maintain that there can and there must.

The other side of "caveat emptor" is "the customer is always right." People in business learn quickly the hard lesson that if what they provide is not what the consumer wants to buy, they will not be able to sell it. Also, in a mass culture, certain conventions of trust are implied. The airline passenger trusts that the engineers who design and build the planes have done a good job—have not cut corners, have not taken risks, have created an airplane that will not fall apart in the air. Similarly, the automotive industry competes for our trust. Which cars are the safest? Which have the best "crash-test" ratings? In some cases, manufacturing standards are mandated by law and supervised by government agencies in order to meet or exceed standards of health and cleanliness. Our food, meat, and milk are inspected and given a government grade. The Occupational Safety and Health Administration mandates certain standards of workplace safety. In a civilized society, certain safety standards are agreed upon and maintained.

However, in other areas, standards are not so clear. That the Enron Corporation was allowed to grow so large, and to fall so far, speaks to an unclarity about ethics and standards. Similarly, the savings and loan scandals of the 1980s showed that financial officers often did not know how to police themselves. These symptoms of values illiteracy continue to show themselves in American culture. Values and ethics are tools that a young person must learn to use. It is up to educators in professional and graduate schools to make an effort to teach civic responsibility. One legacy of the CAVE model in a Political Science Department was that it reconceptualized its approach and changed its emphasis from an abstract study of politics to emphasizing the preparation of students for a life of active and informed citizenship. The study of business too must move from abstract questions of profit and loss to instruction in what is ethical and permissible in personal and professional conduct.

For business schools in the twenty-first century, the question of values and ethics is critical. Let us imagine a business school that does not teach ethics or business law. Some do not; they see no need for such courses. But let us suppose such a school graduates, out of hundreds of gifted, talented, hardworking, and honest students, one or perhaps two individuals who commit some legal infraction and run afoul of the law. Suddenly, headlines in the *Wall Street Journal* focus on the crime, on the punishment, on the jail term of an unethical businessman or -woman.

Suppose this person is a graduate of your business school. What will happen to your recruitment? What will happen to alumni donations? What if your school begins to develop a reputation for graduating businessmen and -women who are less than ethical, who break the law, who go to prison? Can you still apply for and receive grants or government money needed to support your programs? Will the best and most talented of emerging faculty seek to interview for a position? Could the reputation of your institution that has been painstakingly built up over decades be tarnished or ruined in a matter of weeks or months? It could happen.

Business schools that once struggled with whether to offer mandated courses in business ethics find that, after some resistance, students give these courses relatively high marks when the time comes to evaluate them. The reality of the professional school is that students over the age of twenty-one bring varying degrees of experience to the classroom. For example, I offer a course titled Corporate Responsibility. It is not uncommon that students will discuss either in class or with me personally quite troubling moral dilemmas they have encountered in the workplace or in their personal lives. Their life experience has made them sensitive to the values and spiritual dimensions of issues. They often feel the need to talk through issues with a knowledgeable person. Older students do want to learn how to meet these challenges. They consider themselves fortunate if they meet a professor who feels confident in assisting the student in sorting through the confusing web of options and choices. A professor properly trained and committed to the importance of these issues can make a profound contribution to the life of such students. If such students are lucky enough to study in an institution where this concern permeates the environment of the entire professional school, that graduate will be better prepared in the future to seek advice and counsel in future troubling situations.

Themes for a CAVE Model Based in a Business School

Again, we suggest that you begin with themes that we have already tested and that have proved to work. The theme of economic justice can be fruitful for a business school environment. So too can the issue of peace and war. Who profits when war is declared? How much money can and should a society spend on armaments versus education? What happens to a community that depends solely on defense industries for its livelihood? Is there an economic incentive toward war that outdoes any similar incentive toward peace?

Also, as in a medical school and law school, the business school must consider its specific needs and structures. A summer Values Institute may be expanded to three weeks or streamlined into one week or a series of weekend meetings. Faculty stipends for attendance at an institute of whatever length should be seriously considered. Our program is flexible and can be applied to a graduate setting as well as an undergraduate one. Once a dialogue is begun and the faculty commits to the process of our program, you will find that the template we have created can be stretched to cover the specific needs of your institution.

Diverse Needs Within the Academic Context

Most professional schools offering a high-quality education function within the framework of a much larger entity that we call the university.

For instance, a large institution such as Cornell University, Boston College, or Ohio State University operates under the umbrella called the university. In New York, one university such as Syracuse University has many professional schools, including geography, communications, architecture, music, and citizenship and public affairs. On the same campus there will be schools and colleges for the humanities, the arts, and the natural and social sciences. These schools are all part of a much larger university. Thus, within a university there are diverse needs. Where do you begin to meet the challenges implicit in an educational effort designed to discover ways to assist students in facing the values dimensions of issues? Given these diverse contexts such as size and the age of students, where do you begin? If it is overwhelming to think of engaging the entire community of a university of forty-five thousand students in an institution-wide effort, then you need to decide on certain issues.

Where Do We Begin?

Some schools, colleges, and disciplines might be more disposed initially than others to the possibility of implementing some version of the CAVE model. Some aspects of the larger university will be a better place to begin for a myriad of reasons. Where to begin could be in a cluster of colleges or perhaps in a single school giving degrees in journalism, radio, and television. Some fields are made more sensitive for the need for values education by what is happening to professionals in the field. Maybe three or four professional schools within a single university could join forces.

Decide on ways to begin within each college, school, or department. Renewal and reform begin on the local level. Remember the adage: All education is local. Each department and college has its own challenges; some are more open than others. The model and the process work in each situation—they are like chameleons.

Will a Top-Down Approach Work?

Can a president or a provost order the implementation of a CAVE model? We do not advise it. It will not work from the top down because the grassroots preparation has not been completed. The dynamic behind the design of the CAVE model is that people first need to become conscious and aware that there is a values dimension to issues. They then must come to understand why this dimension is important in their own professional field. Next comes the recognition that the values dimension is connected to their own personal and professional lives and finally that it is critical and necessary for them to act on this realization because it is perhaps even more important than the technical dimensions of issues. Only then will they be willing to think about committing themselves to discovering what to do about this realization for themselves and others. It is for this reason that we call it a journey of discovery or a journey of serious inquiry. No one can order you to come to this realization. You must go through the process yourself.

Can the faculty senate, the dean or president's cabinet, or a curriculum committee mandate that an institution follow the CAVE model? Again, the process will not work unless the grassroots preparation has been done earlier. No matter what the goals and objectives of the institution, no matter what its size, unless the model grows from the grassroots, the institution will reject it.

Of course, it does help to have the president or any of the key administrators make it clear that this process of discovery is a priority in the institution and that the institution will work to assist in acquiring the necessary resources and integrating it into the reward and promotion structure of the institution. But unless the model has the right people involved, with the right idea and a deep commitment and the necessary resources, it will not succeed. Then where do you start? Key questions are how, where, when, and who gets this process started.

One Possible Solution

One possible approach is to initiate the program in individual colleges within the larger university system. This approach worked in the Fontys University of Applied Sciences in the Netherlands. The university consists of thirty-six colleges and schools on five major campuses with a total enrollment of 36,000 students and offers both Bachelors and Masters degrees. A member of the Fontys University Board of Trustees had twice visited the Values Program and seen the CAVE model being put into operation at its U.S. site at Le Moyne College. He was so convinced of the necessity and adaptability of the model that when he returned home, he convinced the Fontys University Board of Trustees that its twenty-six separate professional colleges would profit from the program's process and model. The board agreed and began the process by which the Values Program would become better known in the Fontys system. Members of the Fontys faculties traveled to the United States on a number of occasions and met with Krystine Batcho and myself, members of the Working Group on Values, and the Values Program's Board of Directors and actually participated in two separate Values Institutes. The plan was that the idea behind the CAVE model and process would be promulgated throughout the Fontys system, and each college (engineering, pharmacy, journalism, health, and so on) would work in concert with the others to create an appropriate structure for that college. The board provided funding for initial preliminary planning meetings, and out of those meetings grew a plan that included a university chair to coordinate the planning and implementation in the various colleges. As the development of the CAVE model was applied, a Working Group was eventually assembled, and they began to implement the model's components in their own environment. The university's mission statement and strategy document recently approved for the next five years mandates concern for the values dimension as a principal aim in all the schools. One of the ways this is done is to require all students, in addition to an academic major, to complete a minor program elsewhere. One of the most popular minors is "values education, values philosophy."

An Alternative Model

As with the original CAVE model, an individual can gather together a small founding grassroots group. This individual and these group members will be motivated by a concern for a deeply felt critical need in the values and spiritual dimension. Remember, though, that the CAVE model and its Working Group on Values do not interfere with the existing power structure at any particular school. What they do is break down boundaries and discipline barriers and bring in new sources of energy and knowledge. Together, they create new energy in terms of teaching, research, and commitment to the profession and scholarship, which in turn brings in funding and good students.

In what ways does size make a difference? Because all education is local, the question of size may not necessarily be a major obstacle. The question is what it means to engage this community in an institution-wide educational effort. The process of thinking through the institutes for faculty and others will be basically similar: the critical need will remain; the goals and aims of the institute do not change in significant ways.

Conclusion

In this chapter I have focused on why other institutions should consider the CAVE model and the applicability of the CAVE model to three professional schools and colleges, particularly to medical, law, and business schools. Since these schools are usually part of a much larger university system, I have also included some brief remarks pertinent to the university situation. I could have chosen from among many different types of professional schools. I would like to draw some conclusions.

First, the critical need we discovered among our graduates is not confined to a few institutions and places. It exists throughout higher education and professional schools. No institution can escape this fact. Our experience shows us that unless a professional school, or any institution of higher education for that matter, has a persistent and powerful voice that forces the institution to pay attention to the values dimension of issues, it will not happen. It will quickly fall to the margins of the institution's priorities. In this age of cultural drift, something like the Values Program and the CAVE model can bring about a cultural shift. An effective model and process are like the rudder on a ship: without it, the ship quickly loses its ability to maintain direction. It must also be a long-term effort. It cannot be a one-shot deal.

Second, remember the need for initial assessment. A basic assumption of the CAVE model is that all action is based on needs and approaches that can be empirically verified. So a first step before any institution, professional school, or any type of institution begins to implement the model is to do an initial assessment to determine particular needs in relationship to the values dimension among students, faculty, and others. Once these needs are assessed and analyzed, they become a baseline measurement for determining how and why the various ways and approaches that have been discovered and implemented during the process impact the students, faculty, and staff. This first assessment is essential; without it, there is no CAVE model.

Third, the program is universally applicable. If the primary source for this book is the lived experience, reflection, and praxis of hundreds of participants and colleagues not just from my own institution but also from many others, then this model surely touches a sympathetic chord with a diverse group of people from widely varied backgrounds. But the fact that much of this experience occurred in one distinct institution may still cause some to ask how applicable this project is to other institutions. Is it possible that a project based on the East Coast of the United States, in a small to medium-size institution founded in the Catholic and Jesuit traditions, with a student body primarily Catholic and Christian in origin, could have designed a model and process with wide adaptability? My response is to look at the reactions of those individuals who came, saw, looked, tested, and evaluated. In this book I have discussed how representatives from a wide variety of educational and professional institutions discovered that the basic dynamic of the model was sturdy, versatile, and adaptable to nearly every type of educational environment. There is good evidence of the adaptability of this model. An outside reviewer raised concerns when Krystine Batcho and her colleagues applied successfully for a National Science Foundation grant to study our model as it related to the humanities, natural and social sciences, and business disciplines. They were able to convince the NSF of the universal applicability of their proposed study. The Consortium for the Advancement of Private Higher Education was also convinced that this model and process had a wide adaptability. We have made presentations and worked in institutions of higher education and professional schools in such diverse societies as Japan, the Netherlands, Mexico, and Taiwan. In each situation we were able to help people to understand the broad scope of the model and its near universal applicability.

Fourth, we have also found that the model is applicable in institutions with different religious affiliations. We have discovered that the CAVE approach is an effective model for discovering and implementing ways to assist students in meeting the challenges of the spiritual dimensions of issues in their personal and professional lives. We have received a grant from the Lilly Endowment to study the connection between values education and spirituality. This field is a rich area of research for the future.

Finally, based on our lived experience, we recognize that there are one hundred ways to do values education. This finding highlights an important supposition behind the CAVE model: there is more than one way to do values education and values development. If one hundred faculty and staff have been through the experience and understand the importance and the priority of the values dimension to education, then there are now at least one hundred professors in an institution who have committed to becoming part of the process of discovering how best to enact values education and development. Our process does not indoctrinate, nor is it relativistic. Instead, it is a process of serious inquiry. Each faculty member needs to discover how best to provide values education given the strengths and weaknesses of himself, his discipline, and his students. This principle is another aspect of the grassroots and freedom element of the Values Program. It also means that as more and more professors, administrators, and staff understand and commit themselves to the discovery process, they will touch more and more students. Our goal is that all students experience the impact of the institute, not just a small, elite core group.

In some ways the discovery, development, and growth of the Values Program seems to follow many of the same lines of the pedagogy of canal making along the Erie Canal. This book is not about a theory of value and spirituality. It is instead an experiential pedagogy that is practiced. It moved along day by day, inspired by the creativity and tireless efforts of hundreds of people all along the way. They did not do it for their own reward. They did it because they had been caught and fired by a vision and a dream, and they became committed to making that vision and dream a reality. Today, that dream and its experiential pedagogy remain ALIVE. This book is about a model created, implemented, and studied by busy people with limited resources, time, and money. They were able to do it, we were able to do it, so why can't you?

Conclusion
Miles to Go

On the bulletin board in the Values Program office we posted a sign reading:

> Whoever comes is the right people
> Whatever happens is the only thing that could have
> Whenever it starts is the right time
> When it's over, it's over.

The Values Program ran at Le Moyne College from 1988 to 2003: a total of fifteen astonishing years of experiment, growth, change, and development. This pioneering journey of discovery and serious inquiry regularly presented new challenges, and very often we had little or no historical precedents to consult. The sign on our bulletin board was a gift from a colleague. That sense of humor was appreciated because this journey frequently involved careful attention to a quite fragile environment.

Our most memorable success during those fifteen years was that we succeeded in meeting our goals and objectives; our mission was accomplished. We sustained momentum, energy, and focus in the community and engaged the collegewide community in an educational effort for fifteen years through three presidents; countless deans, academic vice presidents, and vice presidents; and other changes in staff from the lowest to the highest level at the college. The CAVE model was not a one-shot deal. It had staying power. In 2003, however, following a change in upper administration at the college, the program as such ceased its activities

206

at Le Moyne. A softening economy had a negative effect on the college budget. Times had changed, and the new administration believed that funds that had gone to the Values Program and to CAVE should be allocated elsewhere. It was time now to return home and to reflect on our experiences.

However, the ripple effect of our vital and successful program continues to expand both within and beyond the boundaries of the institution. The Le Moyne College community was the main laboratory where the CAVE model was instituted and tried. Now it is the place from which the model, the program, and its ideas are disseminated to the wider world. This book and the future companion book by Krystine Batcho are part of that dissemination.

Across Traditional Boundaries

David Schoem pointed out in *Change* magazine that programs that attempt to attend to values issues on a college campus are "usually marginalized with little concern for the core academic mission. Those initiatives are often relegated to 'minor' status or defined as 'tracks'" (2002, 4). In our experience the educational effort that we called the Values Program at Le Moyne College was very different. It managed to be situated at the very center of the institution's academic enterprise. One academic vice president called it "the signature program of the College: it tells people who we are and what we stand for." Another academic vice president was featured in a local newspaper interview explaining the program's appropriateness for Jesuit and Catholic higher education. We succeeded, in Vaclav Havel's words, in creating a space where, in trust, people can gather together (in Vladislav 1987). Our program reached across traditional boundaries to engage faculty, students, staff, and administration in a collegewide experiment in learning and developing. The Middle States Accreditation Report called it a "model of teaching and learning."

The Values Program process offers an umbrella-like structure under which all or most elements within the institution can find a welcoming place. From the very beginning, with the Working Group, we engineered a process where a sense of respect and trust permeated the environment. People's insights were welcomed. No one had a controlling proprietorship in the program. Connected with this environment was the atmosphere of collegiality that was created, an atmosphere where the boundaries of disciplines, departments, and institutional constituencies could be bridged. Very gradually, we created a situation where the faculty compared syllabi, crossed disciplines, and talked about pedagogy.

The dynamic umbrella structure did not dictate a particular agenda or thing to do. Instead, it allowed for creativity and inspiration, as all involved sought to discover and implement ways to enhance values education and values development. This goal was always sought within the larger framework of recognition of the interdependence and connection between so many aspects within the institution. For example, from this process some of the institution's memberships were able to begin to map out the issues inherent in the theme "The Spiritual Dimensions of Higher Education: Attending to the Sacred in Our Midst." This theme is a good example of the ability of the CAVE model to evolve to meet critical needs as they arise. Its umbrella-like structure creates a space that allows members of the community to initiate whatever is needed to provide an environment capable of enhancing what we thought to be important.

Every individual and each community needs a "big vision" to sustain it through the toughest and most diverse of challenges. It needs to be sensitive to and respond to the grassroots and deeply felt needs of students, faculty, and staff. Any program needs to ask itself, Is the vision that sustains this effort one of the "big visions"? Is the program able to adapt to a wide variety of changing needs and circumstances? The vision that grounds the CAVE model demonstrated that it is big enough to engage the entire institution and the communities beyond; it can provide the wherewithal for a flexible, welcoming, and open environment.

Can it adapt quickly to an event such as the terrorist attacks of September 11, 2001? If there is a rape on campus, a significant current event like the deployment of troops, dropping employment figures, or a racial incident that inflames a divided campus, can the program in place include a wide spectrum of perspectives, emotions, opinions? Students and faculty are constantly changing, and their needs and understanding fluctuate. Our experience with the Values Program showed that we did indeed have a program that could adapt to changes of this nature.

A Catalyst, Not Reinventing the Wheel

One key guiding principle was always active: the CAVE model and its programmatic aspects are to act as a catalyst. Its goal is not to take over what is already up and running in the institution but instead, by infusing the values dimension, to bring it to a new and more connected life with other aspects within the larger learning community. Sometimes CAVE spearheaded the events, as in the GTE lecture series "Ethical Issues at the Beginning and End of Life." At other times student affairs would take the lead, as in the student leadership initiative. We were an inclusive, grassroots group and process, organized from the bottom up, not from the top down.

One of our biggest breakthroughs was our discovery of a way to connect and bridge the gap between the communities of student affairs and academic affairs. In the early years, as this model took shape, we felt powerless and marginal in relationship to the administrators and staff who dealt with our students once they had left the classrooms. A student living on campus spent fifteen hours a week in classes with the faculty. Student affairs personnel had very little communication with the professors and academic personnel. It took us nearly five years to win the confidence of certain key student affairs administrators. I am sure this situation is not unique to only one or two institutions. Once we invited a key associate vice president of student affairs to the Values Institute, she was a major catalyst in helping us to break down that barrier. As our program evolved and as we developed more interaction in both the institutes and the Academic Forum, we discovered with joy that we could build this bridge.

The model has shown its adaptability across time, student cohorts, current events, changing institutional needs, and resources. From its programmatic efforts could come cooperation with the learning community, service learning, retreats for students, out-of-class activities, orientation creativity, student personnel changes, changes in teaching pedagogy and course syllabi, and connections within departments, areas, and college constituencies.

It is very important to note that this process was able to attract and engage not just the already converted. Its real strength was its ability to appeal to and motivate those individuals who were often not committed to the wider vision and mission of the institution. Our vision attracted a wide spectrum of individuals.

To achieve such flexibility and inclusiveness is not always easily accomplished in an academic atmosphere. One faculty member remarked that he liked to work with the values programmatic efforts such as the Values Institute, the Academic Forum events, or the Working Group. For him, it was an "oasis" where he came for refreshment, light, encouragement, and energy.

The group's ability to cross borders in the college made its participants feel empowered and part of a meaningful community. I often heard people remark that participating in a values steering group or Working Group helped them to transcend the sometimes-confining role of "yet another committee." We found that people's involvement persisted, and they usually returned because meetings always centered on matters of substance, because they addressed a deeply felt need, because they were interesting, substantive, and attracted a wide diversity of individuals. Father Robert Mitchell, S.J., president of Le Moyne, reflected this sense of hospitality when he introduced me to speak before the college's Board of Trustees with the comment, "In all my years as a college administrator and president, I have never seen anything that had the almost universal support of the faculty as does this program."

Renewable-Energy Resource

This dynamic, alive, and ever evolving structure also provided continuing support for participants. Designed into the very essence of the CAVE model is the idea that it would be a renewable-energy resource for itself. The model in its operation works to renew, or be a catalyst for, the provision of necessary resources. This characteristic is very important, as was shown in Chapter 6 on acquiring resources, especially given the scarce resources available today. From the very beginning, the Values Program made it central to its grassroots identity that it would make a commitment to do more than raise the awareness and consciousness of people to the values dimension. The emphasis was always: What will work? What is necessary to make it work? Resources are always among the responses.

There are critical areas related to resources. Among them are faculty and staff development, the writing of grants, and engaging the wider institution in support of the values mission. We knew this process would never work unless we had adequate resources for faculty development. What practical and theoretical resources would be needed to convince the faculty that this dimension was important and necessary for their professional lives and give them the confidence that this undertaking was legitimate?

Early on we discovered a perceived barrier that exists in nearly every institution of higher education and in the wider society: that "values education" is somehow not "appropriate" or "legitimate" within a university or collegiate setting, that it is not the responsibility of a professor to engage in values education, that it is somehow unprofessional to do so.

The Values Institutes gave to the faculty and staff content, legitimacy, and technique. I have described this process in Chapters 3 and 4 on the CAVE model and the Values Institute, respectively. But they were also very practical. The institutes worked with the faculty and staff to develop ways to make concrete changes in their pedagogy, departmental structures, and priorities. Most important, the collegiality that developed among participants during the institutes provided a community of support during and afterward. Built into the system was ongoing faculty, staff, and administration development.

The CAVE model in action worked at the institutional level to create concrete resources within the societal structures to make real that attention to the values dimension of issues was becoming a priority in the institution. It worked to raise awareness and consciousness at every level; more concretely, it was a catalyst to changing the reward environment for tenure and promotion. Gradually, it became not only acceptable but even noteworthy that one's application for promotion included significant commitment to the values education effort.

Many participants in the Values Institutes and Academic Forums learned to be successful grant writers. Each theme provided a whole new opportunity for creative grant writing. In fact, one of the criteria we used in selecting a theme was its ability to attract funding from a variety of sources. Our success probably was the main catalyst for the institution's decision to hire its first full-time institutional grant writer. The Values Program created, funded, and implemented the only faculty-development programs in the institution over a fifteen-year period. A large part of this element of the program came from resources outside the institution. A collegial spirit began to grow, as coaches, secretaries, residence hall directors and staff, vice presidents, and academic and student deans worked together with the faculty to create the necessary resources for values education. Our goal was eventually to get the commitment of all these people to become part of the discovery process and to train their students in values and spiritual development. Gradually, the "search for meaning and value" became central to the mission statement of the college.

We need to remember as educators that regardless of whether we are aware of it, we are always teaching values. All schools are already involved in values education. We easily accept that certain values are taught in elementary schools. In kindergarten, children learn to share, to play fair, that attendance is important, that certain behaviors are acceptable and certain behaviors are not. Teachers are prompt to encourage courtesy, to discourage bullying, to instruct in classroom etiquette. Sometimes the values that students learn are not as obvious as those lessons of being quiet and attentive when a teacher speaks and learning not to run in the hallway. Students who attend underfunded elementary and secondary schools in urban areas where they must bring their own toilet paper from home, as happened in New York City elementary schools in the fall of 2004, learn a lesson about what is valued in their community. To describe a different type of case, middle-school students who are urged to bring extra notebooks and pencils to school so they can be sent to schoolchildren in Afghanistan learn a different lesson, one of caring and sharing on a global level. Institutions of higher education must see that they too are formers of the young, and they need to be aware and consciously take on this responsibility.

Lifelong Learning

Every educator meets the student attitude: "This is it. In college I will learn all I need. Then I will be done with school." Educators work hard to get students to see that acquiring knowledge and insight is a lifelong process, one that never ends. We must accept that realization. The Values Program succeeded because it subscribed to that long-term vision. It assists the graduate in acquiring a lifelong habit of serious inquiry to meet these issues. No student ever graduates with a degree in "moral and spiritual growth." The goal is the education of the whole person: to assist the person in seeing the importance and necessity of the values dimension of issues. Life is our school, and our lives after we conclude our formal education will include many challenges, moral and otherwise.

Out in the business world of real life, whether an adult finds himself on Wall Street or teaching kindergarten, he or she will still have many lessons to learn and much growth to undertake. And out in the real world, there is not the comforting atmosphere of classrooms, teachers, notes to take, and textbooks to consult.

In our Values Program at Le Moyne we structured our program with this result in mind. We wanted our young people to learn skills in identifying values issues and to acquire the tools to make their own decisions. In our Summer Institutes, our Academic Forums, in all the many and varied activities of our programs, we created a laboratory where teachers discovered a new dimension to their calling, where students could take the lead, where faculty, staff, and the community could be part of programs of inquiry and take part in campuswide discussions. The process we began among our students and colleagues at Le Moyne is a never-ending process. It is also not something we do on our own. It is a communal process.

The CAVE Model . . . Evolving

In order to appreciate a distinguishing aspect of the CAVE model it is important to be very clear about why the word *evolving* is always used to describe the CAVE model. It has not been chosen randomly. Through this word I hope to pinpoint a characteristic at the very core of the CAVE model.

The reality of "evolving" was present at the very beginning when the CAVE model began to take shape and form. It came into being as a result of our shared collective experience as educators. As we began our journey, the participants in the original values group brought with us our specialized backgrounds, perspectives, and approaches from our particular disciplines. All faculty sitting around the table had Ph.D.'s or terminal degrees.

But as it became more apparent to us that we in education were being confronted with a values-related critical need in our graduates, this discovery brought us to a humbling realization: our Ph.D. backgrounds had not prepared us to assist students in their critical need. Our experience of graduate school did not give us the credentials, the know-how, the legitimacy, or the confidence to assist students to a greater sensitivity of the values dimension of issues. Nor did it prepare us to teach them to be more moral.

We all know that being awarded a Ph.D. does not mean that you necessarily have good moral aspects to your psyche or that you know how to deal with the moral and spiritual aspects of an issue. Learning sensitivity, spontaneity, and setting priorities in these realms touches the need to be skilled in the education of the whole person, education involving the mind and the heart.

This profound awareness of our own deficiencies in this area motivated us to make two fundamental choices that would put a stamp on the very essence of the CAVE model. First, we came to a basic assumption: it would be necessary to get input from the students. We would have to create a means of discovering the real needs of our students and our faculty. An underlying assumption of our model is that action should always be based on needs and approaches that can be validated empirically. So for us, assessment was not just conducted after the fact, where we asked and determined if and where we had been successful or unsuccessful. Instead, assessment results would be regularly studied, evaluated, and fed back. This feedback manifested itself in the fine-tuning of the programmatic aspects of the Values Program in order to improve results.

Second, this profound awareness of our own deficiencies in this area motivated us to create and implement the instrument of the Values Institute, one of the legs on the three-legged stool we call the CAVE model. The faculty and staff would need to go back to school. We would need to find a way to "train the trainers"; we would need to discover and implement ways to foster faculty and staff development. One of our goals would be "to encourage faculty and staff to explore the relationship between teaching methods and the development of moral sensitivity in students." It would involve developing and acquiring the necessary attitudes and skills for themselves and then learning how to help students develop those attitudes and skills.

This humbling experience taught us that we did not always know best. This insight is the basis of the grassroots origin of the entire process. It taps into the needs and energies of the many aspects of the institution. We could no longer assume that the faculty, the Jesuits, or any one part of the institution knew best or that professionals are necessarily equipped by their backgrounds to be the best values educators. The models of education that work best are those of cooperation.

For years I described the Values Program as a three-legged stool, its three main components consisting of the Summer Institute, Academic Forum, and the Working Group on Values, joined together by a theme, each functioning to support a stool that was sturdy, strong, and adaptable. I have vivid childhood memories of visiting my grandfather, a dairy farmer, and watching him move from cow to cow as he did his daily milking. His milking stool was a simple yet versatile tool. I can still picture how he could carry it in one hand, effortlessly. As he made multiple other adjustments, he would put the stool down next to the cow he was about to milk, and with one or two movements he would find a level, well-balanced surface where the stool gave him support, strength, and flexibility. The stool worked because it had three sturdy, strong legs welded to a seat, all so simply yet integrally part of its dynamic structure.

So too with the Values Program. It is a sturdy, versatile, and adaptable tool for any educator, educational institution, or business group. Our CAVE model worked and can be replicated in any college, university, secondary school, graduate program, or business environment. From our practical lived experience and reflection on this effort, we are now able, through this book and that of Krystine Batcho's, to put innovative and practical material on the table. We provide this documentation so that the academic community and others may look, research, test, and evaluate. Our challenge as educators is that we must discover and implement ways to integrate an understanding of values and the ethical dimensions of decision making into an increasing technologically based learned experience. The Values Program is one tested answer to this challenge.

Because colleges and universities focus almost exclusively on educating for the marketplace, college graduates, though ready to tackle technical tasks, are unprepared to meet the moral and spiritual challenges of their personal and professional lives. It is imperative that we as educators understand our larger responsibility to the community, to create an environment for our young people where, while they learn the tools that will sustain them over their professional lives, they also understand the values dimensions of their decisions. It is not enough to teach someone to think and to write accurately. They must also learn to ask how they will use these talents. For example, if I seek a job writing advertising copy for the tobacco industry, is that occupation a good use of my talent? Is it a good use of my talent to persuade someone to take up a dangerous, addictive habit? Or, in another scenario, if I am offered a job to write documentation for weapons systems, will I take that job? If I do so, what are my thoughts and feelings about it? Do I take this job only because the salary is attractive? Do I undertake this work because I feel that what I do has the moral value of keeping my country strong in an unstable world? Or will I turn down this job because I do not want to contribute even in a small way to the buildup of arms?

Does my consciousness give me the imagination and the courage to go beyond, "What income do I need to live my life as comfortably as possible? Did my college education provide me with the tools I needed in order to earn that living?" If, for example, I have a talent for dentistry, do I become a dentist who specializes only in lucrative cosmetic work? If I am asked to work without pay one week a year at a clinic for the indigent, do I turn this opportunity down because I do not recognize that there are poor people in my community? Do I turn it down because I believe that the indigent deserve their pain? Do I turn it down because the bill for my country club membership is due? Or do I accept because I feel guilty for my privilege and my high salary? Do I accept because it will be something to brag about at the next gala dinner I attend with my husband? Do I accept because I want to share my gift with those people who are less fortunate? Do I accept because I want to do something to ease the suffering that exists all around me? More important, has my education enabled me even to think the thoughts described above and to recognize these thoughts?

Our goal with the Values Program was and is not to create saints, but to give our graduates tools so that they could think through problems and options. Our point was not to indoctrinate students, but to bring them to recognize that they can trust themselves to learn, to grow, and to make informed decisions. The only approach that is honest is a serious process of inquiry, not one controlled by the institution or any particular ideology. Our goal, which we achieved, is that students become spontaneously alert to the value, spiritual, and moral dimensions of issues and that they acknowledge the importance and necessity of these dimensions. We also seek to assist them in acquiring the skills, the commitment, and the courage to make ethical decisions.

We feel strongly that our students benefited immeasurably from the program we created. To take one small example, the student-led weeklong activities of South Africa–Le Moyne had the potential to make an enormous difference. A student in Syracuse who hears firsthand from a young South African woman about her brother's torture will not read international news in the newspaper again in the same way as someone who has not had this experience. A student who is aware that his professor adopted a child from South Africa will have a different understanding of international problems and of the possibility of making a difference than a student who is not aware of this choice.

Objections to the Model and Difficult Questions

No process develops without setbacks. In our experience we sometimes encountered fundamental questions about the adaptability and the appropriateness of what we were attempting to accomplish.

Presentations at professional conferences and diverse institutions of higher and professional education often forced us to dig more deeply in refreshingly innovative ways. An example is the instance when Krystine Batcho and her colleagues applied to the National Science Foundation. Their proposal involved the study of values education and development as they occurred in their home institution within a variety of distinct disciplines such as the sciences, business, and the humanities. On review, one of the outside evaluators questioned the project's applicability to other institutions. Was it a good expenditure of resources to fund a project based on the East Coast of the United States, in a small to medium-size institution founded in the Catholic and Jesuit traditions, with a student body primarily Catholic and Christian in origin? The grant was awarded after the NSF became convinced of the proposal's broad universal usefulness. Sometimes we heard similar objections as we presented and worked in diverse societies such as Japan, the Netherlands, and Mexico. Each time we were able to help people understand the broad scope of the model and its near universal applicability.

One side of the coin asks questions such as, "Are this program and its model applicable also to public, private, nonsectarian, non-Catholic institutions? Does it have the potential for universal applicability?" On the other side of the coin the question reflects concerns such as, "Are you teaching values, and if so what values do you teach? Can a college with your religious tradition go outside the Catholic doctrine? If so, how can a Catholic college teach values that may go outside Catholic doctrine?" Our first book, *Ambitious Dreams* (Kirby et al. 1990), and this book try to make it very clear that the Values Program's intention is not to "teach values" in the sense of inculcating a particular set of moral values. In response to such a concern, John Carlson, the academic vice president of the college, explained how he understood the purpose of the program. Its goal, he wrote in the local newspaper, is "to enliven in students an awareness of values questions, the ability to deal critically with such questions, and the courage to act upon judgments made" (1991, 13). A key word that he used is *enliven*. The students themselves sensed a similar reality.

An Instrument of Discernment

This book provides individuals and institutions with an understanding of the rationale and operation for the CAVE model. It also presents guidelines, models, and examples for how it might be adapted in other situations. My focus has been more on the practical, the discovery and implementation of ways to assist students with the challenges presented to them by the values dimensions of issues. Our hope is that by working through these ways, students will come to understand the importance, necessity, and priority of values education and the spiritual dimension in their personal and professional lives.

We can be inclined to talk about these issues theoretically, but our program is also practical:

• We identified and articulated a profoundly felt need that is critical to both educational institutions and the wider society. That need is even greater today.

• We created innovative strategies to meet those needs. These strategies are adaptable to different types of schools and colleges.

• Our journey has been distinguished by a number of characteristics that offer valuable insight to others starting out on similar ventures.

• We have both the qualitative and the quantitative data to show that we have been effective in an entire university or collegiate setting.

• Our process has a track record. It is a tried-and-true process that is applicable to other institutions.

Milestones on the Road Ahead

We have always set our sights beyond the Le Moyne campus. Our ultimate goal has always been the education of responsible citizens for the society beyond campus. Our students come to us from that wider world, and they leave us to rejoin that world. Through consulting and through dissemination of our ideas we hope to act as a catalyst to transform other institutions similarly committed to the values education of socially responsible citizens.

Parker Palmer pointed out that the aim of our program was "nothing less than to renew our capacity for community. . . . The grounding of the program is nothing else than—dare I use the word?—truth. . . . The program tries to bring students into truth by teaching them how to participate in humankind's endless, demanding, and exhilarating conversation over what commands our commitment and care" (1990, vi).

Spirituality

The model has demonstrated its continuing ability to evolve to meet changing needs and approaches. After considerable experience and reflection we have discovered that this model is applicable not just for those individuals searching for an adequate response to the challenge of values education but also for discovering and implementing ways to assist students in meeting the challenges of the spiritual dimensions of issues in their personal and professional lives. For example, we began our journey with an emphasis on values education and development in 1986, but by 1990 there were already serious questions being raised about the connection between values education and spirituality. This concern and need resulted in a successful grant by the Lilly Endowment to study that relationship. By 1996 these initial concerns for values education and spirituality had developed into a full two-pronged attack on these challenges. In this ever evolving situation, it is important that we were able to recognize and identify the symptoms, to articulate clearly what was the challenge, to discover and implement a model and a process with the power and the promise to meet the challenge, to develop effective strategies to meet this charge, and to set out the basic suppositions and foundational underpinnings of the basic structure of the program.

Much more work can also be done in the area of connecting the academic and student affairs elements within an institution. A diverse group of professional and academic groups has invited us to explain our model both at their meetings and in their publications. These groups include the American Association for Higher Education, Association of Catholic Colleges and Universities, Association of Practical and Professional Ethics, Society for Values in Higher Education, and Association of Jesuit Colleges and Universities. The fact that the Values Program and its CAVE approach have been featured in various presentations associated with the American College Personnel Association speaks to its adaptability in both the academic and the student affairs areas.

The language and cultural barriers have also not been an issue, as confirmed by our work with such diverse groups as the Universitatis Iberoamericana in Mexico City and Fontys University in the Netherlands.

Wil Derkse, then director of the Radboud Foundation in the Netherlands, wrote to a major worldwide foundation in 1998:

> The Values program meets a critical need in education anywhere; unlike other promising and successful programs I learned about during my visits to Catholic Institutes of Higher Education in 1997 and 1998. The Values Program would be quite easily adaptable to the Western

European context. It would also be very important here in the low
countries; because of the rapid process of secularization and the fading
ideological contexts into one general new-liberal atmosphere of prag-
matic consumerism, more and more signals flare up that people des-
perately are sometimes searching for real values. (n.p.)

The Netherlands has currently developed its spin-off version of the
Values Program. The program has been adapted by the Fontys University
of Applied Sciences in its thirty-six college and schools that offer bachelors and masters degrees. Over 36,000 students are enrolled in the university whose mission statement makes the values dimension of issues a
principal aim of the educational enterprise. Many students elect to take
the newly created values education, philosophy, and ethics program as
their required minor. This program must be taken within a school or program other than where the major is being completed. Another spin-off is
also underway at the University of Tilburg in the Netherlands: According
to their literature the intention is as follows:

> This programme for UvT lecturers addresses the relevance of ethical and
> religious issues to the academic education of students. The object of the
> programme is to strengthen the participants' awareness of the presence
> of religious and ethical questions in the apparent neutrality of a scientific
> programme, to make participants (more) aware of their own motives and
> the basic orientation underlying their actions, to recognize occasions suit-
> able for addressing these questions fruitfully in the teaching process, and
> to reflect on the lecturer's personal position in this. (van Veghel 2004)

The goal is to organize the program for twenty lecturers, to make it an
annual event, "making it possible for us to eventually reach a substantial
number of the total lecturing staff."

With the Values Program we have shown that a group of individuals,
working together, can transform the culture and the experience of a college. We used our individual talents and gifts to create a program that had
a ripple effect far beyond the first Working Group on Values.

The stone we dropped into the pond of the particular institution
created ripples that transformed the educational community where the

Values Program grew and flourished. Now it has the potential for these ripples to travel farther still: to touch the shores of colleges and universities in the Netherlands and elsewhere in western Europe, and anywhere the readers of this book wish to take this vital and durable program.

We have cast our stone into the waters of one college and seen the mingling of the upper and lower strata of the college so that the institution was transformed. With this book we are offering you an opportunity to discover a compass, to chart a new course. We offer you a tested, replicable model for making a positive difference in a world hungry for direction. Won't you take the tools and techniques we describe in this book and use them to make a difference in your college, your university, your business, your world?

References

Index

References

American Association for Higher Education. 1993. *Series on Service Learning in the Disciplines: Service Learning Toolkit.* Issued by Campus Compact.

Bellah, Robert N., et al. 1996. *Habits of the Heart: Individualism and Commitment in American Life.* 1985. Reprint, Berkeley and Los Angeles: Univ. of California Press.

Brandeis, Louis D. 1928. *Olmstead v. U.S.* 277 U.S. 438.

————. 1993. *Oxford Dictionary of American Legal Quotations.* Edited by Fred R. Shapiro. New York: Oxford Univ. Press.

Burger, Warren. 1980. "The Role of Law School in the Teaching of Legal Ethics and Professional Responsibility." *Cleveland State Law Review* 29: 377.

Callahan, Daniel, M.D. 1995. *Setting Limits: Medical Goals in an Aging Society (with an Answer to My Critics).* Georgetown: Georgetown Univ. Press.

Carlson, John W. 1991. "Dean Explains Program." *Syracuse Herald American, Stars Magazine,* Jan. 6.

Colby, Anne, Thomas Ehrlich, Elizabeth Beaumont, and Jason Stephens. 2003. *Educating Citizens: Preparing America's Undergraduates for Lives of Moral and Civic Responsibility.* J. B. Carnegie Foundation for the Advancement of Teaching. San Francisco: Jossey-Bass.

Collins, Bruce D. 1999. "Consider Adding Values, of the Moral Type, in Law School." *Corporate Legal Times* (May).

Curley, Thomas. 1990. "The 1988 Summer Institute." In *Ambitious Dreams: The Values Program at Le Moyne College,* by Donald J. Kirby et al., 19–40. Kansas City, Mo.: Sheed and Ward.

Derkse, Wil. 1998. Letter of recommendation.

de Vries, Paul H. 1990. "The Essential 'Inc-Factor.'" In *Ambitious Dreams: The Values Program at Le Moyne College,* by Donald J. Kirby et al., 185–94. Kansas City, Mo.: Sheed and Ward.

Dolbeare, Kenneth. 1986. *Democracy at Risk: The Politics of Economic Renewal and American Public Policy, a Citizen's Guide.* London: Chatham House Publishing.

Douglas, Mary. 1986. *How Institutions Think.* Syracuse: Syracuse Univ. Press.

Eyler, Janet, and Dwight Giles Jr. 1999. *Where's the Learning in Service Learning?* San Franciso: Jossey-Bass.

Flower, Rob. 1991. *Program for Town Meeting: "Songs of the Hearth: Sacred and Profane."* Syracuse: Le Moyne College.

Fontys University Program Description. Brochure published by the Fontys University of Applied Sciences.

Friere, Paulo. 2000. *The Pedagogy of the Oppressed.* New York: Continuum International Publishing Group.

Green, Thomas F. 1999. *Voices: The Educational Formation of Conscience.* South Bend: Univ. of Notre Dame Press.

Groome, Thomas. 2001. *Educating for Life: A Spiritual Vision for Every Teacher and Parent.* New York: Crossroads.

Hanley, K. R. 1996. Letter to Values Program, Dec. 1.

Hilfinger, M. F., IV, and H. T. Mullins. 1997. "Geology, limnology, and palaeoclimatology of Green Lakes State Park," in *Field Trip Guide for the 69th Annual Meeting of the New York State Geological Association,* Hamilton College, Clinton, N.Y., 127–58.

Hough, M. Catherine, Ph.D. 2006. Personal correspondence, Oct. 14.

Kephart, William, and William Zellner. 2000. *Extraordinary Groups.* 7th ed. New York: Worth Publishing.

King, Martin Luther, Jr. 1964. *Why We Can't Wait.* New York: New American Library.

Kirby, Donald J. 1998. "The Values Program at Le Moyne College." *About Campus* 2, no. 6: 15–21.

Kirby, Donald J., et al. 1990. *Ambitious Dreams: The Values Program at Le Moyne College.* Kansas City, Mo.: Sheed and Ward.

Kirschenbaum, Howard. 1977. *Advanced Values Clarification.* La Jolla, Calif.: University Associates.

———. 2000. "Values Clarification to Character Education: A Personal Journey." *Journal of Humanistic Counseling, Education, and Development* 39, no. 1: 4–20.

Laurence, Peter. 1999. "Can Religion and Spirituality Find a Place in Higher Education?" *About Campus* 4, no. 4 (Nov.–Dec.): 15. Available online at http://www.wellesley.edu/RelLife/transformation/canreligionandspirit.doc.

Le Moyne College. 1986. *Report of the Humanities Core Committee to the Curriculum Committee of the Faculty Senate,* "Introduction and Rationale," 1–3.

Lewis, Harry R. 2006. *Excellence Without a Soul: How a Great University Forgot Education.* New York: Public Affairs.

Marshall, Thurgood. 2007. http://afroamhistory.about.com/od/thurgoodmarshall/a/tmarshallquotes.htm.

McCallum, David, Jr., and Alison E. Molea. 1990. "Two Student Perspectives." In *Ambitious Dreams: The Values Program at Le Moyne College,* by Donald J. Kirby et al., 120–38. Kansas City, Mo.: Sheed and Ward.

Middle States Association. 1996. *Report to the Faculty, Administration, Trustees, and Students of Le Moyne College, Syracuse, N.Y., by an Evauation Team Representing the Commission on Higher Education,* April 14–17.

Miller, William. 1990. "A Mathematician's Perspective." In *Ambitious Dreams: The Values Program at Le Moyne College,* by Donald J. Kirby et al., 97–119. Kansas City, Mo.: Sheed and Ward.

Morrill, Richard. 1980. *Teaching Values in College.* Jossey-Bass Series in Higher Education. San Francisco: Jossey-Bass.

Palmer, Parker J. 1990. Foreword to *Ambitious Dreams: The Values Program at Le Moyne College,* by Donald J. Kirby et al., v–vii. Kansas City, Mo.: Sheed and Ward.

———. 1998. *The Courage to Teach: Exploring the Inner Landscape of a Teacher's Life.* San Francisco: Jossey-Bass.

———. 1998–1999. "Evoking the Spirit." *Educational Leadership* (Dec.–Jan.): 6.

Putnam, Robert D. 2001. *Bowling Alone: The Collapse and Revival of American Community.* New York: Simon and Schuster.

Raths, Louis E., Merrill Harmin, and Sidney B. Simon. 1966. *Values and Teaching: Working with Values in the Classroom.* Columbus, Ohio: Charles E. Merrill Publishing.

Schmidt, Patricia Ruggiano. 1997. Letter to Values Program, Apr. 14.

Schmidt, Patricia Ruggiano, and Ann Watts Pailliotet, eds. 2001. *Exploring Values Through Literature, Multimedia, and Literary Events: Making Connections.* New York: International Reading Association.

Schoem, David. 2002. "Transforming Undergraduate Education: Moving Beyond Distinct Undergraduate Initiatives." *Change* (Nov.–Dec.).

Scribner, Belding H. 2002. "Medical Dilemmas: The Old Is New." *Nature Medicine* 8, no. 10 (Oct.).

Shefrin, Bruce. 1990. "The Academic Forum." In *Ambitious Dreams: The Values Program at Le Moyne College,* by Donald J. Kirby et al., 61–77. Kansas City, Mo.: Sheed and Ward.

Smith, Barbara, Jean MacGregor, Roberta Matthews, and Faith Gabelnick. 2004. *Learning Communities: Reforming Undergraduate Education.* San Francisco: Jossey-Bass.

Sommerville, C. John. 2006. *Decline of the Secular University: Why the Academy Needs Religion*. New York: Oxford Univ. Press.

Steinfels, Peter. 2004. *A People Adrift: The Crisis of the Roman Catholic Church in America*. New York: Simon and Schuster.

"Values Program: A Process for Active Learning in Values Education, The." 1998. Syracuse: Le Moyne College (brochure).

van der Ven, Joannes A. 1998. *Formation of the Moral Self*. Grand Rapids: William B. Eerdmans Publishing.

van Veghel, Harald. 2004. Personal letter to Donald J. Kirby, S.J., early summer.

Vladislav, Jan, ed. 1987. *Living in Truth*. London: Faber and Faber.

Wilgoren, Jodi. 1999. "Exiting Stanford, Noting Many Challenges Ahead." *New York Times,* Sept. 22.

Yaworsky, Krystine Batcho, and William Howard Holmes. 1990. "Power and Promise: Evalution of an Evolving Model." In *Ambitious Dreams: The Values Program at Le Moyne College,* by Donald J. Kirby et al., 161–84. Kansas City, Mo.: Sheed and Ward.

Zlotkowski, Edward. 2001. "Mapping New Terrain: Service Learning Across the Disciplines." *Change* (Jan.–Feb.): 25–33.

———. 2003a. "Integrating Service with Learning." Workshop sponsored by New York Campus Compact, Cornell University, Apr. 11.

———. 2003b. Personal communication, May 1.

Index